"What happened to the apostles after Christ's resurrecti... vanished from history. Or did they? In this classic work Steuart McBirnie scoured all available sources to trace the lives of these men of faith. Read the biographies of those closest to Christ . . . and be encouraged in your faith!"

— DR. CHARLES DYER
Provost and Dean of Education, Moody Bible Institute

THE SEARCH FOR THE
TWELVE APOSTLES

The Twelve

Where did they travel? Preach?
Suffer martyrdom?
What really happened to the
twelve apostles of Jesus?

Dr. McBirnie has followed clues almost 2,000 years old to piece together the inspiring story of the disciples. It is not a story of bones and relics but a dramatic tale of men who knew the Savior, heard the God-breathed word, and courageously carried the message to far reaches of the Roman world.

THE **SEARCH** FOR THE **TWELVE APOSTLES**

WILLIAM STEUART MCBIRNIE

B.A., B.D., M.R.E., D.R.E., PH.D., O.S.J., F.R.G.S.

Tyndale House Publishers, Inc.
Carol Stream, Illinois

CONTENTS

We proclaim to you the one who existed
from the beginning, whom we have heard and seen.
We saw him with our own eyes and touched him with
our own hands. He is the Word of life.

1 JOHN 1:1

The High Adventure of
Some Kinds of Research

In seeking the information contained in this book, my search for the stories of the twelve apostles took me to many famous libraries such as those in Jerusalem, Rome, and the British Museum in London. For years I have borrowed or purchased every book I could find on the subject of the twelve apostles. A five-foot shelf cannot hold them all.

Three times I have journeyed to the island of Patmos and to the locations of the seven churches of the book of Revelation. One whole (and fruitless) day was given to a backroads journey into the high, snowy mountains of Lebanon, up among the famous cedars and elsewhere, to check out a rumor that St. Jude had originally been buried in some small Lebanese village nearby. He was not.

I have personally viewed the many sepulchers which reputedly contain the bones of the Twelve; not that I consider them as having spiritual value, but because I wanted to learn, as an historian, *how* they came to be where they are, hoping that local tradition could be found in the places where the bones are interred that had escaped the history books. This search took me from Germany, to Italy, to Greece, and to almost every Middle Eastern country.

The Vatican very graciously granted me special permission to photograph in all the churches in Rome and elsewhere in Italy. Some of the bodies or fragments of the bodies of the apostles are preserved in that historic land.

Particularly memorable was the awesome descent far beneath St. Peter's Basilica to photograph the bones of the apostle Peter where they rest in an ancient Roman pagan cemetery. One simply cannot imagine, without seeing it, so vast and heavy a church building as St. Peter's sitting squarely over a cemetery filled with beautifully preserved family tombs dating back to the first century before Christ!

Seven times I went to Petra in Jordan, and three times to Antioch in Turkey. I also visited Babylon and made four journeys to Iran in search of the history of the apostles' missions there.

Of course, there were some disappointments. For example, the body of John is today nowhere to be found. I entered his tomb in Ephesus long ago. Recently after many centuries of neglect, the authorities have sealed it and covered it with a marble floor. Though John's body has disappeared some parts of the bones of all the other apostles are believed to exist, and I have seen them.

Travelers to the Bible lands so often pass within a few yards of genuine relics of the apostles and never know it. I had made twenty-six journeys to Jerusalem before learning that the head of James the Elder, several arm bones of James the Just, and part of the skull of John the Baptist are held in veneration in two churches there. And, I might add, with some strong historical records as to their authenticity.

This is not, however, a book about bones. It is about living people who were described by Paul as the founders of the churches (See Ephesians 2:19, 20). We are interested in apostolic bones because they are possible clues as to the whereabouts of the ministry and places of martyrdom of the Twelve.

Now let me face head-on a typically Protestant attitude of skepticism concerning apostolic remains in churches and shrines. I used to suppose that these so-called "relics" were pious frauds, the result of the fervid and superstitious piety of the Middle Ages. Perhaps some are, but after one approaches the whole question with a skeptical mind, and then, somewhat reluctantly, is forced to admit to the strong possibility of their genuineness, it is an unnerving but moving experience.

I suppose the practice of venerating apostolic bones is repugnant to one who, as an evangelical Christian, sees no heavenly merit in praying before the sarcophagi in which they rest. Besides, it does no good to a literal mind to see the gaudy and tasteless trappings which usually festoon the shrines.

But the more one reads of the history of the apostles, and what became of their relics, and the more steeped one becomes in the history and strange (to us) behavior of our Christian ancestors in the Ante-Nicene and Post-Nicene eras, the more the careful preservation of apostolic relics seems to be perfectly in character. To many of those who lived in those times who could not read, an apostolic relic was a visual encouragement to *faith!*

Let it be clearly understood, this book is an adventure in scholarship, not dogmatism. I am keenly aware that absolute proof of every detail recorded here is not possible. But when a researcher checks many sources against each other, when he himself visits the places mentioned, and when he finds many new documents that are not in books, or not commonly found, then he develops a "feel" for the probable or possible.

> To many of our Christian ancestors who could not read, an apostolic relic was a visual encouragement to faith.

This book has been an ever growing labor of love. I became more emotionally committed to the task as the years progressed. On several occasions during the laborious research, arduous journeys, and interminable writing and rewriting, I have had occasion to compare notes with scholars who have written about some of the apostles, and have found not only a gracious willingness to discuss my conclusions but to accept some of them instead of those they had hitherto held.

How does one express an adequate word of appreciation to the many who were so kind in their cooperation, without whom this study could not have been completed? My secretary, Mrs. Fred Pitzer, made this project her own and has saved it from worse faults than those it still may have. My students at the California Graduate School of Theology in Glendale have assisted, and quotations from their research appear often. The same is true of Mr. and Mrs. Robert Schonborn, and of Dr. Miriam Lamb, who is head of research for our Center for American Studies. Mrs. Florence Stonebraker, Betty

Davids and Richard Chase assisted, with Italian translations by Mrs. Marie Placido.

In Jerusalem the libraries of the American School of Oriental Research, the Coptic Church, the Patriarchate of the Armenians (Church of St. James), the Ecole Biblique of the Dominicans, were most helpful in opening their archives for research. In Rome the full cooperation of Monsignor Falani opened many otherwise closed doors. How kind they all were, and many others as well!

Naturally, any errors are not theirs, but mine. Hopefully, if there are any egregious mistakes, some kind correspondent will write to me so that any future editions may be corrected.

A final word about the style of this book: At first I thought to write it for scholars, tearing apart the documentation of every source quoted. But that makes for so dull a book that I was afraid few would read it. I found to my dismay that most "critical" scholars could hardly care less about the post-biblical story of the apostles.

Then, I thought to write it as a narrative with few quotations and little attention to my sources. But in that case scholars would ignore the book as having no proper foundation and lacking concern for critical and historical problems.

As the senior minister of a busy church, I considered writing for pastors. These ministers might appreciate a homiletical boost for a series of sermons on the apostles that might attract the people we are all trying to persuade to attend the church. I have not abandoned this approach altogether, but I did not do much sermonizing in this book.

It even occurred to me that the historical novel might also provide a viable format. But I tend to think as a historian and as a preacher, I lack the imagination to write a novel. Besides, what this book has to offer is analysis, fact and hopefully, *truth*.

So the book is in the form of an interpretation or critical analysis of every bit of knowledge I can find on the subject of the twelve apostles. Mostly I wrote it to become more familiar myself with the apostles and to share that knowledge, and draw some conclusions from it, with as many people as I can; scholars, church members, young people, historians, ministers, and all those who feel as I do, that we need to find ways to make the apostolic age become more alive for us today.

I earnestly hope the reader will find it as interesting and enlightening to read as I found it to write.

WILLIAM STEUART MCBIRNIE

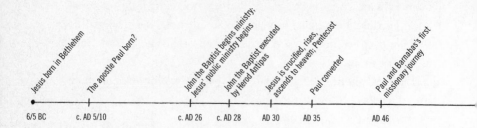

Jesus born in Bethlehem · The apostle Paul born? · John the Baptist begins ministry; Jesus' public ministry begins · John the Baptist executed by Herod Antipas · Jesus is crucified, rises, ascends to heaven; Pentecost · Paul converted · Paul and Barnabas's first missionary journey

6/5 BC · c. AD 5/10 · c. AD 26 · c. AD 28 · AD 30 · AD 35 · AD 46

Introduction

What follows in this book is that which can be known from an exhaustive and critical study of the Biblical, historical and traditional records of the apostles. The author has tried to reduce the legendary to the probable or likely, justifying it with the known historical facts concerning the state of the world in the first century and the documents of subsequent church history, local history, and relevant secular writings.

There is a great deal more information about the apostles available than the casual student might guess. Ten years ago I produced a monograph called *What Became of the Twelve Apostles?* Ten thousand copies were distributed. In that publication I made the following observations:

> Someday a critical scholar needs to take a good look at the mass of legend which has come to us from early medieval times, and even from the last days of Roman power. He needs to try to separate the historical germ from the great over-growth of pure fantasy which one finds in those stories. In a word, a higher criticism of medieval legends needs to be made, and that criticism needs to be carried over into early church history.
>
> I find myself disappointed in the writings of recent church historians who seem to pass over the era of the early church and say only what has been said in a hundred other books on church history written during the past four centuries. It has been so

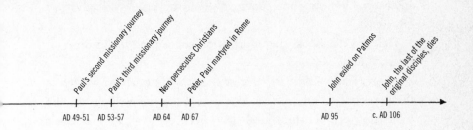

long since I have seen a new fact in a book of church history about the apostolic Age and the age of the church fathers, that I would be mightily surprised if I saw one! But perhaps someday someone will find the probable basis of truth amidst the legendary; and upon this, with perhaps the discovery of new manuscripts, we shall be able to piece together a better history than we now possess.

Since few have done the work of producing a critical study of the Twelve, it has become a challenge to me to do so, for the sake of a renewed interest in the apostolic church.

The source of our material in that earlier publication was primarily obtainable by anyone who would take the trouble to look into the standard books on the subject, such as church histories, sermonic literature, encyclopedias, etc., plus the observations of a few journeys to Rome, Athens, and the Holy Land. But that book was frustratingly limited, incomplete, and sorely lacking in original research.

I visited the Middle East twenty-seven times, then spent ten years of further research which shed much light on the lives of the twelve apostles. Most of these insights have come in very small packages, a bit here, a bit there. I had not even considered writing a subsequent book to the former monograph, but the importance and volume of the material I gleaned from my many personal visits to the places of the ministries and deaths of the apostles, plus their burial sites or tombs, has increased my conviction that this enlarged study *must* be offered.

Here, in this book, the information concerning the histories of the apostles is gathered.

No scholar would dare suggest that anything he has written is the last word on any subject, nor indeed that his writings are the complete story. Yet these ideals have been the goals toward which we have moved.

Insights into the Apostolic Age

There are several insights which the reader should have firmly and constantly in mind as the following chapters unfold.

The early Christians did not write history as such.

Interest in the apostles has waxed and waned in various periods of Christian history. For that reason at certain times more information has been available than at others. New discoveries of historical information are made, then lie dormant in out of print books until a reawakening of interest at a later time brings them to light.

> At first in the apostolic age, the apostles themselves and their converts were too busy making history to bother writing it. Hence, their records are fragmentary.

At first, in the apostolic age, the apostles themselves and their converts were too busy making history to bother writing it. Hence, their records are fragmentary. Further, until the Ante-Nicene Fathers, history as such was not written at all. Even the book of Acts by Luke was not a general history but a polemic written to show the emergence of a Gentile Christian movement from its Jewish matrix, with divine authority and approval.

Surely Luke wanted to defend and validate the ministry of Paul, his mentor! His themes, the acts of the Holy Spirit, the inclusion in God's redemption of the Gentiles, the gradually diminishing role of Jews in the churches, the universality of Christianity, were all the concerns of Luke. It probably did not occur to him that he was writing the prime source of church history! Hence, to a historian of the early church, Luke is both the welcome source of his main knowledge and the cause of his despair at its fragmentary nature.

There were periods of silence in early Christian history.
After Luke and the other biblical writers (particularly Paul who left us a considerable knowledge of early apostolic activities), there is silence for a time. It is as if the Christian movement were in a tunnel, active, but out of sight for a period.

This is not as strange as it may seem. First, the early Christians did not really have a sense of building a movement *for the ages*. To them the return of Christ might well be expected during their generation. They certainly spoke of it often, so they must have looked for the return of Christ daily—at first.

To see this, study carefully the difference in tone between First and Second Thessalonians. In 1 Thessalonians, Paul seemed to dwell at great length upon the *imminence* of the Second Coming. In 2 Thessalonians Paul rebukes those who are over eager by reminding his readers of certain events which must precede or accompany the Second Coming.

It was as if he had looked again at the enormous task of world evangelism and had seen that it would take more than one generation. It was not that Paul lost his faith in the Second Coming, but that he balanced his faith with practicality. In any case, the early Christian movement *was* in a tunnel and out of sight as far as the recording of history is concerned. They were doing, not writing.

The apostles were not considered prime subjects for biography
by the early Christians.
We look at the twelve apostles as the founders of churches, but to the early Christians the Twelve were considered to be leaders, brothers, and dearly beloved friends at first. It took some time for their spiritual descendents to see them as the fathers of the whole church

movement. Their authority at first was in the anointing of the Holy Spirit, not in *ex cathedra* pronouncements on doctrine.

True, the first council of apostles in Jerusalem gave authoritarian pronouncements concerning the admittance of the Gentile converts into the Christian movement. Yet this did not seem to have the ecclesiastical authority then that we attach to it now. We could, in fact, wish there had been more such pronouncements; say, concerning heresy, forms of church government, social matters, etc. But there was nothing much that came *collectively* from the apostles. They simply proclaimed individually what they had heard from Jesus Christ.

We look at the twelve apostles as the founders of churches, but to the early Christians they were considered leaders, brothers, and friends at first.

As they went forth into various parts of the world they carried, no doubt, the authority of their apostolate, but *they* were not the *church*. They founded congregations which were churches. Ecclesiasticism in the highly organized and authoritarian forms it later took was almost unknown to them. The apostles were evangelists and pastors, not ecclesiastics. Their histories, then, are the histories of evangelists, not of prelates. History does not deal as much with evangelists as with rulers. Hence, we have little knowledge about their careers before or subsequent to the dispersion of the Jerusalem Church in AD 69, by which time most of them had left Jerusalem to go on their various missions and many had died.

Secular history largely ignored Christianity in the early centuries.
Almost all history in the first few centuries of the Christian era which has survived is secular, military or political. Josephus did not pay much attention to Christianity though he mentions the death of James. Roman history, except for the writings of Pliny the Younger, hardly notices Christianity until long after the apostolic age. It remains for churchmen such as Hegesippus and Eusebius to give us further details of the travels and history of the Twelve.

The early Christians were humble folk, with some exceptions. Who writes a history of the meek? Therefore we are left with little information about Christianity in general in secular history, except for valuable insights as to the *world* in which the apostles lived. The average reader, however, would be amazed at how much knowledge we do have on the history of this period. Roman history is already well known and more knowledge is daily pouring in from the archeologists who dig up the artifacts of that great epic.

To the avid student of Roman affairs, the world of the apostles is as familiar as the world of a hundred years ago. This does not itself tell us about the actual story of each apostle, but it certainly tells us what was possible or even likely, as well as what was unlikely or impossible.

During the apostolic age, the Roman world was a relatively safe world in which its citizens traveled widely and often. Read in the book of Romans, written by Paul in Corinth, the many names of people whom he knew in Rome, a city which at that time he had not visited. Read the travels of Cicero, sixty years before Christ. Recall the Roman invasions of Britain by Caesar, five decades before the birth of Jesus, and of Claudius in AD 42.

The Roman Empire was a family of nations with a common language under the protection of one government, with roads leading everywhere, from Britain to Africa, from what is now Russia to France, from India to Spain. Paul himself, in the book of Romans, expressed a desire to evangelize Spain, which had been conquered by Rome long before Caesar took it over in 44 BC.

In the era of the apostles there was a wide area of civilization awaiting them, civilized, united, and tied together by transportation and tongue. On that vast stage, and beyond it, we can easily visualize the far-flung apostolic labors. But Roman historians pretty well ignored Christianity in its early days.

> During the apostolic age, the Roman world was a relatively safe world in which its citizens traveled widely and often.

The "search for the Twelve" was at first political or ecclesiastical.
Long after the apostolic age there arose a conflict between the Greek
and Roman divisions of Christianity as to what they called "Primacy."
The Pope claimed it and so did the leader of the Eastern churches. An
issue, for example, was one of Christian art. One group, the Romans,
used images-in-the-round (statues, etc.) as the objects of religious
veneration. The Eastern Greeks preferred *ikons*—images-on-the-flat.
There were other differences, including the removal of the capital of the
Roman Empire from Rome to Byzantium, but mainly it was a political
power struggle which led to the great schism that divided eastern and
western Christianity, as the Roman Empire itself was divided.

At this time, and even before, as the schism was building, both
sides sought apostolic identification with their own religious institutions.

So a great search was made for the *relics* of the apostles. Emperor
Constantine wanted to construct what he called "The Church of the
Twelve Apostles" in Constantinople. In this structure he intended to
house the remains (such as bones or parts of bodies) of the apostles.
He succeeded in securing the remains of Andrew, and also Luke and
Timothy. (The latter two, while not of the Twelve, were close to
them.) Apparently Constantine felt he must leave the bones of Paul
and Peter in Rome though he may have had designs on the bones
of Peter.[1]

He gladly built a basilica to honor the bones of Paul in Rome. But,
one may speculate, the Roman church was also reluctant to part with
the bones of Peter. Constantine apparently did not press the matter,
but he built a church over Peter's resting place, hoping perhaps to
later move his body to Constantinople. In any case, he did not live
long enough to collect all the relics of the apostles for his Church
of the Twelve Apostles. That church building remained unfurnished
except for his own tomb. (Some evidence exists that he sought to
place the apostles' bodies around him in twelve niches while his own
body would lie in the midst as "The Thirteenth Apostle"!) Eusebius
tells the story in "The Last Days of Constantine":

All these edifices the emperor consecrated with the desire of perpetuating the memory of the Apostles of our Saviour before all men. He had, however, another reason for erecting this building (i.e., the Church of the Apostles at Constantinople)— a reason at first unknown, but which afterward became evident to all. He had, in fact, made a choice of this spot in the prospect of his own death, anticipating with extraordinary fervour of faith that his body would share their title with the Apostles themselves, and that he should thus even after death become the subject, with them, of the devotions which should be performed to their honour in this place, and for this reason he bade men assemble for worship there at the altar which he placed in the midst.

He accordingly caused twelve coffins to be set up in this church, like sacred pillars in honour and memory of the apostolic band, in the centre of which his own was placed, having six of theirs on either side of it. Thus, as I said, he had provided with prudent foresight an honourable resting-place for his body after death, and, having long before secretly formed this resolution, he now consecrated this church to the Apostles, believing that this tribute to their memory would be of no small advantage to his own soul. Nor did God disappoint him of that which he so ardently expected and desired.[2]

Planning the Church of the Apostles, Constantine had dreamed of resting there forever in the midst of the Twelve, not merely one of them, but a symbol of, if not a substitute for, their leader. During the months of the church's construction, his agents had been busy in Palestine collecting alleged relics of the apostles and their companions, to be laid up in the church with his body, awaiting the general resurrection.[3]

Robert M. Grant described Constantine's last days in his book *Augustus to Constantine: The Thrust of the Christian Movement into the Roman World*:

At Easter in AD 337, the emperor dedicated the Church of the Holy Apostles in Constantinople, but soon thereafter he was overcome by a fatal ailment. He visited the baths at Helenopolis in vain, and then proceeded to confess his sins in the Church of the Martyrs. At Ancyrona near Nicomedia, he prepared his will, leaving the empire to his three sons, and in the presence of a group of local bishops he was baptized by the bishop with whom he had fought so often, Eusebius of Nicomedia. To this prelate was entrusted the will, the instructions to deliver it to Constantius, Caesar of the east. Wearing the white robe of a neophyte, Constantine died on Pentecost, May 22.

. . . Upon Constantius's arrival, the coffin was carried to the Church of the Holy Apostles and placed among the sarcophagi dedicated to the Twelve. In the presence of a vast throng the bishops conducted an elaborate funeral with a requiem eucharist.

. . . His body rested, however, not in any Flavian mausoleum or with any of the great pagan emperors before him but, by his own choice, among the memorials of the twelve apostles.[4]

The project was started but not completed. However, an official search *was* made for the locations of the bodies of the apostles, and this official *search* was possibly the precipitating cause for the inventory which was made for the apostolic remains or relics.

After this time there arose the practice of the *veneration of relics*. The superstitious awe which these relics evoked was carried to extremes. The bodies of the apostles, the bodies of other "saints," and the various holy relics such as fragments of "the true cross" came into great demand. Healings were claimed by merely touching or kissing these relics and naturally they came to be considered of great value by both the churches and governments of the Middle Ages.

As for a knowledge of the lives of the apostles, this search for relics both helped and harmed a true history. The major relics, including the bodies or portions of bodies of the apostles, give us some hints of the places of the death and burial and hence by tradition or association, the locale of their ministries. We perhaps have successfully traced the history of some of these apostolic remains or relics in the following chapters, up to their locations today.

On the other hand we must recognize that some of these apostolic relics may not be genuine, since wishful thinking or simple mistakes may have led the devout of other, less critical ages than ours, to go astray. This was especially so since there was great church prestige, political preferment, and often much money involved in securing what were believed to be genuine apostolic relics.

Partisans in the great church schism between the east and west undoubtedly sought to associate their possession of apostolic relics as proof of the blessing of the apostles and God *upon them*, witnessing to the fact that *they* had the original and often miracle-working relics in *their* exclusive possession.

Fortunately, that competition has ebbed with the centuries. In quite recent times Pope Paul VI has returned to Greece the head of St. Andrew, to be housed in a new church in the place of his martyrdom in Patras, Greece, under the care of the Greek Orthodox Church. This was a highly conciliatory gesture on the part of the Pope since St. Andrew, having been martyred in Greece, is meaningful to the Greek Orthodox Church. It reduces by one the apostolic relics in Rome, but increases the chances of unity between Rome and Athens very markedly, for whatever that may prove to be worth to those involved.

If one can cut through the maze of the history of relics and trace the presence of fact back to the genuine tradition of apostolic associations in the places of their original martyrdoms and burials, then there is great hope that this may open up the way to confirm or even discover more light on the histories of apostolic labors. This we have attempted to do where possible. Admittedly, this task and its results are open to scholarly criticism and interpretation.

The motivations of the apostles are now more clearly understood.
One great truth about the apostles is unassailable. It has been strengthened by every bit of tradition and history we have studied.

That is, most of the apostles took seriously the great commission of Jesus (as recorded in Matthew 28) and went forth to "Judea, Samaria, and the uttermost parts of the world" to *evangelize* the nations with the Christian gospel. The story of the apostles is thus mainly the story of *evangelism* in the early church.

They set an example for all subsequent Christians that is clear, unmistakable and unswerving. They challenged commoners and kings alike. They did not become salaried ecclesiastics but often worked with their hands to support themselves, so that by any and all means they might share the good news in Jesus. Most, like Paul, sought to preach Christ, "not building upon other men's foundations, but going to the regions beyond."

There was an apostolic strategy of missions.

The lives of the apostles, especially that of Paul, reveal an unusual and brilliant concept of missionary strategy. They always went first to the great cities located on the trade routes. From these centers their disciples and converts then traveled out to the towns beyond and there established churches which in turn established still others. The apostles knew the secret of strategic locations and of delegating responsibility to others, thus multiplying themselves more rapidly than is the case in many modern missionary enterprises.

The Apostles Were Churchmen

Above all, they founded *congregations*. Some modern day evangelism is so apart from the churches that the churches must feed the evangelistic effort, rather than for the evangelistic effort to build the converts firmly into the churches or to give impetus to new churches. This was never the apostolic principle, which is why apostolic evangelism lasted and some modern "populist" evangelism soon passes away.

The apostles enjoined upon their converts the responsibility to *become* the church. Surely this is one lesson that needs to be relearned today. It was Paul who wrote that *Jesus loved the church and gave his life up for it* (Ephesians 5:25).

Why the Twelve?

The apostles of Jesus Christ are heroes whose portraits, as Christians have come to know them, are "larger than life." The Roman and Greek Catholic bestowal of the title, "Saint," upon each of the Twelve (and thereafter upon a flood of others) was partly responsible for making them into demigods. But long before the time the New Testament was collected into one volume called the Canon, the figures of the Twelve had assumed commanding respect. John, in the book of Revelation, speaks of the New Jerusalem which is to have the names of the Twelve inscribed in its foundations. (Incidentally, that inclusion settles the issue of whether Matthias was, after the defection of Judas Iscariot, truly considered by the other apostles as one of the Twelve.)

Why did Jesus choose only twelve chief apostles? Obviously to correspond to the twelve tribes of Israel. He, Himself, as the new and eternal high priest, would stand for the priestly thirteenth tribe, *Levi*. The function of the apostles was to bear witness to the resurrection of Jesus and of His teachings. For this reason, as the election of Matthias to replace Judas confirms, an apostle had to have been with Jesus for a long time and a witness to his teachings.

> To become one of Jesus' apostles, a person had to have been with him for a long time, witnessing his teachings.

Paul stoutly maintained that he also was an apostle, since his conversion, call, and instruction came directly from Jesus, and the *signs* of an apostle were his in abundance. Yet there is no evidence that he was ever admitted to that inner circle of the original Twelve. Some of the original Twelve probably never did fully trust him, and even Peter confessed that he did not always understand the comments of "our beloved brother Paul" (2 Peter 3:15).

The Book of Acts and the Twelve

In a most important sense, the book of Acts, the earliest Christian book of history, is the story of how Christianity, at first a sect within Judaism, was opened to the Gentiles, and how in a short time it became mainly a faith of the Gentiles. From start to finish, the book of Acts shows Christianity as a minority movement among the Jews, soon rejected by most Jews, and Gentilized as the illustrious Paul became the European leader of the Christian movement. Peter remained for a time as the most prominent Jewish-Christian leader, but Christianity after the first century gradually died down among the Jews.

The book of Acts carefully records how Peter, obviously at first against his will, became a grudging apostle to some Gentiles, yet all the while endeavoring to keep Christianity as Jewish as possible. The plan of the book of Acts is as logically and carefully laid out as a lawyer's brief. It proves conclusively that Christianity was intended to, and did, lose its exclusively Jewish character. It was to be much more than a sect or another party within Judaism, such as were the Pharisees, Sadducees, or Essenes.

Those who expect the book of Acts to be the complete early history of Christianity are doomed to disappointment. That is true only incidentally and in a fragmentary way. Its main argument is that God, Himself, tore Christianity loose from its Jewish foundations and made it universal. To do this He used Peter at first, then Paul. The other apostles played only incidental roles in the story of Acts, since it is not a history of the apostles but a history of the emergence of Gentile Christianity.

As valuable and as liberating as this emphasis is, the Bible reader is soon, and perhaps unconsciously, caught up in the personal ministry of Paul. Peter, though prominent at first, is later ignored, as Acts unfolds for the reader the story of Paul and his friends, Timothy, Luke, Barnabas, Silas and others. The book shows Peter and the rest of the Twelve launching the Christian movement, and as having blessed the admission of believing Gentiles into the churches, then portrays again and again the fact that only *some* Jews around the Roman world accepted Christ. As others rejected Christ, in each instance Paul is show as turning to the Gentiles who seemed much more willing to receive the gospel than the majority of the Jews.

This historical insight is necessary to know if we are to understand why we have a great deal of information about John and Peter, and even more about Paul, but know really very little of the other apostles.

Roman and Greek Christianity early became dominant over Judaistic Christianity. Western Christians of the Roman Empire treasured and preserved the writings of John, Peter, and Paul—the three apostles who worked among the Gentiles. The other apostles did not write much, with the exception of Matthew. But Matthew's personality does not come through clearly in his Gospel. The writings, if any, of the remainder of the Twelve are lost.

Mark was the helper and writer for Peter, but Mark was not considered an apostle but an apostolic assistant, as were Timothy, Titus, Epaphroditus, Luke, Barnabas, Silas, Acquilla, Priscilla, and Erastus. Luke wrote about Paul in Acts, and about the apostles and Jesus in his gospel. But Luke was not himself an original apostle. Hence, the New Testament as we have it is the product of Matthew, an apostle, Peter, an apostle, John, an apostle, and Paul, an apostle. Other New Testament authors such as Mark and Luke, were not apostles, but assistants; and Jude and James were not of the original followers of Jesus, but brothers of the Lord, who did not believe until after the Resurrection of Christ.

As for the history of the apostles after the first few years in Jerusalem, except for brief references to them in Acts, we must look into the Epistles, the book of Revelation, the histories and traditions or legends of the early, post-apostolic Christian writers, and to the local traditions of the Christian movement in the places where the apostles labored or died. It is this latter research that has had the least historic treatment and which we will attempt to explore, along with those early Christian traditions and Scriptural accounts which are fairly well (but not universally) known.

Legend, Myth, and Tradition

The word *legend* is in better standing today than it was a short time ago. *Legendary* has often been a word of ill repute for it has meant "mythical" to most people. The word *tradition* stands far higher in the estimation of historians. Scholars today, thanks to literary criticism, historical research, and archeological observations, have more confidence in the existence of a residue of fact amongst the legends and traditions about well-known historical or biblical figures. Blown up and fanciful they may be, legends and traditions are often the enlargements of reality, and traditions may not be exaggerations at all, but actual fact. We have attempted to squeeze some of the water out of those legends which exist about the apostles and also find the elements of the reasonable and possible which are in traditions. It is impossible to be dogmatic about this subject, but surely a fuller knowledge of the lives of all the apostles can now be acquired than has hitherto been generally known.

> Fanciful they may be, legends and traditions are often the enlargements of reality, and traditions may not be exaggerations at all, but actual fact.

The Relevance Today

But *why* should the Christian reader, or the reading public, be interested in the histories of the first apostles of Jesus Christ?

For one thing, any increased knowledge about the apostles will greatly illumine the power-filled early days of Christianity, and perhaps help to recover the secret of the primitive dynamic of the early Christians.

Christians today know, or can know, more about many things than any other generation of believers. Archaeology is a relatively modern science. Textual criticism has secured a clearer biblical text than was ever available before. Yet, unfortunately, much of the power and spirit of New Testament era Christianity is obviously missing in today's churches.

The general public needs to see afresh the dedication of the earliest Christian leaders, and to feel the modern relevance of their timeless methods and ideals. Christianity needs a self-renewal, as do all institutions. From where will this renewal come? That dynamic momentum which early Christians bequeathed, and which has still not entirely run down, was surely, in part, the personal and direct heritage of the twelve apostles and their Christian contemporaries.

The least that a study of this kind should contribute to all Christians is to direct our attention back to the days of a purer, unencrusted, tradition-free Christianity. There is much about the lives of the twelve apostles that can speak to us *existentially* today. Indeed, to discover what the apostles did, or what it is claimed that they did, is to rediscover their motivation and the life-strategy which they followed.

How This Study Began

In a sense this book has taken thirty years of comprehensive and intensive study to write. In 1944, I finished a bachelor of divinity degree at Bethel Theological Seminary in St. Paul, Minnesota, with a major in church history which included over sixty semester credit-hours and a thesis on the same subject. In 1952, I submitted another dissertation on the same subject and was graduated with a doctorate in religious education from Southwestern Baptist Theological Seminary in Fort Worth, Texas.

Since that time, I've read continually on ecclesiastical history and have traveled repeatedly to Europe (thirty-nine times) and the Middle East (twenty-seven journeys) in search of biblical and ecclesiastical information. This rich experience has been a labor of love and has been highly rewarding in terms of the discovery of new facts and fresh insights. It is a false supposition that all useful historic knowledge is to be found only in books, though I've read hundreds of books about the twelve apostles. Much additional information about them could only be gleaned by traveling to places the apostles once knew, and by conversations with people who now live there, who know of traditions not widely found in the books which are readily available to scholars. No one book, to my knowledge, has ever been written that includes all known facts about the apostles until now.

For example, in October 1971, I was an official guest in Iran for the celebration of the 2,500-year memorial to Cyrus the Great. Upon this occasion the opportunity arose to interview the leaders of several of the very ancient Christian movements of Iran who trace their spiritual descent back to the visits to Persia in the first century of at least five of Jesus' apostles! Not only did I obtain new information, but also a wider understanding of the Eastern thrust of early Christianity beyond the borders of the Roman world about which we Christians of the Western tradition know very little. This has been our great loss. The following observations are an illustration of an area of Christian history about which few American Christians know:

> Iran had known Christianity from the earliest times of apostolic preaching. When Christianity was first preached in this part of the world, that is to say, beyond the frontiers of East Roman Empire, namely in the easternmost regions of Asia Minor, north-eastern regions of Ancient Syria and Mesopotamia, the apostles and their immediate successors did not know any boundary between East Syria, Mesopotamia, Armenia and Persia. In fact, the peoples of these countries lived in such a state of close association that the first Christians all belonged to the same stream of evangelization, they shared the same Christian traditions handed down to them by the first apostles and their disciples.
>
> Thus, beginning from the first century, the Christian faith had been preached in Edessa, in the kingdom of Osrohene. It penetrated also Armenia and Persia in the same century. As Tournebize has said: "From Osrohene the faith undoubtedly had shown forth quite early to the East; between Edessa and Armenia the distance was not big." Long before Bar Hebraus, the alliances and frequent interpenetrations between Parthians, Persians, Edessenians, and Armenians had justified the following remark of the famous monophysite patriarch: "Parthians or Persians, Parthians or Edessenians, Parthians or Armenians, all are one."[5]

Later, in November of 1971, I led a group of people from all over America on a historic journey entitled, "The Search for the Twelve Apostles." On this expedition, through Europe and the Middle East, many more of the recorded facts in this book emerged. It can possibly be said that no other group in modern or ancient times has hitherto made so comprehensive a study into the lives and burial places of the apostles *in the actual locations* indicated by history or the traditions associated with the apostles.

There is still more light to be thrown on the subject of the twelve apostles. One thinks, for instance, of the vast archives of ancient and as yet untranslated documents in the Greek Orthodox monasteries or the Vatican Library in Rome. We do not pretend to the scholarship, linguistic ability, or the sheer time which would be necessary to dig for the needles in these huge haystacks. We must await the happy day when others will accomplish these tasks.

But within the limits of present scholarship, original research, and the critical examination of history and traditions, we have, we hope, amassed all that is known, or which reasonably can now be learned about the apostles. We can anticipate with joy that further scholarship which will add to the body of information here presented.

CHAPTER ONE

THE WORLD OF THE APOSTLES

All the believers devoted themselves to the apostles' teaching . . . They worshiped together at the Temple each day, met in homes for the Lord's Supper, and shared their meals with great joy and generosity—all the while praising God and enjoying the goodwill of all the people. And each day the Lord added to their fellowship those who were being saved. Acts 2:42, 46-47.

A strong tide of optimism had begun to well up throughout the vast reaches of the Roman Empire as the year AD 30 dawned. Tiberius Caesar in his palace on Capri did not know it, but a new force was being born that would one day inherit the empire. Under the iron grip of Augustus, the successor to Julius Caesar, peace, even if the oppressive peace of a total conquest, had come to be an accepted way of life for the people of the Roman Empire.

The "Pax Romana"

There were spots of local rebellion which grew hot from time to time, but there was absolutely no doubt that Rome was the saddle that was securely strapped on to Europe, North Africa, and Asia Minor. Augustus and his successor, Tiberius, sat long and firmly in that saddle. Any client king who doubted it, or rebellious province which had the temerity to challenge Caesar soon found out with bloodshed just who rode the world. Further, no one doubted that these affairs would continue, as indeed the future state of the empire of the next three hundred years confirmed. The prolongation of the *Pax Romana* brought prosperity, trade, education, cultural and language homogeneity, and safe travel—an ideal preparation for Christian apostles and missionaries.

There was one perpetually troublesome exception to the *Pax Romana*—the land of Judea. There the Roman legions, as occupation troops, constantly had to be on guard against an implacably hostile population. The Herodian monarchs had ruled since the days of the first Caesar only by the imposed power of Rome. They all understood, if their people did not, that Rome was there to stay and that the *Pax Romana* was undoubtedly the best of all realistically possible conditions.

The various Herods, one after another, had sailed to Rome to visit the dazzling center of power. There they saw the larger picture of the empire and could more easily fit Judea into its small place. But the people they ruled in Rome's name were provincial in the extreme and were able to see no farther than their own borders. To the Israelites, however just and fair they often tried to be, the Romans were hated oppressors, idol-worshipping inferiors, outside the covenant of God, and the proper objects of unceasing attempts at rebellion and assassination. The Romans' haughty contempt for Jewish pride created a resentment that would inevitably lead to the slaughter and dispersion of the Jews. In the end only Rome could win. But rationally or not, among no people in the world of that time did the passion for independence burn so fiercely as it did among the Jews. Most Jews cared little for the safety and prosperity they admittedly gained by being a part of a great cohesive empire.

Their resentment, being nationalistic and ideological, grew primarily as a reaction to the infernal pride of the Romans. To the Jews, nothing Rome could do could possibly be right. To the Romans, granted the right of empire, (which we moderns *cannot* of course

> The *Pax Romana* brought prosperity, trade, education, cultural and language homogeneity, and safe travel—an ideal preparation for Christian apostles and missionaries.

Modern names and boundaries are shown in gray.

THE WORLD OF THE APOSTLES

JERUSALEM

At Pentecost, Jesus' followers in Jerusalem are filled by the Holy Spirit. The Jerusalem church grows.

SAMARIA

Persecution of Christians intensifies. The gospel is spread to other cities in the empire.

SYRIA

Paul becomes a believer. Barnabas brings Paul to the church in Antioch in Syria.

CYPRUS & GALATIA

Paul and Barnabas's first missionary journey is through Cyprus and Galatia.

MACEDONIA & ACHAIA

Paul and Barnabas part ways. Paul visits cities in Macedonia, goes to Athens and Corinth in Achaia, and eventually returns to Antioch.

EPHESUS

Paul's third journey is to Ephesus and other cities in Asia.

JERUSALEM & ROME

Paul is arrested in Jerusalem and under Roman guard begins the long journey to the capital of the empire, where he will appear before Caesar.

grant) the choice was clear: keep Judea pacified or risk the brush fires of rebellion breaking out everywhere else. In order to make their empire viable, the Romans sought to be as just as possible. But, just or not, Rome *would rule* no matter what the people of Israel did or how they felt. The clash of wills between Jerusalem and Rome was the most troublesome political fact of the first century. Eventually it could have but one tragic outcome for Judea.

The peace of Rome, disastrous and painful for the Jews, nevertheless opened up a great share of the world to easy penetration by the newly-risen movement of Christianity. In every Roman city godly Jews were already dwelling. All Israelites, whether from the tribe of Judah proper, or of the remnants of the thirteen tribes, now came to be called Jews. Judah was the royal tribe of David, and Jew is simply an abbreviation for Judah. The *Pay Romana* had spearheaded the return of the exiles from Babylon, who now again possessed the capital, Jerusalem. Judah was the strongest and most persistent of the tribes, and it was the keeper of the temple in Jerusalem, which was the proper geographical focal point of prayer, wherever in the world Israelites were themselves located. So gradually the Israelites of all the tribes who cared about preserving their own national identity, and their ancient Mosaic traditions and religious faith, came to be called Jews.

Intermarriage between the people of the various tribes of Israel in the *diaspora* doubtless helped bind all dispersed Israel toward identification with Judah. Those who did not join this spiritual and nationalistic movement were soon lost, not as whole tribes, but as individuals, as intermarriage with Gentiles or the attrition of death gradually exterminated or eliminated those who were indifferent to their Israelite heritage.

There was not just one single dispersion of the tribes of Israel, though the process began in 725 BC when Assyria carried off many people out of the northern tribes. Instead, there were successive waves of removal from Palestine which scattered the Israelites everywhere. (A colony of Jews which has lived in Cochin, India, since AD 70 came to world attention in the recent years as emigration to the modern state of Israel has finally depleted that section of Indian Jewry. This event reminds us that people traveled much more widely in the first century AD than is commonly realized, a fact that has a bearing on the genuineness of the apostolate of St. Thomas in India during the first century.)

The *Biblical Research Handbook* (volume 2) provides a reminder of the dispersion of the Jews in the pre-Christian era. As the apostles always went first to the Jews in their missions, this passage is very illuminating:

> Armenian and Georgian historians record that after the destruction of the First Temple . . . Nebuchadnezzar deported numbers of Jewish captives to Armenia and the Caucasus. These exiles were joined later by co-religionists from Medes and Judea . . . at the end of the fourth century there were Armenian cities possessing Jewish populations ranging from 10,000 to 30,000. . . .
>
> Monuments consisting of marble slabs bearing Greek inscriptions and preserved in the Hermitage St. Petersburg, and in the museum at Feodosia (Kaffa), show that Jews lived in the Crimea and along the entire eastern coast of the Black Sea at the beginning of the common era, and that they possessed well-organized communities with synagogues. They were then already Hellenized, bearing such Greek names as Hermis, Dionisiodorus and Heracles. In the reign of Julius the Isaurian (175-210) the name "Volamiros" was common among the Jews of the Crimea. This was the origin of the Russian name "Vladimir."[1]

Greek culture had penetrated as far as France, then called the land of the Gauls, by the middle of the first century BC. The various languages of each country were used locally of course, but throughout the Roman Empire both Greek and Latin were widely and universally used. This fact made it possible for Greek philosophy and culture to affect the Roman world profoundly. Later it would provide common literary and linguistic vehicles for the Christian gospel.

The splendid Roman roads, many of which can still be seen today, related the cities of all countries to each other. Over those safe and straight highways and the increasingly viable sea lanes came a busy interchange of goods and customs. These same highways would soon be the paths of the propagation of the faith.

Thus in the first century the Roman world, with all its initial cruelties and harsh conditions, was changing and uniting into the largest and most continually ruled empire the world has ever known. In the Middle Ages, the Mongol Empire briefly ruled a larger area, and perhaps more people, but it left no enduring civilization since it was an empire of destruction which soon faded back into the vast emptiness of Asia from which it had come. Rome brought a culture which remained. Indeed, that culture still remains today, and its influence is as strong as ever.

> Over Rome's safe highways and viable sea lanes came a busy interchange of goods and customs, [future] paths of the propagation of the faith.

Rome had drawn much of her civilization from others, initially from the mysterious Etruscans. But by the first century, the Estruscans had virtually disappeared into history. We cannot read their language even now. Egypt also had given much and would give more. But Egypt had lost the civilization of the Pharaohs and had become Hellenized. Greece itself was still the cultural and medical center of the Roman Empire, but it had become little more than a province which fed its influence into the bloodstream of the empire. Greece was, of course, eventually to triumph over Rome and rise again, not in Athens but in Constantinople. During the first century, however, Rome was the greatest political fact in the world.

This, then, was the world of Jesus and His apostles. On the narrow land bridge between three continents the people of Israel had come and gone, and come again. The Greeks, and afterwards the Romans, had conquered Palestine, but had never really subdued her people. Rebellion continuously simmered. It frequently flared with little provocation into revolution against Rome. The Herodians were quick to take action against their people because if they could not put the rebellion down, the Romans could and would. And when this happened, the Herodians lost face and paid severe penalties to Caesar.

For this reason, the Herodians were zealous to stamp out any sedition before it could be embarrassing to them. It was on a charge of sedition that Jesus was tried and in an illegal trial, which soon got out of hand, was falsely condemned to death for blasphemy and treason, though the Roman governor Pilate had declared Him innocent.

Of course, sedition was only the ostensible reason why Jesus was condemned. As the apostles saw clearly then, and history's long judgment has since confirmed, the greatest reason for his condemnation was the fact that Jesus had lanced through the swollen hypocrisy of the Jewish political and ceremonial religion and the religious bureaucracy of the professional priests, the Pharisees and Sadducees. So all the main Jewish leaders, including the official party of the Herodians called by that name, consented to or sought his death.

When men gain high places and hold them precariously, they often stoop to fatal compromises. When they do so in a semi-religious state they also have a bad conscience. When they are exposed and their real motives are laid bare, they tend to strike back with fangs bared and venom dripping. Jesus aptly called them, "a brood of vipers," and for this, most of all, they lay in wait, coiled, and then struck Him down. Their charges against Him were blasphemy and sedition. Thus Rome was induced to join with Jerusalem to crucify the Son of God.

Jesus' apostles, after the Resurrection, enjoyed a great resurgence of popularity in Judea. The guilt for the death of Jesus lay on the public conscience and the apostles assured those who would repent that this guilt, and all other sinful guilt, had been atoned for by the true Lamb of God. Thousands professed conversion to Christ soon after the Resurrection, and day after day were added to the growing Jerusalem church.

Soon no public or private building could contain their assembly.

Steps were taken by the authorities to discourage the apostles lest Israel be troubled again. But this time there was no stopping them.

Despite martyrdoms, such as those of Stephen and James the brother of John, and the imprisonment of Peter, the church grew, spilled out over Judea, Samaria, and the whole of Palestine. Then it leaped to Antioch in Syria which, during the first century, was the third city of the Roman Empire and the true crossroads of East and West. From Antioch the newly named "Christians" sent forth as missionaries Barnabas, who had come from Jerusalem to shepherd the vigorous church in Antioch, and Saul of Tarsus, whom Barnabas had befriended in Jerusalem and had called from Tarsus to aid him in Antioch. Their missionary destination was Barnabas's nearby island home of Cyprus, and their targets were first the Jews, and then the Gentiles.

They journeyed, after notable triumphs on Cyprus, to the mainland of Asia Minor, which Saul (now called Paul) apparently felt was ripe for the Christian message. The experience of these two eager apostles, first at Antioch and now in Cyprus and Asia Minor, had confirmed that the gospel had indeed been intended for all and could be well received by the Gentiles as well as the Jews. Thus a milestone in Christian history was passed. The process had begun which would tear Christianity loose from its Jewish exclusiveness and make it a universal movement for all men.

Paul and Barnabas did not break the first ground to extend Christianity to the Gentiles. That had been done on the day of Pentecost

MATTHEW WRITES

Jesus came and told his disciples, "I have been given all authority in heaven and on earth. Therefore, go and make disciples of all the nations, baptizing them in the name of the Father and the Son and the Holy Spirit. Teach these new disciples to obey all the commands I have given you. And be sure of this: I am with you always, even to the end of the age."
Matthew 28:18-20

when people from many parts of the Roman world had heard the message, shortly after the ascension of Jesus. But in the Jerusalem church, conversions of the Gentiles were rare and incidental.

The twelve apostles, now reduced by the death of James to eleven, had remained in Jerusalem or at least in Palestine. It seemed they could not bring themselves to the world apostolate which Jesus had commanded. Soon however, Jewish persecution would force some of them out. The nation of Israel was still not willing to accept Jesus as the Christ. Soon the Twelve would also have to turn to the Gentiles. Paul and Barnabas had successfully shown the way. From this time forth, the apostles would go first to the Jews and then, if rejected, turn to the Gentiles. The book of Acts is the record of how Christianity was thus moved by both example and persecution, out of Jerusalem into the rest of the Roman world, with a universal message to both Jews and Gentiles.

While Rome herself was even more hostile to Christianity than was Jerusalem, many Jews and Gentiles everywhere received the new faith. Within the lifetime of the apostles the gospel of Christ had spread over the long Roman roads, as well as by the sea, to such far-off places as Gaul and Britain to the northwest, Alexandria and Carthage on the coast of Africa to the south, Scythia and Armenia (the former Soviet Union) to the north, and Persia and India to the east. In the course of this initial outburst of Christian fervor, the twelve apostles, and many others also called apostles, carried the Christian message great distances and into perilous lands both near and far, even beyond the Roman Empire. There they died, but their message and the churches they founded survived them.

Early in its progress, Christianity recorded histories and legends which tell of the high adventures the apostles had

> Within the lifetime of the apostles the gospel of Christ had spread to such far-off places as Gaul and Britain, Alexandria and Carthage, Scythia and Armenia, and Persia and India.

in the initial years of Christian expansion. Apparently the apostles themselves did not seem aware that their mission was historic so they kept few records which have remained. Such records as we have, apart from the Scriptures, are not without flaw and often lean toward the fanciful. Yet so much more is to be learned about the apostles than the general Christian public knows, or has ever been written by the scholars in a single history. To this end, this account of the lives of the twelve apostles will serve to illuminate the earliest days of the Christian mission. Hopefully it may help to reestablish the apostles as *real people*.

CHAPTER TWO

WHEN DID THE APOSTLES LEAVE JERUSALEM?

From the hundreds of people who followed him from place to place, Jesus chose twelve to be his apostles. *Apostle* means messenger or authorized representative. The one characteristic they all shared was their willingness to obey Jesus.
—*The Life Application Study Bible*

Luke, who wrote the book of Acts, selected as his thesis the emergence of Christianity as a universal faith, not to be held for long in the matrix of Judaism, but liberated, mainly under the pioneering of Paul, so that the gospel might be presented also to the Gentiles. From first to last in Acts, Luke expresses this theme. Christianity, he wrote, began with God and Jesus Christ, His Son. Upon the rejection of Jesus by the Jewish national and religious leadership, the gospel was presented to the Gentiles as was always intended by God. That methodology is reported many times in Acts.

First, Pentecost was an *international* experience. Jews from many nations were in Jerusalem, but surely, so were many Gentiles. "Here we are—Parthians, Medes, Elamites, people from Mesopotamia, Judaea, Cappadocia, Pontus, the province of Asia, Phrygia, Pamphylia, Egypt, and the areas of Libya around Cyrene, visitors from Rome (both Jews and converts to Judaism), Cretans, and Arabs. And we all hear these people speaking in our own languages about the wonderful things God has done!" (Acts 2:9-11) Then Acts records how Philip witnessed to the Ethiopian treasurer, under the direct leadership of the Holy Spirit. The implication of divine approval and authentication of Gentile evangelism is explicit. Luke is making a point that most modern readers miss.

Next, Peter was directly commanded by God to witness to and to baptize Cornelius, the Roman centurion, at Joppa. Paul was meanwhile shown as the persecutor of the Church *motivated by his zeal for keeping the Law of Moses and the Jews themselves from adulteration.* He hauled into prison those Jewish Christians who would forsake Moses for Christ. No one can accuse Paul of not being initially a faithful Jew, though his critics certainly tried.

After Paul's conversion, Luke records, often as an eyewitness, the growing missionary triumphs of Paul, but carefully notes that Paul nowhere broke the Mosaic Law, but in each city always went *first* to the Jewish synagogue to try to win those Jews who would believe. Only then did he go to the Gentiles after the inevitable persecution in the synagogue. As Luke concluded his story in Acts, Paul was in Rome, having first witnessed to the Jewish religious leaders. He was rejected by most, as usual, so he turned to the Gentiles. There the book of Acts ends.

The book of Acts is a limited, but rich slice of apostolic Christian history. It is the record of only some of the apostles and their deeds. It is the story of the mighty acts of the Holy Spirit in the establishment of the early churches. It is a shining vindication of Paul and of his decision to carry the gospel "to the Jews first and afterwards to the Gentiles." To these purposes, all biblical commentaries abundantly agree. But if we stop here, perhaps we have missed the most compelling of all effects which Luke may have been trying to achieve by writing the book of Acts. *This was to encourage all Jewish Christians to consciously go forth to the Gentile world and, like Paul, bear witness directly to it in full confidence of success. And, like Paul, believing confidently that this was the Holy Spirit's intention and that God would bless their efforts in this mission and crown them with success!*

In a word, Acts is a book of successful procedures in international evangelism. The truths contained in it were aimed to stir up those early Jewish Christians who for too long were bound to Jerusalem and Judea or at least to Judaism.

Biblical scholars have long been troubled by the lengthy time some of the apostles spent in Jerusalem after the Resurrection. It was as if some of them clung to the Temple and Judaism for perhaps a quarter of a century, despite the clear commandment of Jesus to disciple *all* nations.

Even when the apostles occasionally were able, or forced, to lead a Gentile to Christ, they themselves soon returned to Jerusalem. Even when the believers were scattered abroad by persecution and sent everywhere preaching, Luke notes that the apostles *were expected* to remain in Jerusalem, which they did. Why? Possibly because they were reluctant to go forth officially to win Gentiles and start organizing Gentile churches. Who knows the agony or timidity these Jewish men had in breaking with Judaism?

> The lengthy time spent in Jerusalem after the Resurrection seems to infer that some of the apostles clung to Judaism, despite Jesus' clear commandment to disciple *all* nations.

The date of the writing of Acts seems certain to have been about the year AD 66. By then the apostles, for the most part, would surely have already left Jerusalem on their world missions.

But the book of Acts covers a considerable period of time, at least thirty-five years. Perhaps the experiences of Paul provided a direct challenge to the early Christians and even to some of the apostles, to get on with the task which belonged to them from the beginning; opening the whole world and all nations to the gospel. The apostolic council in Jerusalem told Paul, "You go to the Gentiles and we will go to the Jews."

Acts may well have been later used as an historical handbook of methods Paul had triumphantly used, how he fared, and the clear proof that the Holy Spirit was visibly willing, despite all obstacles, to bless a mission to the Gentiles. But though we do not suggest that the apostles were shamed into their task of world evangelism by Acts, for the date of writing precludes this conclusion, it might still be possible that some early portions of the book, or at least the experiences of Paul that were later recorded in the book, might have had this effect.

We know nothing of the "Theophilus" to whom Luke addressed Acts. Theophilus is a Greek name to be sure but it simply means "lover of God." Perhaps, with infinite tact, Paul sought to teach some of the "teachers" a lesson they somehow had not yet all learned. If it had been couched as a frontal attack or criticism they could not have accepted it at the hands of Paul, since they were disciples and apostles before he had ever encountered Christ, and were therefore probably reluctant to accept new light on their duties from this late-comer to the faith.

If these conclusions are sound, that means the early parts of the book of Acts were perhaps intended for some apostles (James having been martyred) as a virtual handbook on "successful methods of witnessing to Gentiles," with due credit carefully given to the anointing of the Holy Spirit in all instances. This possibility is strengthened in the various epistles of Paul, particularly in his reference to Peter's reluctance to even eat with Gentile Christians in Antioch when Jewish Christian emissaries from James in Jerusalem arrived on the scene. "I had to oppose him to his face," said Paul, "for what he did was very wrong" (Galatians 2:11).

Paul, in fact, had experienced the reluctance of the apostles to go to the Gentiles in any systematic way and pointed out their strategy as follows: "In fact, James, Peter, and John, who were known as pillars of the church, recognized the gift God had given me, and they accepted Barnabas and me as their co-workers. They encouraged us to keep preaching to the Gentiles, while they continued their work with the Jews" (Galatians 2:9).

Whether or not one of the purposes of the recording of Paul's experiences, which later grew into what is now called the book of Acts, was to encourage and instruct the apostles and other early

Christian workers in their duty to the Gentiles, that was what in fact eventually resulted. Somewhere, sometime, formally or naturally, the apostles one day apparently decided on a world strategy of evangelism, and each went his separate way.

Eusebius tells us the apostles "divided the world" and set forth to all points of the compass. Was this decision prompted or influenced by the experiences of Paul later recorded in Acts? We cannot know with certainty, but it seems likely, at least, that Paul's success could not possibly have been unnoticed, ignored, or uncopied. There is a fragment of early Christian history which indicates there may be some substance to this idea.

> At the beginning of Book III of his *History of the Church*, after having described the Fall of Jerusalem, Eusebius says that 'the inhabited world' was divided into zones of influence among the Apostles: Thomas in the region of the Parthians, John in Asia, Peter in Pontus and Rome, Andrew in Scythia. This statement contains a certain measure of historical truth, particularly for John, but it is difficult to verify for the others. One fact, however, gives support to it. The apocryphal writings of the *New Testament* are divided into cycles: the cycle of Peter, the cycle of Thomas, the cycle of Philip, the cycle of John. These cycles seem to refer to definite geographical areas, and it seems, in particular, that the Judaeo-Christian mission at the beginning of the second century took several different forms: the Mesopotamian, linked to James and Thomas; Asiatic Christianity, which depends on Philip and John; the Petrine group comprising Phoenicia, Pontus, Achaea and Rome.[1]

A study of what became of the apostles, then, must take into account the possibility that the experience of Paul later recorded in Acts may have served as a catalyst to hasten the decision of the Apostles to go into all the world and preach the gospel. A study of the date of the book of 1 Peter certainly allows time for the book of Acts to have been completed by AD 64. This is mentioned because it is clear from

1 Peter 1:1 that Peter made missionary journeys to Asia Minor before the conclusion of Paul's first Roman imprisonment in AD 64.

But even if Peter became an earlier witness to the Gentiles (despite Galatians 2:9) this does not mean *all* the *other* apostles had also left Jerusalem by AD 64, which is the earliest possible date of the writing of Acts. Nor does it imply that, even if all the apostles had left Jerusalem itself long before AD 64, they had necessarily engaged in a *ministry to the Gentiles* wherever they may have gone, for Jews were found everywhere. To have achieved this, even among some of the apostles, would be a worthwhile purpose for the experiences of Paul to be told and later incorporated in Acts.

In any case, once they had been launched into the far reaches of the Roman Empire, the apostles lit a fire that shines in most of the world to this day.

CHAPTER THREE

SIMON PETER

A servant girl noticed [Peter in the high priest's courtyard.] She said, "This man was one of Jesus' followers!" But Peter denied it. "Woman," he said, "I don't even know him!" After a while someone else looked at him and said, "You must be one of them!" "No, man, I'm not!" Peter retorted. About an hour later someone else insisted, "This must be one of them. . . ." But Peter said, "Man, I don't know what you are talking about." And immediately, while he was still speaking, the rooster crowed. At that moment the Lord turned and looked at Peter. . . . And Peter left the courtyard, weeping bitterly. Luke 22:56-62

O f all the human personalities whom Jesus remade, Simon Peter is the one (next to Paul) about whom we know the most, and the man who seems most like ourselves. As Dr. Stalker has said, "He [Christ] managed the tumultuous and fluctuating elements of his [Peter's] character as a perfect rider does a high mettled horse. He transformed a nature as unstable as water into the consistency of a rock."

The first meeting Jesus had with Simon, He addressed him,

> *Thou art Simon the son of Jona: thou shalt be called Cephas,*
> *which is by interpretation, A stone.* John 1:42, KJV

A great deal of misunderstanding has arisen from the disputes over the real meaning of this word *stone*. Dr. Scofield's footnotes are correct when he comments as follows: "There is in the Greek, a play upon the words *Thou art Peter* (Petros—literally, 'a little rock' or 'pebble') and upon this Rock (Petra) I will build my church. He does not promise to build His church upon Peter, but upon Himself, as Peter himself is careful to tell us" (1 Peter 2:4-9). That there may be no misunderstanding at this point, let the apostle Paul settle the issue once and for all as to what the Foundation of Christianity is:

> For no one can lay any foundation other than the one we already have—Jesus Christ. 1 Corinthians 3:11.

Had Paul ever understood that Peter was the foundation of the church which Christ organized in Jerusalem, he would not have said there is no other foundation but Christ Himself.

Peter's Home in Capernaum

The discovery of Peter's house is a triumph of modern archeology. For most of the twentieth century, with some interruptions, Italian archeologists have been digging and restoring the town of Capernaum. The site is one of the most visited spots in Galilee and yet many tourists who go there do not recognize even yet the real link to the lives of the apostles which has been found there in Peter's actual home. Ancient church history tells the story and has provided the vital clues for the discovery of the history of Peter's house.

> In his Panarion—a treatise on heresies—St. Epiphanius mentions the difficulties encountered in establishing a Christian community in Kfar-Nachum which was still wholly Jewish till the middle of the fourth century. Only when Count Joseph—a convert to Christianity and Governor of Tiberias—managed to obtain from the Emperor Constantine The Great [just a few years before his death in 337] an Imperial decree to build a church on the traditional site of St. Peter's house in Kfar-Nachum—could preparations for this building start. And even then the actual work on site did not begin until 352. In the course of time this modest church was superseded by a splendid basilica frequently mentioned in texts of the Pilgrims who visited it and appreciated its beauty.[1]

In his *New Memoirs of St. Peter by the Sea of Galilee* Virgil Corbo reports:

> From the very first day Jesus visited Capernaum, the building was marked out as 'the home of Simon and Andrew' (Mark 1:29). Here, on the morrow, Jesus healed the mother-in-law of Peter. Here, near the door, he cured a great number of other sick people (Mark 1:33). Subsequently, it is made clear that he passed the night under this roof (Mark 1:35). The house of hospitality is next described as surrounded by such a crush of people seeking Jesus that there was no room even outside (Mark 2:2). To this home Jesus returned after his journeys round the Lake, and after the official election of the twelve apostles (Mark 3:19). It was here that he imparted his more intimate teaching (Mark 7:17). There, one day, his mother appeared, together with his 'brethren' (Mark 3:31).
>
> It was in this very home that Jesus embraced a little child, to give the Twelve a lesson in humility (Mark 9:33-37). Here occurred the miracle of the healing of the paralytic (Mark 2:1-12). The last time the house is mentioned in Mark is when Jesus came back from a tour of preaching (Mark 10:10).
>
> In this list of events in Jesus' life at Capernaum, we make mention only of those involving the house of Simon Peter and Andrew. It has been our good fortune to bring to light this very building, so specially blessed by the presence of Christ.[2]

The archaeologist continues with the detailed description:

> The octagonal basilica was erected as a place of worship, not for any ordinary needs of a Christian community, but as a memorial. It stood over the ruins of a house which, from very ancient times, bore proofs of veneration on the part of the Christian community of Capernaum which was of Jewish origin. All this had been long attested by tradition and was proven true by our excavations.

The latter show most clearly that, beneath the octagonal basilica, there lay buried a complex of small buildings of great antiquity. The architect of the basilica took care to site the central octagon directly above a room which was held in great reverence, and even to follow its very dimensions. At the same time, while removing the upper parts of the ancient buildings, he took care to preserve the latter substantially when he filled in earth round about them. In this respect, one discovery was most striking. To preserve a doorstep which would normally have been built into the foundations, the architect placed a little bridge over it. Thus, we owe this unknown planner a deep debt of gratitude. Designing his octagonal basilica, and placing its floors a metre and a half above those of the ancient dwelling, he could have obliterated the previous structure completely. Instead, he providentially preserved for all posterity its venerated remains.[3]

The archaeologists who have long and painstakingly excavated the house of Peter in Capernaum have unearthed a great deal of interesting and vital information which is not generally known.

The archaeological excavation beneath the pavements of the Byzantine church has not only brought to light a network of habitations of the first century of our era, but has demonstrated with the same evidence also the evolution of a cultic character which made itself known in these habitations around the largest room of the complex. The sacred character of this hall is known from ancient Christian tradition, which has reached us through the testimony of pilgrims; today we know this independently of the testimonies, also from the testimonies of the archaeological excavations, which we will present in a complete manner to scholars in the final publication of these researches.

Peter the Deacon reports an ancient text ascribed to Egeria. "In Capharnaum, however, a church has been made out of the house of the prince of the Apostles; its walls are standing until today as they were. There the Lord cured the paralytic." A writer known as "Anonymous of Piacenza" (570 A.D.) writes, "We likewise came into Capharnaum into the house of blessed Peter, which is now a basilica."[4]

Father Corbo describes the rooms of Peter's house:

The principal and largest room of a very poor habitation was venerated by the Jewish Christians of the first generation and in the following centuries by adapting some dependencies into a place of reunion and of prayer in order to preserve in this place the sacred character which it derived both from the person of the proprietor Peter and also from the consecration given to it by the long stay of the Lord. So whilst around this hall the cult of the primitive Jewish Christians of the community of Capharnaum was centered, the other surrounding rooms continued to throb with the ordinary life of men. The house of Peter, in the following centuries, continued to be indeed the house of the Lord and the house of men.

Among the objects found on the floor of the house church I mention two fishhooks and behind the east wall of the central octagon a small axe for cutting stones.[5]

Father Corbo sums up the conclusions of the findings at Capernaum:

Having reached the end of this report we consider it useful to sum up in a few points the principal discoveries which we made in these first two campaigns of excavation in the area of the Christian church at Capharnaum, constructed over the house of St. Peter.

1) A complex of habitations of the first century of our era has been found in the entire area of the excavation.

2) In this complex of very poor habitations one hall was venerated in a special way from the first century onwards by the local community of Jewish Christians, who transformed

this area into a place of cult, whilst they continued to live in the other rooms next to this one.

3) From the late Roman period (about the fourth century onwards) the community of Jewish Christians of Capharnaum enlarged the primitive house church by adding to the venerated hall an atrium on the east and dependencies on the north by enclosing the entire small *insula* of the house of Peter within a sacred precinct.

4) The belief of the community of Jewish Christians of Capharnaum and of pilgrims in the sanctity of the place, indicated as the house of St. Peter by tradition, finds expression in incisions of symbols and graffiti on the walls of this venerated hall.

5) A church with a central plan (two concentric octagons with a portico on five sides and sacristies and subordinate loci on three other sides) was constructed at Capharnaum towards the middle of the fifth century over the venerated house of St. Peter.[6]

The Conversion of Peter

Peter was brought to Christ by his brother Andrew. They were both fishermen, plying their trade on the Sea of Galilee. Peter was a young man when he first met Jesus Christ, and certainly he was interested in the Messiah. When his brother Andrew announced that he had found the Messiah, Peter eagerly dropped his nets and went along to see for himself. Then he returned to his trade.

It was sometime later that Jesus came to the shores of Galilee and there found Peter who had talked with Him before. There the invitation of Christ came, "Come, follow me, and I will show you how to fish for people!" (Matthew 4:19). Peter and Andrew straightway left their nets and boats and followed Jesus. Peter was married and his mother-in-law apparently lived with him and his wife.

Peter's Personality

Much has been made of Peter's temperament. He was not particularly modest, but usually was self-assertive. He frequently stood in

the early days at the forefront of the apostles and was their spokesman. It remained only for Paul to outshine him. But Peter always
remained firm in the affection of the early Christians as the first
among the great Christians. Though the record indicates that John
and Paul were also highly regarded, nevertheless, in the lists of apostles in the Scriptures, we find the name Peter preceding the rest of
the twelve.

Peter was impulsive. He often acted first and thought second.
He quickly dropped his net at the invitation of Christ. When Jesus
walked across the water, Peter stepped over the side of the boat and
walked on the water toward Him. After the Resurrection, Peter threw
himself into the sea and swam impul-
sively to shore, not waiting for the slow
rowing of the boat.

Peter's character was not at first as
firm as it might have been. He was the
loudest in his avowals of loyalty to Christ
the night before Jesus was seized. That
night, with all the rest, he forsook Him
and cursed His name. Then in another
impulsive reversal, after Jesus looked at
him, Peter went out and wept bitterly.

Peter was a rare combination of courage and cowardice, of great strength
and regrettable instability. Christ spoke

Peter was a rare
combination of courage
and cowardice, of
great strength and
regrettable instability.
He sinned as grievously
as Judas. The only
difference was that
Peter repented and
Judas did not.

more often to Peter than to any other of His disciples, both in blame
and praise. No other disciple is so pointedly reproved by our Lord as
Peter, and no disciple ever ventured to reprove his Master but Peter!
However, by degrees and under the teaching and example and the
training of Christ, Peter's overly tempestuous character was gradually
brought under control, until finally after Pentecost it became the
personification of faithfulness to Christ.

There was one redeeming factor about Peter's character and that
was his exquisite sense of sin. He was extremely sensitive and tender

in his spirit in this respect. It was Peter who said, "Oh, Lord, please leave me—I'm too much of a sinner to be around you" (Luke 5:8). Peter sinned as grievously as Judas did. Judas sold Jesus. Peter cursed Him. There is no essential difference, except that Peter repented and Judas did not. It is revealing to read from Peter's own epistle the following words written in the evening of his life.

> I am warning you ahead of time, dear friends. Be on guard so that you will not be carried away by the errors of these wicked people and lose your own secure footing. Rather, you must grow in the grace and knowledge of our Lord and Savior Jesus Christ. All glory to him, both now and forever! Amen."
> 2 Peter 3:17-18

Facts the New Testament Reveals about Peter

In the book of Acts, note that Peter takes a unique and early position of importance in the church in Jerusalem. In fact the first division of Acts is composed largely of the "Acts of Peter," just as the second division of the book contains the stories of the "Acts of Paul." The book of Acts was originally written to show the transition of Christianity from a Jewish sect to a world faith. Therefore, the story of Peter is told there so that we might see how Peter, who had the leadership position in the early church, carried the gospel beyond the boundaries of the Jewish world into the Gentile world. Then the story is transferred to Paul who became uniquely the apostle to the Gentiles.

It was Peter who prompted the choice of the twelfth disciple to take the place of Judas. It was he who spoke to the assembled multitude on the day of Pentecost. It was he who performed the healing miracle on the lame man. In Galatians 2:9, Paul speaks of Peter with James and John as "pillars" of the church. It was Peter who defended the cause of the gospel when the Jewish authorities took action against the apostles. He exercised church discipline in the congregation in the case of Ananias and Sapphira. He also spoke out against Simon, the magician who sought to buy the gift of the Holy Spirit.

The book of Acts emphasizes the faith of the common people in the miraculous power of Peter. They considered his shadow capable of effecting a healing. Peter was delegated by the Twelve in Jerusalem to go to Samaria to look into the genuineness of the spiritual renewal which was going on there under the direction of Philip. Following this, Peter appeared in missionary activities in Lydda, Joppa, and Caesarea, where he is especially mentioned as having been led to baptize the household of the Gentile, Cornelius.

Finally Peter appeared at the apostolic council where he defended the inclusion of Gentiles in the Christian movement. From this point Peter disappears from the narrative in Acts. Paul mentions him in his epistles only in regard to Peter's mistake in Antioch when he feared the Jewish Christians from Jerusalem who demanded separation from the Gentile Christians on the part of Jewish Christians. Paul says in his statement that Peter was to blame and that therefore he, *Paul, had to oppose him to his face!* Peter apparently backed down before Paul's fierce logic.

We are on certain ground in tracing Peter to Corinth after Paul had founded the church there and before Paul wrote his epistles to the Corinthians. Jean Danielou observes:

> In Corinth the memory of Peter was closely associated with that of Paul by the bishop Dionysius. It is evident from the *Letter* that Clement of Rome wrote to the members of the Church at the beginning of the second century that there were links between Corinth and Rome, with which Peter and Paul were also associated. The *Letter* shows that the town was torn by discord, the presbyters against another party, perhaps that of the deacons.[7]

In the *Epistles of Ignatius* there is a reference to Peter at Antioch. Eusebius quotes the passage:

> About this time flourished Polycarp in Asia, an intimate disciple of the Apostles, who received the episcopate of the church

at Smyrna, at the hands of the eyewitnesses and servants of the Lord. At this time, also, Papias was well known as bishop of the church at Hierapolis, a man well skilled in all manner of learning, and well acquainted with the Scriptures. Ignatius, also, who is celebrated by many even to this day, as the successor of Peter at Antioch, was the second that obtained the episcopal office there.[8]

The church historian Jean Danielou discusses the presence of Peter at Antioch:

> It remains true that if the Church of Antioch was not typically Petrine, it had many ties with Peter; we have seen that he had stayed there at a very early date. The Petrine apocryphal writings were popular in Antioch, as Theophilus and Serapion show. The *Ascension of Isaiah* is the first work to mention Peter's martyrdom. Antiochene Judaeo-Christianity thus appears as representing the Petrine position. We have also noticed its links with the Phoenician sector, which was specially dependent on Peter. The same links are to be found in the other regions which came under Peter's influence and which were in communication with Antioch.
>
> Eusebius tells us that Pontus and the neighbouring regions of Bithynia, Cappadocia and Galatia were dependent on Peter; other facts confirm this. The *First Epistle of Peter* was addressed to the Christians of these regions. That may be the source of Eusebius's information, but this hypothesis is far from certain, since there is other evidence for the link. Pontus and Cappadocia are geographically an extension of North Syria and it was in that direction that Syria usually expanded. In a letter of Dionysius, Bishop of Corinth in the middle of the second century, we see the links between Corinth and Pontus. Now Corinth was in Peter's sphere of influence. In the Paschal controversy, the bishops of Pontus were in agreement with the Bishop of Rome and in disagreement with the Asiatic bishops.[9]

There is widespread confirmation that Peter did indeed make Antioch his headquarters. Catholic scholar Hugo Hoever writes in his *Lives of the Saints,* "Church historians affirm positively that St. Peter founded the See of Antioch before he went to Rome. Antioch was then the capital of the East. St. Gregory the Great states that the Prince of the Apostles was Bishop of that city for seven years."[10]

In the memorial book called *Souvenir of India* in an article by V. K. George entitled "The Holy See of Seleucia—Ctesiphon," the traditions of the church of the East are recorded.

> Meanwhile, the Apostles set out to preach the Gospel. The first missionary field of the Apostles was the Jews. They were their own racial kinsmen. They were the people who were waiting for the coming of the Messiah. Hence the work among them was very easy. "The Apostles had only to add a few articles to their existing faith that the Messiah had come; that he had died for their sins and risen for their salvation; that he had ascended into heaven and had sent His Holy Spirit to his disciples; and that he was to be worshipped as God."
>
> At that time Mesopotamia was one of the strongest centers of Jews. It was there that the "Lost Tribes" were living. They were very rich and influential and they had commercial settlements in many places on the coast of India, Ceylon, Malaya and on the farthest coast of China. We see that Jesus Himself had sent the seventy apostles to Mesopotamia during his ministry on earth.
>
> And therefore it was natural that the Apostles chose that area for their first missionary activity. *St. Thaddeus,* (Mar Addai) went to Edessa to fulfill the promise of Our Lord to King Abgar of Edessa. St. Peter also preached the Gospel in Babylon and the Holy Bible proves it: "The chosen Church which is in Babylon and Mark, my son, salute you" (1 Peter 5:13). *St. Thomas* had worked among the Jews of Mesopotamia and later on went in search of their small colonies on the coast of India and reached

Cranganore in 52 A.D. *St. Bartholomew* and Mar Mari of the Seventy were also the founders of this Church.

As in the Roman Empire, so also in the Persian Empire, Christianity had the beginning in important cities and spread into the interior. Thus Antioch, Corinth, Ephesus, Alexandria, Rome, etc., in the Roman Empire and Edessa, Arbil, Seleucia-Ctesiphon, etc., in the Persian Empire became strong Christian centres.[11]

The Coptic Church historians agree with the Roman Catholics:

Moreover, Eusebius asserts that the church of Antioch was founded by St. Peter, who became its first bishop even before his translation to the See of Rome. According to tradition, he presided for seven years over the newly established Antiochene church, from 33 to 40 A.D., when he nominated St. Euodius as his vicar before departure to the West. While the circle of preaching the Gospel was widened toward the East in Edessa, Nisibis and distant Malabar by the Apostle Thomas and Mar Addai (St. Thaddaeus), the fall of Jerusalem in the year 70 A.D. could only have increased the number of Christian Jewish emigrants to Antioch.[12]

Here we must part company with Eusebius. There is no evidence that Peter was in Rome as early as AD 44. It is much more likely that he was in Babylon, as the Eastern churches claim. In the book of Romans, Paul makes no reference to Peter. The book of 1 Peter comes from Babylon according to the plain statement of the writer. Peter could hardly have been in Rome until after the epistle of Romans was written since he apparently stopped over in Corinth after Paul was there, as Paul states in 1 Corinthians.

There are, as we have noted, Paul's references in 1 Corinthians that indicate that Peter had visited Corinth and preached there for a while. Apparently Peter took his wife with him on his journey as we learn in 1 Corinthians 9:5. Having been in prison twice in the city of Jerusalem, Peter left and went into other parts of the world. His epistle notes that it was written in "Babylon." Many have wondered if this did not mean Rome which was frequently called Babylon by the early Christians.

The actual city of Babylon, however, still was of importance. It was a great center of Jewish colonists and was a powerful center when Peter ministered there for a time. The Eastern churches trace their lineage to Babylon, and hence to Peter, to this day. In Acts 12:17, we are told that Peter "went to another place." We do not know if this was Babylon, nor, if he went, how long he stayed. But the tradition of the Eastern churches is united that he did indeed go to Babylon, from which he wrote his first epistle.

There was no need to use Babylon as a symbol of Rome as there was later when John wrote the book of Revelation. John

PETER WRITES

"There is wonderful joy ahead, even though you have to endure many trials for a little while. These trials will show that your faith is genuine. You love [Jesus Christ] even though you have never seen him. Though you do not see him now, you trust him; . . . The reward for trusting him will be the salvation of your souls." 1 Peter 1:6-7, 8-9

was writing literature deliberately designed to pass the Roman censors but obviously Peter was not. According to Galatians 2:9, a decision had been reached by the apostles in Jerusalem to the effect that Paul and his fellow-workers were to keep preaching to the Gentiles, while the missionaries from Jerusalem (Peter and others) went to the circumcised (that is, the Jews).

Thus Peter was identified from the beginning with the Jewish party within Christianity as Paul was identified with the Gentile party, though there are many evidences that both men went over the line and dealt with people of the other group. One should not imagine, however, that Peter considered himself the opponent of Paul, despite Paul's arguments as recorded in Galatians. Peter, himself, no doubt stood nearer to Paul than did the other members of the Jerusalem church. Likewise, there is no evidence that Paul ever recognized the primacy of Peter in his relationship to Paul. And in Corinth, Paul did not permit a "Cephas party" any more than he did any other party.

Did Peter Evangelize the Area to the North of Rome?

In his exhaustive but not generally accepted study of early Christianity, George F. Jowett outlines the various speculations and traditions about the apostle Peter. In his book *The Drama of the Lost Disciples*, he creates a scenario based upon various apocryphal and doubtful sources:

> Peter fled direct to Britain. This is affirmed by Cornelius in Lapide in his work *Argumentum Epistolae St. Pauli ad Romanos*, in which he answers the question as to why St. Paul does not salute St. Peter in his *Epistle to the Romans*. He replies: "Peter, banished with the rest of the Jews from Rome, by the edict of Claudius, was absent in Britain."
>
> Peter, acting as a free-lance missionary, stemming from Avalon, preached in Britain during the Caradoc-Claudian war. While in Britain he became well acquainted with the members of the two branches of the Royal Silurian House of Arviragus and Caractacus. He knew the children of Caractacus years before they went into Roman captivity. Years after, when the British family became well established in Rome, he was naturally attracted to the home of the Pudens at the Palatium Britannicum. The visits of both Peter and Paul, with the family of the Pudens, is referred to in Scripture. Other ancient records state that the children of Claudia and Rufus Pudens were raised at the knees of Peter and Paul and other disciples, particularly naming St. Paul, for reasons stated in a former chapter.
>
> There is plenty of evidence to show that Peter visited Britain and Gaul several times during his lifetime, his last visit to Britain taking place shortly before his final arrest and crucifixion in Nero's circus at Rome.
>
> In Gaul, Peter became the Patron Saint of Chartres, by reason of his preference to preach in the famous Druidic rock

temple known as *The Grotte des Druides*. This is considered to be the oldest Druidic site in Gaul, on which is built the oldest cathedral in France.

Of his visits in Britain we have the corroboration of Eusebius Pamphilis, A.D. 306, whom Simon Metaphrastes quotes as saying: "St. Peter to have been in Britain as well as in Rome."

Further proof of Peter's sojourn in Britain was brought to the light of day in recent times when an ancient, time-worn monument was excavated at Whithorn. It is a rough hewn stone standing 4 feet high by 15 inches wide. On the face of this tablet is an inscription that reads: "Locvs Sancti Petri Apvstoli" (the Place of St. Peter the Apostle).

The eminent Dean Stanley, writing in his works of the beloved Apostle, claims that the vision that came to St. Peter, foretold his doom: "Knowing that shortly I must put off this my tabernacle, even as our Lord Jesus Christ hast shewed me" (2 Peter 1:14), appeared to St. Peter on his last visit to Britain, on the very spot where once stood the old British church of Lambedr (St. Peter's), where stands the present Abbey of St. Peter, Westminster. Shortly afterwards Peter returned to Rome, where he was later executed.

The first church dedicated to Peter was founded by King Lucius, the British King, who was the first by royal decree to proclaim Christianity the national faith of Britain in Winchester A.D. 156.

The church was erected A.D. 179, to the affectionate memory of St. Peter, in commemoration of his evangelizing labours in Britain. It is still known as "St. Peter's of Cornhill" and bears the legend on its age-worn walls relating the historic fact and dates by the order of King Lucius, the descendant of Arviragus, preserved to this day for all to see and read.[13]

Jowett may be suspected of placing too much reliance on late or doubtful documentation, but there are some who agree with him. J. W. Taylor observes:

Two other traditions of first-century Christian missions, but belonging to a slightly later period, demand some attention as also bearing on Western Christianity.

The first is the tradition of "St. Maternus," and is connected with all the old country of the Treviri and Tungri beyond the Alps.

Here, and especially at Trier (or Tréves), the Romans had formed important colonies some fifty years before the coming of Christ; and although, as in Britain, there were frequent uprisings against the power of Rome, the Romans maintained their supremacy for two hundred years or more.

Nowhere so far north are the Roman remains and ruins so rich, so fine, and so remarkable as they are in Tréves today.

And the first Christian mission to Tréves is represented as partly Roman and partly Hebrew, as coming direct from Rome by the authority of St. Peter, and in the course or channel of Roman colonization.

In some of these points it differs entirely from those we have been considering. The tradition also has other points of very considerable interest. It runs as follows:

Three Saints—Eucharius, Valerius and Maternus—all of whom had been pupils of St. Peter at Rome, were sent by him to Trier to preach the gospel of Christ.

Eucharius was appointed as bishop, and Valerius and Maternus as his assistants. Maternus was of Hebrew birth, and came from the little town of Nain in Palestine, being "the only son of his mother," whom Christ had raised from the dead. But no special honour was at this time accorded him. He was the least of the three missionary disciples, one of the "personal witnesses" who, as long as they lived, accompanied the other evangelists in most of their distant journeys.

But though ready to take the lowest place among his Greek and Roman companions, Maternus appears to have been most active in his apostolic labours. For while all three—Eucharius,

Valerius and Maternus—are associated with the foundation of the church at Trier and Cologne (the scene of their chief labours at Trier being a little outside the present city, on the site of the old St. Matthiaskirche), Maternus alone is represented as pushing forward and reaching the farthest settlement of Tongres, where he is said to have built a little church which he dedicated to the Blessed Virgin—the first church beyond the Alps dedicated to her name and memory ('Ecclesia Tungrensis prima cis Alpes beatae Mariae Virgini consecrata').[14]

One could wish that Taylor was on firmer and more widely confirmed historical ground. But there certainly is no reason why Peter could not have visited Great Britain. Many believe he did. Like most other Christians in the world, the British believers of the early Middle Ages sought to claim a number of apostles as having had some association with their forebears. The more one studies the early history of Britain, the more possible this claim appears. Those who have a classical education (that is, studies in the Latin classics) often apparently tend to draw most of their impressions from the war chronicles of Julius Caesar. They are perhaps forgetting that *The Gallic War* is not only history but also Caesar's personally slanted political propaganda. The Britons offered stout and intelligent resistance to the Roman conquest as Caesar found out to his dismay, something primitives could not have done.

Archaeological discoveries in Britain confirm that a viable civilization had developed there as far back as the time of the Phoenicians whose traces have been found in England. It is Caesar who has pictured them as painted savages very much like American Indians before Columbus. This impression is absolutely wrong. Perhaps the civilization of Britain was not as far advanced as Taylor and Jowett would like to believe. But the use of the wheel and the knowledge of metallurgy which existed in Britain long before the time of Caesar (circa 60-40 BC) clearly indicates civilization far in advance, for example, of that of the Aztecs at the time of the conquest of Cortez (AD 1519) who used neither wheels nor iron.

Considering this relatively advanced civilization, it is not difficult to believe that some of the apostles visited England. Did they not believe that theirs was the commission to take the gospel *to the ends of the earth*? Whether they did or did not go to England is not provable, but it is not unlikely or impossible.

Peter and Rome

The common tradition that Peter founded the church at Rome is unverifiable. Paul could hardly have named so many Roman Christians in the last chapter of Romans if there had not been churches there long before any possible visit of Peter. Jean Danielou observes however:

> Was Paul's the only mission to the West? The Acts tells us that in 43, after the death of James, Peter left Jerusalem "for another place" (Acts 12:17). He is lost from sight until 49 when we find him at the Council of Jerusalem. No canonical text has anything to say about his missionary activity during this time. But Eusebius writes that he came to Rome about 44, at the beginning of Claudius's reign (*HE* II, 14, 61). It seems certain that Rome was evangelized during the period from 43 to 49. Suetonius says that Claudius expelled the Jews in 50, because they were growing agitated "at the prompting of Chrestos." This shows that discussions between Jews and Judaeo-Christians were taking place, leading to conflicts which came to the ear of the emperor. In fact at Corinth in 51 Paul met some converted Jews driven from Rome by Claudius: Aquila and Priscilla. In 57 Paul addressed the community of Rome, already considered important. In 60 he found communities established in Puteoli and in Rome.[15]

However, as we have pointed out, Peter was probably in Babylon from AD 44 to 49 rather than in Rome. We cannot imagine the silence of Acts if Peter had been in Rome during that time. In any case this period (AD 44–49) seems to be the only time which Peter could have been in Babylon, which was located on the great Roman highway as the next great city to the east of Antioch.

There is no serious attempt by any reputable modern scholar to find the presence of Peter in Rome before Paul wrote the book of Romans to the band of Christians that had already grown to some size in that capital city of the first century world. On the other hand, Peter had to die and be buried somewhere and Christian tradition has been in agreement from the earliest times that it was actually in Rome that Peter died. No less a Protestant theologian and historian than Adolph Harnack wrote that, "to deny the Roman stay of Peter is an error which today is clear to every scholar who is not blind. The martyr death of Peter at Rome was once con-tested by reason of Protestant prejudice." The Protestant theologian H. Lietzmann has come to the conclusion that the testi-mony from the year 170 concerning the graves of the two apostles at Rome must be correct. That is, that the two apostles (Peter and Paul) were actually buried in two places in Rome.

> Peter had to die and be buried somewhere. Christian tradition has been in agreement from the earliest times that Peter died in Rome.

Perhaps one authoritative word has been written by Oscar Cullmann. In his book, *Peter. Disciple. Apostle. Martyr*, he presents an argument based upon First Clement 5:24, in which he inferred from this text that the martyrdoms of Peter and Paul took place in Rome.

Excavations of St. Peter's Basilica in Rome

Since the end of World War II great interest has been focused upon the excavations under the church of St. Peter in Rome. It has now been officially announced by the Pope that the grave of Peter has been found. Most scholars today accept the Roman stay of Peter. It is possible that Revelation 11:3-13 contains a cryptic account of the martyrdom of Paul and Peter in Rome. That this passage is both historic and prophetic is evident. The historical aspect of it may be a reference to the death of Paul and Peter in Rome, though this text seems to point primarily to a future fulfillment.

Near the close of the gospel of John there is a hint given as to the manner of Peter's death. It agrees with the tradition which has been long with us that Nero had Peter crucified head-downward on the Vatican Hill. Jesus says to Peter:

> *When you were young, you were able to do as you liked; you dressed yourself and went wherever you wanted to go. But when you are old, you will stretch out your hands, and others will dress you and take you where you don't want to go.* John 21:18

It is universally recognized that these words are intended as a prediction of the martyrdom of Peter for the following verses tell us that these words speak of the kind of death that Peter was going to die to glorify God. The phrase "stretch out your hands" may indicate the manner of execution, which is crucifixion.

Finally, it must be noted that in the entire scope of the very earliest Christian literature there is complete silence concerning the death of Peter. We certainly do not even have the slightest reference that points to any other place besides Rome which could be considered as the scene of his death. And in favor of Rome, there are important traditions that he did actually die in Rome. In the second and third centuries when certain churches were in rivalry with those in Rome it never occurred to a single one of them to contest the claim of Rome that it was the scene of the martyrdom of Peter.

In *The Christian Centuries* Danielou shares an allusion to St. Peter's visit to Rome by writing, "A certain Paron puts his house (aedes) at the disposal of St. Peter, as well as its inner garden, which could hold five hundred persons."[16]

Perhaps we can get a realistic impression about Peter's final days in Rome from Jowett:

> Maliciously condemned, Peter was cast into the horrible, fetid prison of the Mamertine. There, for nine months, in absolute darkness, he endured monstrous torture manacled to a post.

Never before or since has there been a dungeon of equal horror. Historians write of it as being the most fearsome on the brutal agenda of mankind. Over three thousand years old, it is probably the oldest torture chamber extant, the oldest remaining monument of bestiality of ancient Rome, a bleak testimony to its barbaric inhumanity, steeped in Christian tragedy and the agony of thousands of its murdered victims. It can be seen to this day, with the dungeon and the pillar to which Peter was bound in chains.

This dreaded place is known by two names. In classical history it is referred to as Gemonium or the Tullian Keep. In later secular history it is best known as the Mamertine. At this time it is not out of place to pause in our story to describe this awesome pit, if only to provide us who live so securely today with a slight reminder of what the soldiers of Christ suffered for our sake, so we may be quickened the better to appreciate the substance of our Christian heritage.

The Mamertine is described as a deep cell cut out of solid rock at the foot of the capitol, consisting of two chambers, one over the other. The only entrance is through an aperture in the ceiling. The lower chamber was the death cell. Light never entered and it was never cleaned. The awful stench and filth generated a poison fatal to the inmates of the dungeon, the most awful ever known. Even as early as 50 B.C. the historian Sallust describes it in the following words:

"In the prison called the Tullian, there is a place about ten feet deep. It is surrounded on the sides by walls and is closed above by a vaulted roof of stone. The appearance of it from the filth, the darkness and the smell is terrible."

No one can realize what its horrors must have been a hundred years later when Peter was imprisoned in its depths.

In this vile subterranean rock the famed Jugurtha was starved and went stark raving mad. Vercingetorix, the valorous Druidic Gaulish chieftain, was murdered by the order of Julius Caesar.

It is said that the number of Christians that perished within this diabolic cell is beyond computation—such is the glory of Rome.

One can re-read the denouncing words of the noble Queen Boadicea, with profit. She branded them for what they were. These people of the Roman purple, who scorned all their enemies as barbarian, were the greatest and most cruel barbarians of all time.

How Peter managed to survive those nine long dreadful months is beyond human imagination. During his entire incarceration he was manacled in an upright position, chained to the column, unable to lay down to rest. Yet, his magnificent spirit remained undaunted. It flamed with the immortal fervour of his noble soul proclaiming the Glory of God, through His Son, Jesus Christ. History tells us the amazing fact that in spite of all the suffering Peter was subjected to, he converted his gaolers, Processus, Martinianus, and forty-seven others.

It is a strange and curious circumstance that the chair, or throne of Pius IX, at the Vatican Council, was erected directly over the altar of Processus and Marinianus. (sic)

Peter, the Rock, as he predicted, met his death at Rome by the hands of the murderous Romans, who crucified him, according to their fiendish manner. He refused to die in the same position as our Lord, declaring he was unworthy. Peter demanded to be crucified in the reverse position, with his head hanging downward. Ironically enough, this wish was gratified by the taunting Romans in Nero's circus AD 67.[17]

The Legends of Peter and Paul

Legends, unlike traditions, have at best only grains of truth in them and those grains may be impossible to find. However, there is a persistent legend regarding Peter and Simon the sorcerer which, at least has its beginnings in the historical account in the book of Acts where

Peter denounced Simon for trying to purchase the Holy Spirit. The legend about the aftermath is as follows:

> The magician, vanquished by a superior power, flung his books into the Dead Sea, broke his wand, and fled to Rome, where he became a great favorite of the Emperor Claudius, and afterwards of Nero. Peter bent on counteracting the wicked sorceries of Simon, followed him to Rome. About two years after his arrival he was joined there by the Apostle Paul. Simon Magus having asserted that he was himself a god, and could raise the dead, Peter and Paul rebuked his impiety, and challenged him to a trial of skill in the presence of the emperor. The arts of the magician failed; Peter and Paul restored the youth to life and on many other occasions Simon was vanquished and put to shame by the miraculous power of the Apostles. At length he undertook to fly up to heaven in sight of the emperor and the people; and, crowned with laurel, and supported by demons, he flung himself from a tower, and appeared for a while to float thus in the air, but St. Peter, falling on his knees commanded the demons to let go their hold, and Simon, precipitated to the ground, was dashed to pieces.[18]

The same book records the early church fathers' beliefs in the stories of Peter and Simon the magician:

> There can be no doubt that there existed in the first century a Simon, a Samaritan, a pretender to divine authority and supernatural powers; who, for a time, had many followers; who stood in a certain relation to Christianity; and who may have held some opinions more or less similar to those entertained by the most famous heretics of the early ages, the Gnostics. Irenaeus calls this Simon the father of all heretics. "All those," he says, "who in any way corrupt the truth, or mar the preaching of the Church, are disciples and successors of Simon, the Samaritan magician." Simon gave himself forth as a god, and

carried about with him a beautiful woman named Helena, who he represented as the first conception of his—that is, of the divine—mind, the symbol or manifestation of that portion of spirituality which had become entangled in matter.[19]

So notable a figure as Peter would, of course, have more legends created about him than the Simon the magician story. Another example that Anna Jameson notes:

> The Apostle Peter had a daughter born in lawful wedlock, who accompanied him in his journey from the East. Being at Rome with him, she fell sick of a grievous infirmity which deprived her of the use of her limbs. And it happened that as the disciples were at meat with him in his house, one said to him, "Master, how is it that thou, who healest the infirmities of others, dost not heal thy daughter Petronilla?"
>
> And St. Peter answered, "It is good for her to remain sick." But, that they might see the power that was in the word of God, he commanded her to get up and serve them at table, which she did; and having done so, she lay down again helpless as before; but many years afterwards, being perfected by her suffering, and praying fervently, she was healed. Petronilla was wonderfully fair; and Valerius Flaccus, a young and noble Roman, who was a heathen, became enamored of her beauty, and sought her for his wife; and he being very powerful, she feared to refuse him; she therefore desired him to return in three days, and promised that he should then carry her home. But she prayed earnestly to be delivered from this peril; and when Flaccus returned in three days with great pomp to celebrate the marriage, he found her dead. The company of nobles who attended him carried her to the grave, in which they laid her, crowned with roses; and Flaccus lamented greatly.
>
> The legend places her death in the year 98, that is thirty-four years after the death of St. Peter; but it would be in vain to attempt to reconcile the dates and improbabilities of this story.[20]

We are on firmer historical ground in the records of the church fathers regarding the death of Peter himself.

> Thus Nero publicly announcing himself as the chief enemy of God, was led on in his fury to slaughter the Apostles. Paul is therefore said to have been beheaded at Rome, and Peter to have been crucified under him. And this account is confirmed by the fact, that the names of Peter and Paul still remain in the cemeteries of that city even to this day. But likewise, a certain ecclesiastical writer, Caius by name, who was born about the time of Zephyrinus bishop of Rome, disputing with Proclus the leader of the Phrygian sect, gives the following statement respecting the places where the earthly tabernacles of the afore-said Apostles are laid. 'But I can show,' says he, 'the trophies of the Apostles. For if you will go to the Vatican, or to the Ostian road, you will find the trophies of those who have laid the foundation of this church. And that both suffered martyrdom about the same time, Dionysius bishop of Corinth bears the following testimony, in his discourse addressed to the Romans. "Thus, likewise you, by means of this admonition, have mingled the flourishing seed that had been planted by Peter and Paul at Rome and Corinth. For both of these having planted us at Corinth, likewise instructed us; and having in like manner taught in Italy, they suffered martyrdom about the same time." This testimony I have superadded, in order that the truth of the history might be still more confirmed.[21]

There is much evidence that Peter chose Mark as his secretary or *amanuensis*.

> Peter's claim to literary fame rests more firmly on his relation to the Gospel of Mark. Papias of Hierapolis recorded the fact that "Mark, the interpreter of Peter, wrote down carefully what he remembered, both the sayings and the deeds of Christ, but not in chronological order, for he did not hear the Lord and he did

not accompany him. At a later time, however, he did accompany Peter, who adapted his instruction to the needs [of his hearers], but not with the object of making a connected series of discourses of our Lord. So Mark made no mistake in writing the individual discourses in the order in which he recalled them."

On this authority it is believed that Mark served as translator for Peter when he preached in Rome. As Peter told and retold his experiences with Jesus, Mark interpreted them again and again to Christian groups. This frequent repetition gave Mark an almost verbatim memory of Peter's recollections. After the death of Peter, Mark, realizing the value of Peter's first-hand account, recorded what he remembered so clearly in the document we know as the first of the Gospel records. Matthew and Luke obviously used Mark's Gospel in the writing of their lives of Jesus. In this manner Peter became the source for our earliest Gospel and thus to a large extent supplied the material for the first written record of our Lord. If this reconstruction of events is accurate, Mark's Gospel can be considered Peter's personal remembrance of his life with Jesus. As such it remains one of Peter's greatest contributions to the Christian Church.[22]

John's Gospel hints at the manner of Peter's death—that Emperor Nero had Peter crucified head-downward on the Vatican Hill.

Seventeenth century writer Dorman Newman wrote in *The Lives and Deaths of the Holy Apostles* that "Peter was led to the top of the Vatican Mount near the TYBUR and crucified with his head downwards. His body was embalmed by Marcellinus the Presbyter after the Jewish manner, then buried in the Vatican near the Triumphal Way. Over his body a small church was erected. It was destroyed by Heliogalachis."[23]

Dorman Newmann apparently had sources unavailable to us which possibly cast more light on Peter's burial:

His [Peter's] body was removed to the cemetery in the Appian Way, 2 miles from Rome where it rested obscurely until the Reign of Constantine [who] rebuilt and enlarged the Vatican to the honor of St. Peter.

The appearance of St. Peter was as follows: His body was slender of a middle size inclining to tallness. His complexion pail [sic] and almost white. His beard curled and thick but short. His eyes black but flecked with red due to frequent weeping. Eye brows thin or none at all.[24]

Robert Grant's Roman history *Augustus to Constantine*, contains an interesting insight regarding controversies about the propriety of the early Christians' veneration of apostolic burial places.

The Montanist Proclus argued that the tombs of the four daughters of Philip, all prophetesses in New Testament times, were still to be seen at Hierapolis in Asia. Gaius replied that he could point out the "trophies" of the Apostles (Peter and Paul) who founded the Roman church; they were on the Vatican hill and by the Ostian Way.

This interest in tombs was fairly widespread among Asian Christians and was certainly present at Rome as early as the middle of the second century. It did not spring into existence at that time, for in the *New Testament* itself we read of the burial of John the Baptist and of the martyr Stephen. Ignatius of Antioch expected wild beasts to be his tomb, but this was a special case. Polycarp of Smyrna was carefully buried, even though a reference to an annual commemoration in the late second century may be an interpolation in the story of his martyrdom.[25]

The head of Peter is said to be entombed in the Cathedral of St. John Lateran. The guidebook furnished to pilgrims there makes the following statements regarding this traditional resting place, but it gives no explanation of how the head of Peter came to be there. "The central Altar is called the Papal Altar, because only the Pope can celebrate Mass there. . . . Behind the grille, aloft, in bust of silver gilt, are preserved the relics of the heads of St. Peter and St. Paul."[26]

Archaeological Discoveries of Peter's Relics

One story concerning the burial of Peter appeared in December 1971 in *National Geographic*. This account, quoted by permission, provides Catholic archaeological and ecclesiastical conclusions regarding the burial place of St. Peter. This report is interesting not only because of its conclusions, but because it provides an authoritative description of the steps by which those conclusions were reached.

> Tradition holds that he was crucified upside down in Nero's Circus near Vatican Hill. His body was given to his friends, and he was buried close by.
>
> . . . When Julius II pulled much of it down and began the church that is there today, the tomb of St. Peter was lost to view. Historians thought Peter's bones were gone, his tomb sacked long before by Saracens.
>
> . . . In 1939, while excavations were being made for Pius XI's tomb, Pius XII gave orders that the digging was to be extended in a search for the tomb of St. Peter. This 'village' was one of the great discoveries. The houses and simpler tombs under them dated from the first to the third centuries A.D. They proved beyond doubt that Constantine had built St. Peter's over a cemetery.
>
> But an even more exciting discovery was involved. A Roman presbyter named Gaius, who lived in the second and third centuries, had seen a grave memorial to St. Peter, and had mentioned it in a letter, a fragment of which has come down to us. Right under the papal altar, early in the excavations, a small ruined monument was found. This could well be the memorial Gaius had seen. At its foot was a slab like a gravestone let into the ground. The excavators raised it. They found a grave, but it was quite empty. Some bones were discovered nearby. For

several years they were believed to be the bones of Peter, but anthropological study established that they were actually the bones of more than one person.

Inscription leads to a startling find
The drama builds as the article continues:

> That would have been that, except for one obstinate and learned woman, Margherita Guarducci. She is a professor at the University of Rome, and she deciphers ancient inscriptions.
>
> She spent six years studying the scribblings made by Christian pilgrims on two old walls above the empty grave. One graffito on the older wall, when deciphered, delivered an electrifying message: "Peter is within." In the other wall was a recess lined with marble. To her it was clearly an ossuary, a niche for someone's bones. Had any been found?
>
> The professor got hold of a workman who seemed to remember that something had been found there years ago, but he thought it was a piece of wall with a graffito. Undaunted, she searched St. Peter's storage rooms. There in a box marked for graffiti, she found bones.
>
> The bones, she learned were indeed from the ossuary in the ancient wall. Ten years before, a monsignor, during his daily inspection of the excavations had put the bones in a plain wooden box and deposited it in storage.

Pope Paul resolves a scholarly dispute
Journalist Aubrey Menen concludes the article:

> Professor Guarducci had the bones examined by Professor Venerando Corrnti, an anthropologist of the University of Rome, who, as she puts it, "entirely bore out what could be expected for the bones found in the only niche built by Constantine in his monument to St. Peter."
>
> It was plain to her what had happened. When Constantine had erected the first St. Peter's, he had cautiously moved the

bones of the saint from his grave to this hiding place, a few feet away, to protect them from deterioration and grave robbers.

That the bones Professor Guarducci found are those of St. Peter, she has no doubt. They are the bones of a man of 60 or 70, and in a box with them were bits of earth and shreds of purple-and-gold cloth. The age tallies with Peter's traditional age at the time of his crucifixion. Tradition says that he was buried in plain earth. And when Constantine had the bones removed to the niche, it would have seemed only fitting to have had them wrapped in precious purple-and-gold cloth.

Scholars disputed these conclusions; some still do. But Pope Paul VI settled the question for the Catholic world. Speaking in St. Peter's on June 26, 1968, he announced that the bones of the saint had been found.

Today the bones are back in the niche of the tomb, hidden from public view.[27]

I had the privilege to be granted permission late in November 1971 to study and photograph the burial place of St. Peter's bones deep beneath the huge basilica of St. Peter's. Beyond any doubt, this huge church building is indeed built upon a very extensive and well-preserved first-century AD Roman cemetery, and the photographs reveal the name of Peter clearly inscribed in ancient Latin in the place where the apostle's bones were discovered.

Edgar J. Goodspeed quotes Clement and Eusebius concerning the last hours of St. Peter's life.

Peter's parting words to his wife as she was being led out to martyrdom are recorded by Clement of Alexandria in his *Miscellanies* and repeated by Eusebius in his *Church History*: "They say that when the blessed Peter saw his own wife led out to die, he rejoiced because of her summons and her return home, and called to her very encouragingly and comfortingly, addressing her by name and saying, 'O thou, remember the Lord!' "[28]

CHAPTER FOUR

ANDREW

Andrew, Simon Peter's brother, was one of [the] men who heard what John [the Baptist] said and then followed Jesus. John 1:40

A ndrew was a native of Galilee, born in Bethsaida. Later he lived by the sea in Capernaum. Josephus, toward the end of the first century, wrote charmingly about this area, which was near the city which he governed and later surrendered to the Roman army.

Alongside Lake Gennesareth is a stretch of country with the same name, wonderful in its characteristics and in its beauty. Thanks to the rich soil there is not a plant that does not flourish there, and the inhabitants grow everything: the air is so temperate that it suits the most diverse species. Walnuts, most winter-loving of trees, flourish in abundance, as do palms, which thrive on heat, side by side with figs and olives, for which a milder air is indicated. One might deem it nature's crowning achievement to force together into one spot natural enemies and to bring the seasons into healthy rivalry, each as it were laying claim to the region. For not only does it produce the most surprisingly diverse fruits; it maintains a continuous supply. Those royal fruits the grape and the fig it furnishes for ten months on end, the most ripening on the trees all year round; for apart from the temperate atmosphere it is watered by a spring with great fertilizing power, known locally as Capharnaum.[1]

Today the land of Galilee is precisely the same in every respect as in the days of Josephus and Andrew. One has no trouble in fitting the biblical scenes into the lush hillsides and blue waters that are virtually unchanged in appearance in the long centuries since Andrew lived there.

Andrew was the first apostle whom Jesus chose. He was, in a way, a successor to John the Baptist. As John the Baptist introduced Jesus to the nation, so Andrew is noted for having introduced Jesus to individuals.

Andrew was the son of a woman named Joanna and a fisherman named John, and had a brother called Simon who was later called Peter. Actually Andrew's father's name was not John as we say the word today, but Jonah, the same as the famous prophet. It is not commonly known, but Jonah's native village, Gath-Hepher, was near Nazareth. Jonah, the prophet, had been the most illustrious citizen ever to have lived near Nazareth.

Bethsaida, where Andrew was born, was twenty-five miles east of Nazareth, located on the northern shores of the sea. It was highly appropriate that the head of a family in which the tradition of fishing was passed from father to son should be called Jonah. Just as the name Smith originally referred to a man's occupation, so the name Jonah was apparently often given in those days to men who followed the fishing trade. Another Jonah, whom we call John the apostle, was also initially a fisherman.

Apparently, Andrew thought more about matters of the soul than about fishing, for he left his fishing nets to follow John the Baptist. He walked a long way down the Jordan valley to come to the place where John was preaching, to Bethany, across the Jordan River from Jericho. Here Andrew found that voice of authority in the spiritual matters for which he had been seeking. He was not content with the spiritual wickedness, compromise, and graft which he had found in the cities of Galilee and Judea. But John the Baptist was a man after his own heart: an outdoorsman, rough, homely, who practiced the simple virtues and who lived the life of a man to whom the flesh mattered little and worldly acclaim even less. This was a man one could follow!

So Andrew busied himself serving John the Baptist. He learned from him that some day, soon perhaps, the promised King would arrive. To Jewish minds this coming king was known as the Messiah, which is translated via a Greek word, *Christos*, meaning "The one anointed to become king, who has not yet come to rule."

After Andrew had heard John preach, and had seen the throngs of people flocking out of the cities of Judea seeking spiritual aid, and after he had assisted John in baptizing many because they wished to die to the old way of life and become alive to a new one, Andrew was prepared for an event which would shortly change his life too.

Andrew was the first apostle whom Jesus chose. As John the Baptist introduced Jesus to the nation, so Andrew is noted for having introduced Jesus to individuals.

One day, amid a growing antagonism on the part of Herod toward the popular John the Baptist (which was eventually to result in John being thrown in prison and finally executed), there came among the crowd seeking baptism, Jesus of Nazareth.

When John the Baptist saw his cousin Jesus, he stopped his preaching and turned the attention of the crowd toward that lonely, solitary figure and said: "Look! The Lamb of God who takes away the sin of the world! He is the one I was talking about when I said, 'A man is coming after me who is far greater than I am, for he existed long before me' " (John 1:29-30). Andrew, who heard these words, had been seeking more than just the message of John, for John's message was delivered within the framework of the old revelation. John was the last of the prophets. But now, *here was the One whom John had preached would come.* Here was the Christ! So Andrew immediately left John and attached himself to Jesus. It is likely that John, the future apostle, who was also first a follower of John the Baptist, also followed

Jesus at this time. Andrew then found his brother Simon Peter and later Philip, and introduced them to Jesus.

At this stage Andrew was not yet a disciple of Jesus. He was merely a follower—that is, an interested onlooker who was willing to go along to observe. Jesus took Peter, Andrew, Philip, and John back to Nazareth with Him, after the forty days of temptation by Satan in the wilderness following His baptism. There they were permitted to accompany Him to a family feast in honor of a marriage at Cana of Galilee, just six miles from Nazareth. In Cana they saw Jesus perform His first miracle.

Then Jesus took them on a preaching tour up into Galilee, and later down to visit Jerusalem where they saw Him cleanse the Temple. But not during any of this time were they yet His disciples. Finally, they returned to Galilee and went back to their old task of fishing. We do not know how much time passed, but one day Jesus came to the coasts of Galilee into Capernaum and there found Andrew and Peter.

We have often heard Peter referred to as "the big fisherman." That he was, but so was Andrew. We have often heard the words of Christ to Peter quoted; "Come, follow me, and I will show you how to fish for people!" (Matthew 4:19). But we must remember that these words were spoken to Andrew as well as to Peter. Andrew merited this title even more than Peter. Or to be fair to both, let us say that Peter became the fisherman of men *en masse* and Andrew was a fisherman for *individuals*.

Now at last Andrew had been enrolled as a disciple of Christ and for Andrew there followed approximately two and a half years of instruction. His name was inscribed upon the original list of the twelve apostles. He was present at the feeding of the five thousand by the Sea of Galilee, where he introduced Jesus to the boy who had the five loaves and two fish.

He was also present at the Feast of the Passover and introduced many to the Master.

On the Mount of Olives Andrew was present with Peter and

inquired diligently about the coming destruction of Jerusalem and the end of the age. His name is listed as an apostle in the book of Acts. That is the last record we have of him in the Bible.

Yet we must realize that Andrew was present and ministered to the church in Jerusalem. Each time we read a reference to that church and the elders or apostles, we must also read in Andrew's name, for he belongs there.

Just when Andrew left Jerusalem is not known. Perhaps he went out as a missionary of his own accord, or perhaps he was driven out by the persecution which arose.

The Later Ministry of Andrew

There are some impressive traditions about the later ministry of Andrew. One, recorded by Eusebius (*HE* III, 1, 1), is that he went to Scythia, which is southern Russia, in the area around the Black Sea. Andrew was known for a long time thereafter as the patron saint of Russia, and this adoption of Andrew as the holy patron was based upon the early tradition that he had preached the gospel in Russia. Early apocryphal works agree:

"*The Acts of St. Andrew and St. Bartholomew* gives an account of their mission among the Parthians."[2]

According to Budge's book *The Martyrdom of St. Andrew* the apostle was stoned and crucified in Scythia.

Another strong tradition places his ministry in Greece. There, according to tradition, he was imprisoned, then crucified by order of the proconsul Aegeates, whose wife, Maximilla, had been estranged from her husband by the preaching of Andrew. Supposedly Andrew was crucified on a cross which instead of being made like the one upon which Jesus died, was made in the form of an "X." To this day that type of cross is known as St. Andrew's Cross.

There is a third tradition about the ministry of Andrew which describes him as spending time in Ephesus and in Asia Minor, where John is supposed to have written his Gospel from a revelation given to Andrew.

Goodspeed writes:

> To Andrew, tradition has assigned Scythia, north of the Black Sea, as his mission field, but the *Acts of Andrew*, written probably about AD 260, describes his labors as taking place chiefly in Greece or in Macedonia, where his martyrdom occurs at Patras as described in his *Acts*.[3]

Supposedly Andrew was crucified on a cross made in the form of an "X." To this day that type of cross is known as St. Andrew's Cross.

At first glance it would seem that these three traditions are contradictory. But perhaps they are mutually complementary. After all, Andrew had to minister *somewhere* in the world, and if he did not die in Jerusalem it is very possible that he went to Asia Minor to be with his old friend, John. Or if for a while he went on beyond Asia Minor to Scythia—that too is reasonable. Scythians are mentioned in the New Testament. Then perhaps Andrew returned to Asia Minor because it is the natural land-bridge between Russia and Greece. It is entirely possible that Andrew labored for a while in and around Ephesus and then finally went to Greece in his later years.

There in the southern part of Greece he may well have, as tradition says, so angered the governor by winning his wife to faith in Christ that the governor, in seeking revenge, caused this preacher of the Cross to die himself upon a cross in Patras. It was not at all unusual in the first century for noble people, especially the wives of nobles, to be converted to Christianity. There is nothing in this tradition that is impossible or incredible.

There are some medieval forgeries, however, about the life and ministry of the apostle Andrew which are beyond belief. At least they probably do not have much truth in them. There is the story that it was revealed to him that the apostle Matthias, (the one chosen to succeed Judas), had been imprisoned by cannibals. Andrew was commissioned to go and set him free. After a miraculous voyage, he arrived on the scene and was instrumental in releasing Matthias and then converting the entire cannibal population to Christianity, except for a few incorrigibles, by means of spectacular miracles.

Now such a story is plainly a legend. Nevertheless, there may be indeed a grain of truth in the fact that Andrew, true to his character as a personal soul winner and interested in rescuing people, may have actually helped one or the other of the apostles, perhaps even Matthias, to be rescued from some difficult situation. And he might thereby have won Matthias's captors to Christ. Andrew may actually have had some sort of adventure with cannibals in Russia, although not in the fantastic extremes as described by this legend.

At the time of the Emperor Justinian, relics of the apostle Andrew were found in Constantinople. This city was a depository of Christian relics from southern Russia, and Asia Minor, as well as Greece. In fact, the relics of martyrs were often transported to this chief city of Greek Orthodox Christianity. A modern authority, Michael Maclagen recounts that "Constantine began in 336 a shrine to the Holy Apostles. The edifice was completed by his son and consecrated in about 356. It contained the relics of St. Timothy, St. Luke, and St. Andrew."[4]

A few bones reputed to be those of Andrew were transported to Scotland by a Christian named St. Regulus, in the fourth or fifth century. There they were buried at a place which was later called, "St. Andrews." Today the apostle is the patron saint of Scotland, and St. Andrew's Cross is the official symbol of that Christian country. He is also claimed as patron saint by Russian Christians, and Greek Christians.

Dorman Newman reports the details of the life and death of St. Andrew as they were known to him in 1685:

> St. Andrew went to Scythia and to Byzantium where he founded churches. Thence to Greece and finally to Patrae a city of Achaia where he was martyred. Aegeates, proconsul of Achaia,

after debate, ordered Andrew to forsake his religion or be tortured fiercely. Each begged the other to recant. Aegeates urged Andrew not to lose his life. Andrew in return urged Aegeates not to lose his soul.

After patiently bearing scourging, Andrew was tied, not nailed, to a cross that his sufferings might be prolonged. He exhorted the Christians and prayed, saluted the cross which he had long desired as the opportunity to show an honorable testimony to his Master. Andrew hung upon the cross two days, exhorting all who witnessed. Some people importuned the Proconsul but Andrew besought the Lord that he might seal the truth with his blood. He died upon the last day of November though in what year no certain account may be recovered.[5]

It must be added, despite Newman, that the date of AD 69 is generally accepted as the year of the martyrdom of St. Andrew in Patras.

Mary Sharp indicates the Roman Catholic tradition of the fate of Andrew's relics:

> The relics of St. Andrew: Head in St. Peter's, Rome; some are in Sant' Andrea al Quirinal, Rome, the rest are in Amalfi. They were stolen from Constantinople in 1210 and taken to the Cathedral of Amalfi near Naples. In 1462, Pope Pius II transferred the head to St. Peter's, Rome.[6]

In 1964, Pope Paul VI gave the skull of St. Andrew to the Greek Orthodox Church in Patras, Greece, where Andrew was martyred. In November, 1971, I journeyed to Patras, Greece, to photograph the reliquary containing the skull of St. Andrew, now kept in an old church building covering a well of water said to have been there at the time of the apostle. In a beautiful silver reliquary, resting in an altar, is the skull the Pope returned from Rome to Patras. A new Cathedral was built nearby to house the sacred relic. The Greek Orthodox priest in the church was the soul of kindness and permitted the photographs to be taken.

The original gold reliquary, which was shaped like the face of the apostle by the Roman Catholics while they had custody in Rome of the relic, had been destroyed by a deranged person in Patras several years ago. Greek Orthodox doctrine prohibits the duplication of the human form or visage "in the round," preferring flat pictures (ikons) as less likely to resemble pagan gods. The deranged person was discovered to have removed the skull of St. Andrew unobserved, and to have smashed the gold reliquary in which it was delivered from Rome in 1964. The new silver reliquary now used is a lavishly decorated, round container, without a likeness of a human face.

In the church of St. Andrew's in Patras there is a book written in Greek which adds light on the story of Andrew. I am indebted to the Reverend Mark Beshara, one of my graduate students at the California Graduate School of Theology and an Orthodox minister, for his excellent original translation from which the following is quoted:

JOHN WRITES

Jesus climbed a hill and sat down with his disciples around him. . . . Jesus soon saw a huge crowd of people coming to look for him. Turning to Philip, he asked, "Where can we buy bread to feed all these people?" . . . Andrew, Simon Peter's brother, spoke up. "There's a young boy here with five barley loaves and two fish. But what good is that with this huge crowd?"

> Holy Tradition says that Andrew went to the foothills of the Caucasus Mountains (present day Georgia in Russia), and he preached to the race of Scythians as far as the Caspian Sea.
>
> He finally reached Byzantium (present day Istanbul) and there he ordained Bishop Stachys.
>
> Andrew was imprisoned and stoned and suffered much for Christ. In Sinope he was under the threat of being eaten alive by cannibals. In spite of this he continued his Apostolic task

of ordaining priests and Bishops and spreading the Gospel of Jesus Christ the Saviour.

From Byzantium he continued to Greece for his main Apostolic journey. He travelled to Thrace and Macedonia down through the Corinthian Gulf to Patros. It was in Patros that Andrew was to preach the Gospel of Christ for the last time.

Aigeatis, the governor of Patros became enraged at Andrew for his preaching and ordered him to stand before the tribunal in his attempt to do away with the Christian Faith. When Andrew resisted the tribunal the governor ordered him crucified. Andrew remained tied to the cross with thick ropes for three days and his last words were: "Accept me, O Christ Jesus, Whom I saw, Whom I love, and in Whom I am; Accept my spirit in peace in Your Eternal Realm."

A Christian named Maximilla took down Andrew's body from the cross and buried it. When Constantius, the son of the Emperor Constantine, himself became the Emperor, he had the body of Saint Andrew removed to the Church of the Holy Apostles in Byzantium (Istanbul) where it was placed in the Altar. The head of Saint Andrew remained in Patros.

In 1460 A.D. the head of Andrew was taken to Italy and placed in the Church of Saint Peter for safekeeping after the Turks had swept through Byzantium (Istanbul). It remained there in Italy until 1964 when Pope Paul VI had it returned to the Episcopal See of Patros. Three representatives of the Pope accompanied the head which was placed in a reliquary and was carried by Cardinal Bea from the Basilica of Saint Constantine, who still guards it to this day.[7]

Some indication of the means by which the relics of St. Andrew were dispersed is to be found in *Sacred and Legendary Art*:

At the time that Constantinople was taken, and the relics of St. Andrew dispersed in consequence, a lively enthusiasm for this apostle was excited throughout all Christendom. He had been previously honored chiefly as the brother of St. Peter; he obtained thence-forth a kind of personal interest and consideration. Philip of Burgundy (AD 1433), who had obtained at great cost a portion of the precious relics, consisting chiefly of some pieces of his cross, placed under the protection of the Apostle his new order of chivalry, which according to the preamble, was intended to revive the honor and the memory of the Argonauts. His knights wore as their badge the cross of St. Andrew.[8]

Perhaps the relics of St. Andrew have more evidence for genuineness than those of any other apostle. We can trace them clearly through the centuries and down to the present: in Rome, Amalfi, and most importantly now in Patras, on the west coast of Greece, facing Italy. Before long a great cathedral will house the sacred head of the apostle, honoring it and his martyrdom in the very place where he was executed for his faith.[9]

CHAPTER FIVE

JAMES, THE SON OF ZEBEDEE

[Jesus] saw two other brothers, James and John, sitting in a boat with their father, Zebedee, repairing their nets. And he called them to come, too. They immediately followed him, leaving the boat and their father behind. Matthew 4:21-22

Of the three men who comprised the inner ring of the disciples, Peter, James, and John, we know the least about James. Despite the relative silence of the Scriptural account of James, he was noteworthy among the apostles. Perhaps the most unusual thing about his life was the manner and time of his death, for he was the first of the apostles of Christ to become a martyr. Judas and James are the only two of the original twelve disciples whose deaths have a Scriptural account.

James was the elder brother of John, the beloved disciple. With John, he was a partner with Andrew and Peter in the fishing trade along with Zebedee, his father. They owned several boats and employed hired servants, and therefore, this fishing company must have been quite affluent. There is also some evidence that James was a first cousin to Jesus Christ and had been acquainted with Him since infancy.

James received his call to follow Christ when Jesus was walking by the Sea of Galilee.

One day as Jesus was walking along the shore of the Sea of Galilee, he saw two brothers—Simon, also called Peter, and

Andrew—throwing a net into the water, for they fished for a living. . . . A little farther up the shore he saw two other brothers, James and John, sitting in a boat with their father, Zebedee, repairing their nets. And he called them to come, too. They immediately followed him, leaving the boat and their father behind. Matthew 4:18, 21-22

Now John had been a disciple of John the Baptist but left him to follow Jesus. But there is no reference to James being first a disciple of John the Baptist. After a period of companionship and a probationary period with Jesus, James is referred to as being present at the healing of Peter's mother-in-law at Capernaum. Following this he was ordained as one of the twelve disciples of Christ, and from that time forth he occupied a prominent place among the apostles. With Peter and John he became part of the innermost circle among the disciples. These three, apart from the other apostles, were present at the raising of Jairus's daughter, the Transfiguration, and the agony in the garden of Gethsemane.

It is interesting to note that these three disciples, who were to suffer so much for the cause of Christ, should witness the raising of the dead to give them courage to die; the transfiguration of Christ that they might know the reality of the spiritual world; and the agony in the Garden that they might understand that they, too, must suffer agony for Christ. Note that it was Peter who would carry the gospel cause so prominently forward as the first leader of the apostles. It was John who would some day outlive the rest of the apostles and die a natural death, after having completed five books of the New Testament, and having fulfilled a great ministry in Asia Minor as the leading voice of Christianity in the world almost up to the year AD 100.

> James was the first of Christ's apostles to become a martyr. He and Judas are the only two of the original twelve disciples whose deaths have a Scriptural account.

In contrast to these two who were the greatest leaders among the apostles, it is James whose life was cut off while the church was young. As the first of the apostles to die a martyr's death, it is significant that Christ permitted him to share the intimate secrets of His agony in the Garden and His transfiguration.

Shortly after the Transfiguration, when Jesus set His face to go to Jerusalem, and on the way was passing through Samaria, the wrath of James and John, his brother, was kindled by the hostile reception given to Jesus by the people of a small village through which they traveled.

> They said to Jesus, "Lord, should we call down fire from heaven to burn them up?" But Jesus turned and rebuked them. Luke 9:54-55

It was probably this hot-headed impetuosity and fanaticism that won them the surname, Boanerges, which is translated, "Sons of Thunder." This name was bestowed on them when they were first called as disciples.

It was not long after this when the mother of James and John asked Jesus to guarantee her sons the privilege of sitting one on His right hand and the other on His left hand when He came into His glory. The other ten disciples were moved with indignation and Jesus rebuked this ungodly ambition. The outcome of this is told in Mark 10:42-45:

> So Jesus called them together, and said, "You know that the rulers in this world lord it over their people, and officials flaunt their authority over those under them. But among you it will be different. Whoever wants to be a leader among you must be your servant, and whoever wants to be first among you must be the slave of everyone else. For even the Son of Man came not to be served but to serve others and to give his life as a ransom for many."

James was one of the four who questioned the Lord Jesus concerning the last things when Jesus delivered His address on the Mount of Olives as they stood overlooking the Temple. James was also there when the risen Christ appeared for the third time to the disciples and the miraculous catch of fish was made at the Sea of Tiberias.

James was murdered by King Herod Agrippa I, about the year AD 44, shortly before Herod's own death. The account is found in Acts 12:1-2:

> *About that time King Herod Agrippa began to persecute some believers in the church. He had the apostle James (John's brother) killed with a sword.*

Thus did James fulfill the prophecy of Christ that he, too, should drink of the cup of his Master.

> *Jesus said to them, ". . . Are you able to be baptized with the baptism of suffering I must be baptized with?" "Oh, yes," they replied, "we are able!" Then Jesus told them, "You will indeed drink from my bitter cup and be baptized with my baptism of suffering."* Mark 10:38-39

Legends of St. James the Great

The Acts of St. James in India tells of a missionary journey of James and Peter to India. According to the *Martyrdom of St. James*, he preached to the twelve tribes scattered abroad, and persuaded them to give their first-fruits to the church instead of to Herod.

The Apostolic History of Abdias connects James with two magicians called Hermogenes and Philetus. The latter was converted by James and was on the verge of leaving the former. Hermogenes cast a spell upon Philetus, who sent word to James for help. James sent his kerchief and by it Philetus was freed from the spell. Hermogenes sent devils to fetch James and Philetus, but the devils were powerless against them. James sent them back to bring him Hermogenes bound, which they did. James released him from the devils and Hermogenes became a Christian, spending the rest of his years in charity, performing miracles for the benefit of his fellow men.

One legend about James is related by Eusebius who took it from the seventh book of the lost *Hypotyposes* of Clement of Alexandria. It tells of the one who led James to the final judgment seat in Jerusalem and when he heard James's testimony he was moved and confessed that he also was a Christian. He begged James to forgive him, and they were both led away and beheaded together.

The artists of the fourteenth and fifteenth centuries adopted the stories of James as the themes of many of their paintings, thus the fame of the apostles spread far and wide. Some interesting legends developed in the long history of Spain. *Sacred and Legendary Art* relates some of them:

> According to the Spanish legend, the Apostle James was the son of Zebedee, an illustrious baron of Galilee, who, being the proprietor of ships, was accustomed to fish along the shores of a certain lake called Genesareth, but solely for his good pleasure and recreation: for who can suppose that Spain, that nation of Hidalgos and Caballeros, would ever have chosen for her patron, or accepted as the leader and captain-general of her armies, a poor ignoble fisherman? It remains, therefore, indisputable, that this glorious Apostle, who was our Lord's cousin-german, was of noble lineage, and worthy of his spurs as a knight and a gentleman;—so in Dante.
>
> But it pleased him, in his great humility, to follow, while on earth, the example of his divine Lord, and reserve his warlike prowess till called upon to slaughter, by thousands and tens of thousands, those wicked Moors, the perpetual enemies of Christ and his servants. Now as James and his brother John were one day in their father's ship with his hired servants, and were employed in mending the nets, the Lord, who was walking on the shores of the lake, called them; and they left all and followed him; and became thenceforward his most favored disciples, and the witnesses of his miracles while on earth. After the ascension of Christ, James preached the Gospel in Judaea;

then he traveled over the whole world, and came at last to Spain, where he made very few converts by reason of the ignorance and darkness of the people.

Then St. James, having founded the Christian faith in Spain, returned to Judaea, where he preached for many years, and performed many wonders and miracles in the sight of the people; and it happened that a certain sorcerer, whose name was Hermogenes, set himself against the Apostle, just as Simon Magus had wickedly and vainly opposed St. Peter, and with the like result. Hermogenes sent his scholar Philetus to dispute with James, and to compete with him in wondrous works; but, as you will easily believe, he had no chance against the Apostle, and, confessing himself vanquished, he returned to his master, to whom he announced his intention to follow henceforth James and his doctrine. Then Hermogenes, in a rage, bound Philetus by his diabolical spells so that he could not move hand or foot, saying, "Let us now see if thy new master can deliver thee": and Philetus sent his servant to St. James, praying for aid. Then the Apostle took off his cloak, and gave it to the servant to give his master; and no sooner had Philetus touched it, than he became free, and hastened to throw himself at the feet of his deliverer.

Hermogenes, more furious than ever, called to the demons who served him, and commanded that they should bring to him James and Philetus, bound in fetters; but on their way the demons met with a company of angels, who seized upon them, and punished them for their wicked intentions, till they cried for mercy. Then St. James said to them, "Go back to him who sent ye, and bring him hither bound." And they did so; and having laid the sorcerer down at the feet of St. James, they besought him, saying, "Now give us power to be avenged of our enemy and thine!" But St. James rebuked them, saying, "Christ hath commanded us to do good for evil." So he delivered Hermogenes from their hands; and the magician, being utterly confounded, cast his books into the sea, and desired of St. James that he would protect him against the demons, his former servants. Then St. James gave him his staff, as the most effectual means of defence [sic] against the infernal spirits; and Hermogenes became a faithful disciple and preacher of the word from that day.

But the evil-minded Jews, being more and more incensed, took James and bound him, and brought him before the tribunal of Herod Agrippa; and one of those who dragged him along, touched by the gentleness of his demeanor, and by his miracles of mercy, was converted, and supplicated to die with him; and the Apostle gave him the kiss of peace, saying, "Pax vobis!" and the kiss and the words together have remained as a form of benediction in the Church to this day. Then they were both beheaded, and so died.

And the disciples of St. James came and took away his body; and, not daring to bury it, for fear of the Jews, they carried it to Joppa, and placed it on board of a ship: some say that the ship was of marble, but this is not authenticated; however, it is most certain that angels conducted the ship miraculously to the coast of Spain, where they arrived in seven days; and sailing through the straits called the Pillars of Hercules, they landed at length in Galicia, at a port called Iria Flavia, now Padron.

In those days there reigned over the country a certain queen whose name was Lupa, and she and all her people were plunged in wickedness and idolatry. Now, having come to shore, they laid the body of the Apostle upon a great stone, which became like wax, and, receiving the body, closed around it: this was a sign that the saint willed to remain there; but the wicked queen Lupa was displeased, and she commanded that they should harness some wild bulls to a cart, and place on it the body, with the self-formed tomb, hoping that they would drag it to destruction. But in this she was mistaken; for the wild bulls, when signed by the cross, became as docile as sheep, and they drew the body of the Apostle straight into the court of her palace. When Queen Lupa beheld this miracle, she was confounded, and she and all her people became Christians. She built a magnificent church to receive the sacred remains, and died in the odor of sanctity.

But then came the darkness and ruin which during the invasion of the Barbarians overshadowed all Spain; and the body of the Apostle was lost, and no one knew where to find it, till, in the year 800, the place of sepulcher was revealed to a certain holy friar.

Then they caused the body of the saint to be transported to Compostela; and, in consequence of the surprising miracles which graced his shrine, he was honored not merely in Galicia, but throughout all Spain. He became the patron saint of the Spaniards, and Compostela, as a place of pilgrimage, was renowned throughout Europe. From all countries bands of pilgrims resorted there, so that sometimes there were no less than a hundred thousand in one year. The military Order of Saint Jago, enrolled by Don Alphonso for their protection, became one of the greatest and richest in Spain.[1]

How Likely Is It that James of Zebedee Went to Spain?

It is most unlikely that James would have visited Spain during his lifetime though a better case can be made for the possibility that some of his body relics or bones may have been transported there in the seventh century. In the introduction to the notable book, *The Great Pilgrimage of the Middle Ages* by Vera and Hellmut Hell, Sir Thomas Kendrick relates the historical traditions:

> In the early ninth century, perhaps somewhere about the year 810, three bodies, believed to be those of the Apostle, St. James the Greater, and two of his disciples, were found in the far north-western corner of Spain by Theodomir, Bishop of Iria Flavia (Padron); they lay in a long-forgotten tomb in wild

country about twelve miles from the Bishop's seat. At the time of the discovery the reconquest of Spain from the Moors had begun, and the kingdom of the Asturias, in which the find had been made, was an outpost of Christendom, bravely giving hope to the rest of Europe that the advance of Islam had been successfully stopped on the south side of the Pyrenees.

Then came the announcement. It was made first by the Bishop and then by the King of the Asturias, Alfonso II (791-842), and they let it be known that the discovery had been made as a result of heavenly guidance. In other words, at this time when danger threatened western Europe, St. James had suddenly offered the potent encouragement of his bones (no small thing in that relic-obsessed age) to sustain the courage of Christians fighting on the battle-front against Islam.

It was certainly an astounding thing to have happened, and it is said that Alfonso II informed the Pope, Leo III, and Charlemagne, of the wonderful event; but, be that as it may, some will think that the sequel to the discovery was even more astounding. Over the deserted necropolis where St. James lay rose the town of Santiago de Compostela, which by the twelfth century was bracketed with Rome and Jerusalem as a necessary place for far-travelling pilgrims to visit.

We want to know why it was so easy to believe that the body of St. James had been found in that tomb. The Apostle had no long-established hold on the affections of the Spaniards. It was not until the seventh century that they had any reason to suppose that St. James had preached in Spain during his lifetime, and even then the reason was no more than a one-word scribal error in an apocryphal list of the Apostles' mission-fields. At first, very little notice indeed was taken of this.

The subsequent honour paid to St. James through-out Europe and the crowds of Pilgrims journeying to his tomb can, fortunately, be studied without answering the question whether it really was the Apostle whom Bishop Theodomir of

Iria Flavia found in a forgotten Galician grave. Argument on that point continues to this day, and is, indeed, ingeniously carried a stage farther by the authors of this book. Real bones assumed to be those of St. James and his two disciples were found in a real tomb, and all we have to do is to marvel at the result of the discovery. Let it be noted, however, that even as early as the twelfth century there were pilgrims who were not quite sure that the *bout du pelerinage* was all that it claimed to be.

For the Bollandists accepted as a fact that the Apostle had conducted a mission to Spain during his lifetime. It was a matter that had been doubted and St. James's prestige had suffered. . . . But the Bollandists had come to the rescue (after agonizing inquiry by William Cuypers), and Spain's renowned ecclesiastical historian, Enrique Florez, agreed with their verdict, and Benedict XIV endorsed it.

It was not until 1879 that they were found again behind the High Altar, a sensational discovery causing one of the workmen to faint and become temporarily blind. Elaborate tests were applied to the mingled remains of St. James and his two disciples, and the skeleton of the apostle was identified with the help of a missing portion preserved in a reliquary in the cathedral of Pistoya. In a bull that bears the date of All Saints' Day in 1884, Pope Leo XIII declared that Santiago [St. James] in person had been found in that cathedral at Compostela where for over a thousand years the faithful had known the glorious Apostle lay in his grave.[2]

In the same magnificent book the authors have traced a history of the relics of St. James.

We can assume with reasonable certainty that St. James died in the year 44, since he was executed in Jerusalem during the rule of Herod Agrippa I (Acts 12, 2). Thus his original grave must have been situated near Jerusalem. In the year 614 the Persians occupied the Byzantine territories in Syria and Palestine, and some scholars (Tillemont) believe that the body of James was brought to Galicia at that time. Another suggestion (Gams) is that the body was transferred rather earlier, in the sixth century, in the time of the Emperor Justinian, who presented the relics to the monastery of Raithiu in the Sinai peninsula. Alternatively, a number of chroniclers between the eighth and twelfth centuries (e.g. the *Breviarium Apostolorum*) say that he was buried at "Achaia Marmorica" (spelt in several different ways). So far this name has not been identified conclusively with any known town or place.

The discovery of the relics of St. James in Santiago occurred in the first quarter of the ninth century (during the reign of Alphonso II, 791—842, and before the year 842), that is before the first destruction of the shrine of St. Menas, but at a time when there must already have been some concern for its security. Thus it may be assumed that the relics of St. James were conveyed to Galicia in the early part of the ninth century at the very latest. It is also possible that the transfer was made before 711 (the Arab invasion of Spain), but it is unlikely to have occurred during the Arab occupation of the Iberian peninsula. It was not until the early part of the ninth century that the Asturian kingdom in the north of Spain attained sufficient stability to have any hope of reconquering the remainder of the country. The first alternative is supported by the face that the references to Achaia Marmarica as the burial place of the saint date from the eighth century.

If these conjectures are correct, then it is possible that the route by which the relics were taken from Jerusalem to Santiago could have passed through Sinai and the town of Menas. In this case the most likely time for them to have crossed over to Spain would have been early in the ninth century, that is, shortly before the construction of the first church in Santiago under the reign of Alfonso II.[3]

A modern authority William Barclay, in his book *The Master's Men*, states the most telling argument against the visit of James to Spain.

> Considering the early date of his martyrdom the connection of James with Spain is impossible, however much we would wish it to be true; and the whole story is one of the unexplained mysteries of legend. In art James is depicted with a copy of the Gospels in one hand, and a pilgrim staff and script in the other, to show symbolically how far-travelled an evangelist he was.[4]

However, Asbury Smith in his study of the apostles, *The Twelve Christ Chose*, opens the door to the remote possibility that James might have visited Spain.

> James is not mentioned in the Gospel of John, a fact of interest if we accept John, the brother of James, as its author. The Gospel of John is the only source of information about Philip, Andrew and Nathanael Bartholomew. Yet strangely enough, John tells nothing of James, his brother, and conceals his own identity under the cloak of 'the beloved disciple.' The usual explanation of these omissions is the reticence of John; but, even so, they seem unnatural and difficult to understand. This is one of many portions of the Bible record about which more knowledge is needed.
>
> The process by which the country was Christianized is not clear. Paul in his letter to the Romans spoke of his desire to carry the Gospel to Spain. Most scholars believe that his martyrdom prevented him from fulfilling this desire, but there are some who think that he did go to Spain. The Spanish tradition, however, is that the Apostle James founded the Christian Church there. Although his early death makes this conclusion almost untenable, the legend has exercised great influence on the Spanish people. Historians generally assign the beginning of Christianity in Spain to the second or third century. But

no one can be sure about this early period, for there are no trustworthy sources of information.[5]

J. W. Taylor, in *The Coming of the Saints*, seems eager to accept the theory of James being a missionary pioneer to Spain.

St. Peter and St. John were together at Jerusalem during the years immediately following, but nowhere do we read of the presence of St. James with them. This is remarkable, because he had been constantly with them before this. Sole sharer with them of the special revelation on the Mount of Transfiguration, sole sharer with them, again, of the final conversation in the Garden of Gethsemane, his absence from their company afterwards, and especially when 'Peter and John went up together into the Temple at the hour of prayer' (Acts 3:1), needs emphatically some explanation. The only possible conclusion is, that their constant companion in the older days must have been absent from Jerusalem.

Now, there are some very old traditions, reaching back to the earliest centuries, which, if accepted, thoroughly explain this phenomenal silence regarding one of the chief of the Apostles.

In these St. James is represented as a distant traveler in the West in the very earliest years after Christ, and as a missionary pioneer in Sardinia and in Spain.

These traditions about St. James are so old and so definite, however improbable they may appear to be, that I make no apology for reproducing their more prominent features. They represent the Apostle as coming from the East and preaching the Gospel both in Sardinia and in Spain; as then returning to Jerusalem for the keeping of the Passover Festival or Easter at Jerusalem, and as suffering martyrdom during this visit to the Church and to his friends in Palestine.

His body is reputed to have been taken care of and brought from Palestine to Spain by loving disciples, who buried him in Spanish ground among the people to whom he had first preached the Gospel of the Kingdom.

A fact mentioned by contemporaneous historians—both Tacitus and Josephus—makes this mission antecedently more probable than it appears to be at first sight.

About A.D. 19 we are told by Tacitus (*Annals*, vol. ii, c. 85) that 4,000 youths, "affected by the Jewish and Egyptian superstitions" were transported from Italy to Sardinia. These are spoken of as "4,000 Jews" by Josephus (*Antiquities*, bk. svii, cap. 3), and it is evident that their banishment and forcible enlistment (for they were used as soldiers in Sardinia) made a profound impression on the Jews in Palestine.

Some have supposed that these banished Jews were already believers in Christ or followers of the teaching of St. John the Baptist. This is hardly probable; but it is quite possible that many of them may have been old followers of Judas the Galilean (Acts 5:37), who had been living as prisoners in Rome during all the succeeding years. If so, they, or the families from which they came, would be personally known to 'James and John'. They would indeed be "lost sheep of the House of Israel," and would have a special and urgent claim on the sympathy of the great Apostle.

The active belief in the legend or tradition of the Spanish mission of St. James appears to date from about A.D. 820 when the body of the Saint was 'discovered' by Theodosius, bishop of Tira. Around the reputed body of St. James there gradually grew the shrine, the cathedral, the city, and finally the pilgrimages of 'Santiago di Compostela'. The original cathedral was consecrated in A.D. 899, and this was destroyed by the Moors under El Mansui in

James's body is reputed to have been brought from Palestine to Spain by loving disciples who buried him among the people to whom he had first preached the Gospel.

997. The later cathedral was founded in 1078 on the site of the one which had been destroyed. But long before the supposed discovery—or rediscovery—of the body of St. James, we have evidence that the essentials of the tradition were held by Spanish inhabitants and Spanish writers. From immemorial times, or at least from A.D. 400, we find references to the tradition in old Spanish Offices.

In the latter part of the next century or beginning of the seventh (about A.D. 600) there are three distinct references confirming the tradition of the preaching of St. James in Spain in the writing of Isidorus Hispalensis (vii, 390, 392 and v, 183), but this author writes of his body as having been buried in "Marmarica" (Achaia). The tradition is again confirmed by St. Julian, who ruled the Church of Toledo in the seventh century (*Acta Sanctorum*, vol. 33, p. 86), and by Freculphus, who wrote about A.D. 850 (bk. ii, cap. 4). The summing-up of the Bollandists in the *Acta Sanctorum* appears to be decidedly in favour of the thesis that the reputed Spanish mission of St. James is reliable and historical.[6]

No one seems to have done a more thorough job of research than J. W. Taylor on the apostolic age, but it seems obvious that this scholarly writer is a bit too anxious to prove a case. However tempting this may also be to us, we simply dare not share all of Taylor's enthusiasms. Neither, on the other hand, has honest scholarship the right to reject them out of hand.

The best of the Bible encyclopaedias (*The International Standard Bible Encyclopaedia*) indicates James was slain by Herod Agrippa I about AD 44. The editors make this theological comment: "Thus did James fulfill the prophecy of our Lord, that he too should drink of the cup of his Master" Mark 10:39. The same source quotes the following apocryphal literature:

According to the *Genealogies of the Twelve Apostles* (cf. Budge, *The Contendings of the Apostles,* vol. II, 49) Zebedee was of the house of Levi, and his wife of the house of Judah. Now, because the father of James loved him greatly he counted him among the family of his father Levi, and similarly because the mother of John loved him greatly, she counted him among the family of her father Judah. And they were surnamed 'Children of Thunder,' for they were of both the priestly house and of the royal house.' *The Acts of St. John*, a heretical work of the second century, referred to by Clement of Alexandria in his *Hypotyposis* and also by Eusebius (*HE*, III, 25), gives an account of the call of James and his presence at the Transfiguration, similar in part to that of the Gospels, but giving fantastic details concerning the supernatural nature of Christ's body, and how its appearances brought confusion to James and other disciples (cf. Hennecke, *Handbuch zu den neutestamentlichen Apokryphen*, (423-59). The *Acts of St. James in India* (cf. Budge, *Contendings of the Apostles*, 295–303) tells of the missionary journey of James and Peter to India, of the appearance of Christ to them in the form of a beautiful young man, of their healing a blind man, and of their imprisonment, miraculous release, and their conversion of the people.[7]

Hugo Hoever, nearly a hundred years ago, summed up the beliefs of Christian scholarship during his era: "On account of early zeal of James and John, Our Lord styled them Boanerges, or sons of thunder. . . . St. James preached the Gospel in Spain and then returned to Jerusalem, where he was the first of the Apostles to suffer martyrdom. By order of Herod Agrippa he was beheaded at Jerusalem about the feast of Easter, 44 A.D."[8]

The very authoritative *A Traveller's Guide to Saints in Europe* offers this conjecture: "Most scholars think it's unlikely that he visited Spain, but state that this does not dispose of the claim that the relics at Santiago are his."[9]

The *Encyclopaedia Brittanica* does not reject utterly the claim of an association of James with Spain, but affirms James' official martyrdom about fourteen years after the death of Christ (Acts 12:2) under Herod Agrippa I, the grandson of Herod the Great. It adds, "There is a tradition open to serious difficulties and not unanimously admitted, that James preached the gospel in Spain and that after his death his body was transported to Compostela."[10]

A rival tradition is held by the writer of the *Armenian Patriarchate of Jerusalem*. This authority affirms that the Cathedral of St. James in Jerusalem, the seat of the Armenian Patriarchate, now stands upon the site of the house of James the Less. [In a later chapter of this book I have demonstrated that whatever historicity there may be to this claim, it is unlikely to be the burial place of James the Less, but rather the burial place of James the brother of Jesus.] However, the following affirmation is interesting as a contrary claim regarding the present location of the body of James the Great. "The Cathedral contains the Shrine of St. James the Major (the Apostle and brother of St. John). The head of the Apostle is buried in this Shrine."[11]

In another volume, *The Treasures of the Armenian Patriarchate of Jerusalem*, the following claim is made:

> The St. James Cathedral stands on the spot where according to tradition the head of St. James the Major, brother of John, who was beheaded by Herod Agrippa in 44 A.D. was buried (under the northern wall of the present church). At present the grave is within the Cathedral. According to tradition a chapel was built on the spot of the decapitation of St. James the Major as early as the first century. However, there are many evidences that the foundations of the first church built upon these sacred spots were laid in the fourth century.[12]

The same authority adds:

> According to Armenian tradition, after the destruction of the monastery in which the body of the martyred Apostle, James the Younger, was originally buried, his relics were removed to the Cathedral of St. James and placed on the spot where the

principle altar now stands. This Cathedral is believed to be the site on which the head of the Apostle James the Great, brother of John the Evangelist was interred. These traditions were usually adduced to underscore the Armenian institution's historic association with the two Apostles whose relics they have jealously guarded for many centuries.[13]

What Happened to the Body of James?

The answer to this can be deduced from the evidence in hand as to the life, martyrdom, and subsequent fate of the body of James: Admittedly the story of James the Great is a mixture of certainty and conflicting traditions. We suggest the following *hypothesis* to harmonize the information while scholarship awaits further discoveries.

James lived for fourteen years after the resurrection of Jesus. Considering the ease with which inhabitants of the Mediterranean basin could travel from one end of the sea to the other, as far back as the time of Hannibal of Carthage, and considering the even greater facility of travel at the time of Julius Caesar (circa, 60–40 BC) who visited Spain at least three times, we can see no formidable difficulties against the possibility of James visiting the Jewish colonies in Spain. It is not unlikely that James would preach to the Gentiles except for those who had become proselytes in the Jewish synagogues in Spain.

One important branch of Judaism, the *Sephardim*, has been more closely identified with Spain than with any other European country. James would hardly have considered his missionary responsibility to have included a mission to Gentiles since, if he went to Spain at all, it is likely that the brevity of his preaching career (fourteen years) would have taken him only to the far-flung Jewish colonies in Spain.

The apostle Paul had not yet broken the Christian movement loose from official Judaism at the time James would have had to have left Judea, if indeed he went to Spain. However, the absence of the name or the record of activities of so prominent an apostle as James the Great in the book of Acts, after the first listing of the apostles in the first chapter of Acts, could have some significance. We can hardly accept the notion that James traveled to India and to Spain as well. Since we cannot utterly rule out a visit to Spain during the fourteen silent years of the history of this apostle and since it is reasonable to believe that James was a special target of the Herodian persecutors of the church, there is no *formidable* historical obstacle to a possible visit by James to Spain.

Thus James *might* have gone to Spain to preach to the Jewish colonists and slaves there. We do not know why he should have chosen to go to the Jews in Spain. Upon his return to Jerusalem from Spain, it might well be possible that James could have been accused by Herod Agrippa I of spreading sedition among the Jewish slaves in Spain. Doubtless, Herod was unpopular in Judea because he had sent those Jewish captives into slavery. Or it could have been that he did not seem to raise enough objections against Rome for having enslaved them. Most probably however, the Jewish slaves in Spain were enemies of both Herod and Rome.

Anyone from Judea who made the long journey to Spain and who was observed or overhead speaking to the slaves might very well, upon his return, have been considered by Herod as a potential enemy of his throne.

With the rapid growth of the Christian movement in Jerusalem itself, Herod might have seen all or some Christian leaders as potential insurrectionists. He might well have thus accused James of spreading sedition and had him beheaded as a manifest enemy of the state. He would not have been without sympathizers among the priesthood or ruling groups of the Jews by his act against James. By AD 44 Jewish religious and political leadership was no longer tolerant of Christianity, even if during its earliest years it might have been considered too small to be potentially dangerous.

I can't see any reason why James could not have indeed fallen victim to Herod's fears and wrath on just such a charge as sedition. If Herod was determined to stamp out Christianity, or at least immobilize it to please the Jewish ruling circles, it would not have been untypical of him to suborn various "witnesses." Or it may be entirely possible that the preaching about a Messiah who had come, *and who would return* won for James many followers and believers among the Jewish slaves in Spain. If so, this would have resulted in the Romans having trouble with those Jewish slaves and this disturbance might have been laid primarily at the feet of James. One need not even theorize that false witnesses would be necessary. The resultant death of James due to a mere suspicion of illegal activities was a hallmark of all the Herods.

Admittedly, we cannot go beyond postulation to prove this theory. But it is entirely possible that a number of Jewish slaves in Spain were indeed converted to Christ by James, and have based on this their miraculous tales concerning the visit of James which might well have been the foundation of a later association of James with Spain. Such a visit was entirely in character with what we know of the personality of James. He was a zealous Jew who could have been filled with compassion for the salvation of those doubly unfortunate Jewish slaves in Spain. He would have wanted them for Christ and have felt keenly their separation from the main body of Israel.

The Death of James

Upon the death of James it is certain that his friends and fellow apostles buried his body somewhere in Jerusalem. A family tomb near the present location of the Armenian Patriarchate might well have been the depository of his body and severed head. It is not impossible that the head might have been preserved in that location and, when a later church was built, have been interred there.

It is certainly not impossible that with the increase in the early medieval practice of the veneration of apostolic relics, some of the bones of the apostle, perhaps the body, might have been taken to Spain to escape the invading Persians. The head might well have been kept in Jerusalem, because a reliquary containing the skull could have been quite easily hidden regardless of invading and pillaging Persian soldiers. The body, apart from the head, could well have been sent to Spain for safekeeping. One can easily imagine the Armenian Christians long ago prudently deciding to separate the relics of the apostle James so that at least some of them might be preserved regardless of the possibility of some being lost in the process. Even to this day such places in Spain as the Escorial claim fragments of the bodies of almost all of the apostles. The fragmentation of relics was an almost universal practice in the early Middle Ages and there is no sound reason for denying the possibility that some major portions of the relics might be in St. James at Compostela in Spain to this day.

As we have stressed, this possibility must be labeled as a postulation because we possess no facts which can either confirm or seriously challenge it. It is not likely that any shall be found, so we must be content with theory. I, for one, having confirmed the fact of the practice of the fragmentation of apostolic relics, and having visited both Spain and Jerusalem, see no reason to doubt the possibility that the bones of James the son of Zebedee are located partly in Spain and partly in Jerusalem to this day.

CHAPTER SIX

JOHN

When Jesus saw his mother standing [near the cross] beside [John] the disciple he loved, he said to her, "Dear woman, here is your son." And he said to this disciple, "Here is your mother." And from then on [John] took her into his home. John 19:26-27

Like all other biblical biographies, that of John is fragmentary. We do, however, know considerable information about him.

He was one of the sons of Zebedee, a fisherman of Galilee, and of Salome who was probably a sister of Mary, the mother of Jesus. He grew up in Galilee and was a partner with his brother and with Andrew and Peter in the fishing business. Along with Andrew, he was a disciple of John the Baptist (John 1:34-40). He accompanied Jesus on His first tour in Galilee and later, with some of his business partners, quit the fishing industry to become a disciple of Christ. He was with Jesus at the wedding in Cana of Galilee (John 2:1-11) and was also present in Jerusalem during Jesus' early Judean ministry.

We are told John owned a home in Jerusalem; probably the interview with Nicodemus was held at his home. He was sent out as one of the twelve on a preaching mission.

With Peter and James, he was present at the raising of Jairus's daughter (Mark 5:37), and at the Transfiguration (Matthew 17). They were nearest to the Lord at the agony of Gethsemane. John was, therefore, the most intimate of Christ's disciples. He and his brother were called "Sons of Thunder" when they sought to call down fire from heaven on a Samaritan village whose inhabitants had refused them hospitality. (Mark 3:17). On another occasion, John exhibited his zeal, intolerance, and exclusiveness when he exclaimed, "Teacher, we saw someone using your name to cast out demons, but we told him to stop because he wasn't in our group" (Mark 9:38). John's mother expressed the ambition of her sons when she requested for them the chief places in the kingdom (Mark 10:35).

At the Last Supper John occupied the privileged place of intimacy next to Jesus (John 13:23). At the trial of Jesus he was present in the court because he was known to the family of the high priests. He had probably become acquainted with prominent people in Jerusalem through his work as a business representative for his father's fishing business. John was present at the Crucifixion and there Jesus Christ gave him the responsibility for His mother, Mary (John 19:26). He was with Peter during the time of Jesus' burial in the tomb and came with him as one of the first visitors to see the empty tomb. John's greatest act of faith was when he saw the empty grave clothes; as he testifies, "He saw and believed" (John 20:8).

> John's greatest act of faith was when he saw the empty grave clothes; as he testifies, "He saw and believed" (John 20:8).

John was with Peter at the gate of the Temple when a lame man was healed (Acts 3:10). He was also with Peter on the mission to Samaria to impart the Holy Spirit to the new converts (Acts 8:12). He, along with Peter and James, the Lord's brother, are called "pillars" in the Jerusalem church.

Many have identified John as "the disciple whom Jesus loved" (John 12:23; 19:26; 20:2; 21:7, 20).

We learn from the beginning of John's Gospel that he lived for a long time after the beginning of the Christian era. His epistles reveal that he rose to a position of influence within worldwide Christianity, and shortly before the destruction of Jerusalem moved to Ephesus in Asia Minor. At this strategic location he became the pastor of the church in Ephesus and had a special relationship to other churches in the area, as we know from his letters to the seven churches in Asia. His brother, James, was the first of the apostles to die. John, on the other hand, was the last to die. Almost all the other apostles met violent deaths, but John died peacefully in Ephesus at an advanced age, around the year AD 100.

The Later Life of John

When John was living in Ephesus it is believed that Mary, the mother of Jesus, was living with him there for a few years. Nicephorus in the *Ecclesiastical History*, (2, 2), says John stayed in Jerusalem and cared for Mary like a son until the day of her death. However, this is a tradition which has less weight than the one which says that Mary was taken to Ephesus and died there. The matter would not be important except that there are two places currently on exhibit where she is said to have died. There is a tomb in Jerusalem, and in Ephesus there is the "House of St. Mary." Though the tomb in Ephesus has not been found, the weight of archaeology seems to indicate that it was once there. Two guide books at the ruins of ancient Ephesus indicate that this is the case.[1]

Irenaeus, himself a native of Asia, who knew Polycarp, a disciple of John, several times recalls the teaching of John in Ephesus and says he lived there until the time of Trajan.[2]

While in Ephesus John was exiled to Patmos, a penal colony off the coast of Turkey. This is confirmed by Eusebius, Chapter XVIII, i.

> According to early tradition, the sacred text of the book of *Revelation* was given to St. John and set down while he was in the cave that is now known as the cave of the Apocalypse, which cave is now hidden within, and below, the buildings of the Monastery of the Apocalypse. This monastery was built in the 17th century to house the Patmias—a theological school that was established at that date, and its structures have been very little altered since then. The buildings constitute an ensemble of cells, class-rooms,

John's brother, James, was the first of the apostles to die whereas John, the last, died peacefully in Ephesus at an advanced age.

flowered courtyards and stairways, with chapels dedicated to St. Nicholas, St. Artemios and St. Anne—this last one being built in front of the open side of the cave. The holy cave, or grotto, itself has long since been transformed into a small church dedicated to St. John the Theologian. In the grotto, signs remain that long tradition holds and bears witness to St. John's presence—in one corner there is the place where he laid his head to rest; near it the place where he rested his hand to raise himself from the rocky floor on which he slept; not far away the place where he spread his parchment; and, in the roof of the cave, the triple fissure in the rock through which he heard 'the great voice as of a trumpet.' The cave is small, and the light is dim; it is a place that draws one to meditation, prayer, worship contemplation . . . a place of which a man might say, "How fearful is this place! This is none other than the house of God, and this is the gate of Heaven."

An apocryphal writing of considerably later date than the book of Revelation, attributed to the hand of Prochoros, a "disciple" of St. John, offers us some details on St. John's sojourn on Patmos. This document bears the title "Travels and Miracles of St. John the Theologian, Apostle and Evangelist, set down by his disciple Prochoros." It probably dates from the 5th century. Some scholars place it in the 4th, however, while others place it as late as the 13th century. All the local island traditions are derived from this text, which provides a lengthy account of how St. John wrote his Gospel on Patmos. This tradition was disseminated widely from the 11th century onwards, but today we can only treat it with the greatest skepticism. The same text also recounts the miracles of St. John performed before coming to Patmos, the difficulties he encountered on the island, and the final success of his apostolate; and there is in particular an account of how he came into conflict with a pagan magician called Kynops, whom in due course he overcame. And still today there are Patmians willing to point out the various places mentioned in the account. Fishermen will point out Kynops petrified in rock from beneath the calm waters of the bay of Scala, and monks will show you the frescoes illustrating this same scene in the outer narthex of the big monastery of St. John the Theologian at Chora.

From the 4th Century A.D. onwards, Patmos came to be one of the chief centres of pilgrimage in the Christian world. There are many columns and capitals now built into the main church and other parts of the big Monastery, and into other churches on the island as well, that originally came from churches built in the 5th and 6th centuries. But from the 7th century onwards, Patmos came to be abandoned like the majority of the Aegean islands, for this was the period of the upsurge of Islam and of great navel battles between Arabs and Byzantines.[3]

Eusebius records that John was released from Patmos and returned to Ephesus:

But after Domitian had reigned fifteen years, and Nerva succeeded to the government, the Roman senate decreed that the honours of Domitian should be revoked, and that those who had been unjustly expelled should return to their homes, and have their goods restored. This is the statement of the historians of the day. It was then also, that the Apostle John returned from his banishment in Patmos, and took up his abode at Ephesus, according to an ancient tradition of the church.[4]

One of the most interesting stories of John is also recorded by Eusebius:

About this time also, the beloved disciple of Jesus, John the Apostle and evangelist, still surviving, governed the churches in Asia, after his return from exile on the island, and the death of Domitian. But that he was still living until this time, it may suffice to prove, by the testimony of two witnesses. These, as maintaining sound doctrine in the church, may surely be regarded as worthy of all credit: and such were Irenaeus and Clement of Alexandria. Of these, the former, in the second book against heresies, writes in the following manner: "And all the presbyters of Asia, that had conferred with John the disciple of our Lord, testify that John had delivered it to them; for he continued with them until the times of Trajan." And in the third book of the same work, he shows the same thing in the following words: "But the church in Ephesus also, which had been founded by Paul, and where John continued to abide until the times of Trajan, is a faithful witness of the Apostolic tradition."

Clement also, indicating the time, subjoins a narrative most acceptable to those who delight to hear what is excellent and profitable, in that discourse to which he gave the title *What Rich Man is Saved?* Taking therefore the book, read it where it contains a narrative like the following:

Listen to a story that is no fiction, but a real history, handed down and carefully preserved, respecting the Apostle John. For after the tyrant was dead, coming from the isle of Patmos to Ephesus, he went also, when called, to the neighbouring regions of the Gentiles; in some to appoint bishops, in some to institute entire new churches, in others to appoint to the ministry some one of those that were pointed out by the Holy Ghost. When he came, therefore, to one of those cities, at no great distance, of which some also give the name, and had in other respects consoled his brethren, he at least turned towards the bishop

LUKE WRITES

The members of the [religious Jewish] council were amazed when they saw the boldness of Peter and John, for they could see that they were ordinary men with no special training in the Scriptures. They also recognized them as men who had been with Jesus.
Acts 4:13

ordained (appointed), and seeing a youth of fine stature, graceful countenance, and ardent mind, he said, "Him I commend to you with all earnestness, in the presence of the church and of Christ." The bishop having taken him and promised all, he repeated and testified the same thing, and then returned to Ephesus.

The presbyter taking the youth home that was committed to him, educated, restrained, and cherished him, and at length baptized him. After this he relaxed exercising his former care and vigilance, as if he had now committed him to a perfect safeguard in the seal of the Lord. But certain idle, dissolute fellows, familiar with every kind of wickedness, unhappily attach themselves to him, thus prematurely freed from restraint. At first they lead him on by expensive entertainments. Then going out at night to plunder, they take him with them.

Next, they encourage him to something greater, and gradually becoming accustomed to their ways in his enterprising spirit, like an unbridled and powerful steed that has struck out of the right way, biting the curb, he rushed with so much the greater impetuosity towards the precipice. At length, renouncing the salvation of God, he contemplated no trifling offence, but having committed some great crime, since he was now once ruined, he expected to suffer equally with the rest.

Taking, therefore, these same associates, and forming them into a band of robbers, he became their captain, surpassing them all in violence, blood, and cruelty. Time elapsed, and on a certain occasion they sent for John. The Apostle, after appointing those other matters for which he came, said, "Come, bishop, return me my deposit, which I and Christ committed to thee, in the presence of the church over which thou dost preside."

The bishop at first, indeed, was confounded, thinking that he was insidiously charged for money which he had not received; and yet he could neither give credit respecting that which he had not, nor yet disbelieve John. But when he said,

"I demand the young man, and the soul of a brother," the old man, groaning heavily and also weeping, said, "He is dead." "How, and what death?" "He is dead to God," said he. "He has turned out wicked and abandoned, and at last a robber; and now, instead of the church, he has beset the mountain with a band like himself."

The Apostle, on hearing this, tore his garment, and beating his head with great lamentation, said, "I left a fine keeper of a brother's soul! But let a horse now be got ready, and some one to guide me on my way." He rode as he was, away from the church, and coming to the country, was taken prisoner by the outguard of the banditti. He neither attempted, however, to flee, nor refused to be taken; but cried out, "For this very purpose am I come; conduct me to your captain."

He, in the meantime stood waiting, armed as he was. But as he recognised John advancing towards him, overcome with shame he turned about to flee. The Apostle, however, pursued him with all his might, forgetful of his age, and crying out, "Why dost thou fly, my son, from me, thy father; thy defenseless, aged father? Have compassion on me, my son; fear not. Thou still hast hope of life. I will intercede with Christ for thee. Should it be necessary, I will cheerfully suffer death for thee, as Christ for us. I will give my life for thine. Stay; believe Christ had sent me."

Hearing this, he at first stopped with downcast looks. Then threw away his arms; then trembling, lamented bitterly, and embracing the old man as he came up, attempted to plead for himself with his lamentations, as much as he was able; as if baptized a second time with his own tears, and only concealing his right hand. But the Apostle pledging himself, and solemnly assuring him, that he had found pardon for him in his prayers at the hands of Christ, praying, on his bended knees, and kissing his right hand as cleansed from all iniquity, conducted him back again to the church. Then supplicating with frequent prayers, contending with constant fastings, and softening down his mind with various consolatory declarations, he did not leave him as it is said, until he had restored him to the church. Affording a powerful example of true repentance, and a great evidence of a regeneration, a trophy of a visible resurrection.[5]

The Scripture's record of John ends with the seven letters to the seven churches mentioned in the first two chapters of the book of the Revelation. St. Augustine states that John preached to the Parthians—the people who lived on the borders of what is now Russia and Iran, and near the eastern regions of Turkey.

Tertullian in *De Praescriptione* says that John was with Peter in Rome and for a time was in danger of his life. The legend is that he was tortured by being boiled in oil but was delivered miraculously. This story does not seem to have much foundation in historical fact but the Church of San Giovanni in Olio seems to have been built on the spot in Rome to honor the Apostle's escape.

Also there is a tradition that in Rome an attempt was made to poison John, but that when he took the cup, the poison disappeared in the form of a serpent. Thus the Roman Catholic symbol for this Apostle is a cup with a serpent issuing from it.[6]

While in Ephesus John wrote his Gospel. Eusebius tells the circumstances:

JOHN WRITES

I, John, . . . am your partner in suffering and in God's Kingdom and in the patient endurance to which Jesus calls us. I was exiled to the island of Patmos for preaching the word of God and for my testimony about Jesus. Revelation 1:9

The fourth of the Gospels was written by John, one of the disciples. When exhorted by his fellow-disciples and bishops, he said, 'Fast with me this day for three days; and what may be revealed to any of us, let us relate it to one another.' The same night it was revealed to Andrew, one of the Apostles, that

John was to write all things in his own name, and they were all to certify.[7]

Church history records few moments of humor but surely one must be the picture that Eusebius gives in this passage concerning one Cerinthus, a noted heretic in the days of John. Eusebius quotes as his authority, Irenaeus, and relates that he said that "John, the Apostle, once entered a bath to wash; but ascertaining Cerinthus was within, he leapt out of the place and fled from the door, not enduring to remain under the same roof with him. John exhorted those within to do the same, 'Let us flee lest the bath fall in, as long as Cerinthus, that enemy of the truth, is within.' "[8]

In dealing with that same Cerinthus, St. Jerome wrote several paragraphs about John, indicating that John wrote the Gospel against the heresy of Cerinthus. The entire selection from St. Jerome is worth reading:

John, the Apostle whom Jesus most loved, the son of Zebedee and brother of James, the Apostle whom Herod, after our Lord's passion, beheaded, most certainly of all the Evangelists wrote a *Gospel*, at the request of the bishops of Asia, against Cerinthus and other heretics and especially against the then growing dogmas of the Ebionites, who assert that Christ did not exist before Mary. On this account he was compelled to maintain His divine nativity. But there is said to be yet another reason for this work, in that when he had read Matthew, Mark and Luke, he approved indeed the substance of the history and declared that the things they said were true, but that they had given the history of only one year, the one, that is, which follows the imprisonment of John and in which he was put to death. So passing by this year, the events of which had been set forth by these, he related the events of the earlier period before John was shut up in prison, so that it might be manifest to those who should diligently read the volumes of the four Evangelists. This also takes away the discrepancy which there seems to be between John and the others. He wrote also one Epistle which begins as follows "That which was from the beginning, that we declare unto you."

In the fourteenth year then after Nero, Domitian having raised a second persecution, he was banished to the island of Patmos, and wrote the *Apocalypse*, on which Justin Martyr and Irenaeus afterwards wrote commentaries. But Domitian having been put to death and his acts, on account of his excessive cruelty, having been annulled by the senate, he returned to Ephesus under Nerva Pertinax and continuing there until the time of the emperor Trajan, founded and built churches throughout all Asia, and, worn out by old age, died in the sixty-eighth year after our Lord's passion and was buried near the same city.[9]

Another tradition concerning John is also handed down by Jerome. It says that when John was evidently an old man in Ephesus he had to be carried to the church in the arms of his disciples. At these meetings he was accustomed to say no more than, "Little children, love one another!" After a time the disciples wearied at always hearing the same words and they asked, "Master, why do you always say this?" "It is the Lord's command," was his reply. "And if this alone be done, it is enough!"

We are aided to catch the spirit of the aged apostle in a poem by the poet Eastwood in which he describes the last hours of John's life.

What say you, friends?
That this is Ephesus and Christ has gone
Back to His kingdom? Ay, 'tis so, 'tis so;
I know it all: and yet, just now I seemed to stand once more
    upon my native hills
And touch my Master . . .
Up! Bear me to my church one more
There let me tell them of a Saviour's love:
For by the sweetness of my Master's voice
I think he must be very near.

. . . So, raise up, my head:
How dark it is! I cannot seem to see.
The faces of my flock \Is that the sea
That murmurs so, or is it weeping? Hush!
"My little children! God so loved the world\
He gave His son: so love ye one another,
Love God and men. Amen."[10]

There is a firm tradition that John lived until the reign of Nerva, 68 years after the resurrection of Jesus. [11]

Clement of Alexandria writes that "during his last days John appointed bishops in the new Christian community"[12] while Irenaeus writes that "Polycarp and Papias were his disciples."[13]

Visiting the Tomb of St. John

The local guide books available to the visitor to Ephesus have been written with scholarship. They tell of the history of the tomb of St. John.

The disciples of St. John built a chapel over the tomb of the Evangelist which became a centre of Christian worship. So many pilgrims visited the chapel that by the sixth century the Emperor Justinian and his wife Theodora agreed to build a monument worthy of St. John in place of the previous construction which was of little artistic value. Justinian's church, 130 metres long, with three naves, was built in the shape of a cross. The wide central nave was covered with six large domes: the narthex was covered with five smaller ones. The main dome and central section of the church was supported by four square pillars. The tomb of the Apostle was in a room under the part of the floor immediately beneath the large dome. According to tradition the dust from this room had healing powers, which brought many sick people to the tomb during the Middle Ages.

The floor of the church was covered with mosaics. The monograms of Justinian and Theodora can be clearly distinguished on the capitals of some of the columns. On the 26th of September, the probable date of the Evangelist's death, commemorative ceremonies were held. Illuminations and processions attracted large crowds from the surrounding districts. Second century coins found at the Saint's tomb prove that already, in the earliest times, it was a place of pilgrimage.

North of the ruins of the Basilica of St. John we see opposite us, like a crown on the highest point of the Seljuk Hill, the Citadel with its fifteen towers. This castle is a Byzantine building but a large part was repaired during the time of the Aydinogullari. A tower and the walls in the southern part of the building are characteristic of that period. The Citadel may be entered on the western side. It contains a church, a mosque and cisterns. According to tradition, the Gospel of St. John, he who saw so well the world about him, was written on this hillside.[14]

More or less the same story is told in another book by the same title:

From the very beginning of Christianity the communities of Christians accepted this place [Ephesus] as a spot of pilgrimage and performed their homage. Later on this church was destroyed by the acts of God and was built again enlarging the old one by Emperor Justinian. This doomed church had a fine yard surrounded with pillars. It had two storeys and consisted of six big and five small domes. The domes were covered with mosaics. In excavations some coins were found belonging to the second half of the 1st century B.C. This proves that the tomb of St. John used to be visited by many a man at that time. Holy wells, the places of which hymns used to be sung, and ashes which cured every kind of illness, were under the roof of these domes.

The curing water flourishing near the tomb of St. John had a special value for the pilgrims of that period. For about four or five years St. John lived together with his rival Artemis! Though the temple of Artemis was plundered more often than not, nobody touched St. John, because St. John was the great messenger of human and of holy loves and a follower of Christ and of His Holy Mother. His tomb, just like the Temple of St. Mary on the hill, was erected to fit a disciple. His memory will never be neglected by the western believers of the faith.[15]

Describing the inside of the Church of St. John, Keskin explains:

Its reconstructions show us that this church was just in the middle of the walls of Ayasuluk Hill and used to control around it. The grave of St. John is the place barred. Since the Middle Ages it was believed that, just like the holy water of St. Mary's Fountain, a kind of cure-all, ashy-like dust issued here. For this reason this place was a focus of pilgrimage for the Christian world in that period. Over the grave of St. John, at first, a small church, and then a large one, were constructed by Justinian in the 4th Century A.D.[16]

Eusebius confirms the location of the tomb of St. John by this quotation from Polycrates: "The place of his burial is shown from the Epistle of Polycrates who is Bishop of the Church of Ephesus, which Epistle he wrote to Victor, Bishop of Rome . . . thus . . . 'John, that rested on the bosom of our Lord . . . he also rests at Ephesus.'"[17]

In 1953, when I first visited the ruins of Ephesus, I found them in great disrepair. At that time, the floor of the Basilica of St. John was missing but the entrance to the tomb could be entered. In 1971, the occasion of the my last visit, the floor of the church had been restored and wrought iron railings had been placed around the entrance to the tomb. Apparently the bones of the Apostle have disappeared. An English-speaking Turkish guide said that they had been removed to the British Museum.

Certainly a large number of marble carvings from the nearby Temple of Diana had indeed been removed to the British Museum by the

English archaeologist, Wood, when he made the notable discovery of that famous building. Evidently the Turks are not very happy about its removal and they tend to blame the disappearance of anything they cannot find on the British. But a personal visit to the British Museum and a conference with the authorities there indicate that they have no record of any such find by Mr. Wood, nor do they have the relics of St. John.

This is a strange denouement. Some relics of all other apostles still exist, but the grave of John, which is perhaps the best attested of any apostolic tomb by history and archaeology, contains no relics, nor are there any historical traces or traditions of what may have become of them!

CHAPTER SEVEN

PHILIP

[Jesus] found Philip and said to him, "Come, follow me." . . . Philip went to look for Nathanael and told him, "We have found the very person Moses and the prophets wrote about! His name is Jesus, the son of Joseph from Nazareth." John 1:43, 45

How did a Jew get such a name as the Greek, *Philip*? The name means "lover of horses." The Philip best known to history is that of Philip of Macedon, father of Alexander the Great. Alexander conquered Palestine and left behind him a lasting Greek influence, especially in northern Galilee. In the first century there was a local king in the province of Ituraea, (named after the original Philip, no doubt) called Philip the Tetrarch, who raised the status of Bethsaida to be the capital of the province. Philip the apostle was probably named in honor of the tetrarch, who had, some ten years before the future apostle's birth, done so much for that region and Bethsaida where he was born. The Greek influence in Philip's life and ministry is most significant. Historian E. A. Wallis Budge says Philip was of the tribe of Zebulon.

Jesus found Philip and said to him, "Come, follow me!" (John 1:43). This young, liberal Jew, certainly with some Greek influence in his background, could be useful to the Master who would command His gospel to be taken to the Greeks as well as the Jews.

Philip went out immediately to find his friend Nathaniel. "We have found the very person Moses and the prophets wrote about! His name is Jesus, the son of Joseph from Nazareth" (John 1:45).

It was Philip who later introduced certain Greeks to Christ. (See John 12:20-33.) He was mentioned at the feeding of the five thousand, and again at the Last Supper. (John 6:5-7) It is impressive that all the references to Philip are in John's Gospel. John was a fellow Galilean, who lived in the neighboring village of Capernaum on the shore of the sea. He was, no doubt, a close friend to Philip.

According to Anna Jameson in *Sacred and Legendary Art*:

After the ascension, [Philip] travelled into Scythia, and remained there preaching the Gospel for twenty years; he then preached at Hierapolis in Phrygia, where he found the people addicted to the worship of a monstrous serpent or dragon, or of the god Mars under that form. Taking compassion on their blindness, the Apostle commanded the serpent, in the name of the cross he held in his hand, to disappear, and immediately the reptile glided out from beneath the altar, at the same time emitting such a hideous stench that many people died, and among them the king's son fell dead in the arms of his attendants: but the Apostle, by Divine power, restored him to life. Then the priests of the dragon were incensed against him, and they took him, and crucified him, and being bound on the cross they stoned him; thus he yielded up his spirit to God, praying, like his Divine Master, for his enemies and tormentors.[1]

JOHN WRITES

Some Greeks who had come to Jerusalem for the Passover celebration paid a visit to Philip, who was from Bethsaida in Galilee. They said, "Sir, we want to meet Jesus." Philip told Andrew about it, and they went together to ask Jesus.

Jesus replied, " . . . Anyone who wants to be my disciple must follow me, because my servants must be where I am. And the Father will honor anyone who serves me." John 12:20-23, 26

Jean Danielou affirms:

> Papias had written some *Expositions of the Oracles of the Lord*,
> in which he had collected traditions about the Apostles from
> people who had known them, and he tells us, in particular, that
> he has heard the daughters of the Apostle Philip speaking in
> Hierapolis; so we can believe as certain the information he gives
> us that the Apostle Philip lived in Hierapolis. Later the Mon-
> tanist Proclus declared that it was not the Apostle Philip but
> the deacon of the same name, the person described in the *Acts*
> as having stayed in Caesarea, whose four daughters remained
> virgins and uttered prophecies. (*HE* III, 31, 4). But Polycrates
> of Ephesus, at the end of the second century, confirms what
> Papias says, and it is certainly the Apostle Philip who died at
> Hierapolis (*HE* III, 31, 3). Two of his daughters had remained
> virgins and also died at Hierapolis; the others married (*HE* III,
> 29, 1) and one died at Ephesus (*HE* III, 31, 3).

> Other facts seem to confirm this link between Philip and
> Phrygia. This region is close to that of the Apostle John. It is
> remarkable that Philip plays a specially important part of the
> *Gospel of John*, written at this time, toward the end of the first
> century.

> Moreover a *Gospel of Philip* has been found at Nag Ham-
> madi. It is Gnostic in Character and certainly of later date,
> but its contacts with the Asiatic theology of Irenaeus and the
> Asiatic Gnosticism of Mark the Magus are very remarkable.
> There also exists the apocryphal *Acts of Philip* which praises
> virginity. Finally it should be noted that Hierapolis received
> no letter either from Paul or John, whereas the neighboring
> cities of Colossae and Laodicea received letters; perhaps this is
> because Hierapolis was Philip's fief.[2]

On five occasions I visited the amazing remains of the Turkish
city of Hierapolis, the former health resort where Philip's tomb is
still to be found. A great chemically impregnated spring of lukewarm

water still sparkles out of the rocks and forms an enormous crystallized falls over the side of a mountain, almost as large as Niagara. In biblical days this was a spa, visited by sick people from all over the world of that time. It no doubt served as a strategic mission spot from which to spread the gospel to many visitors, and thence many lands. There is no reason whatever to doubt that Philip ministered effectively in this Roman-Greek city, nor that he did, indeed, die here. He was ideally suited for a ministry to Greek-speaking people, and died in an area that was at that time still largely Greek in culture, though ruled by Rome.

> Philip was ideally suited for a ministry to Greek-speaking people, and died in an area ruled by Rome but largely Greek in culture.

Robert Grant writes: "The Montanist Proclus argued that the tombs of the four daughters of Philip, all prophetesses in New Testament times, were still to be seen at Hierapolis in Asia."[3]

Traditions Concerning the Ministry and Burial of Philip

There have been some spirited arguments as to whether or not Philip ever visited France. There is little doubt that Philip died at Hierapolis which is close to Laodicea and Colossae, both biblical cities. The church history of the Byzantine era indicates a great deal of Christian activity in these three towns.

As Christianity spread throughout Asia Minor (now Turkey) it is evident that much missionary work soon made Asia Minor a nominally Christian country. Since Colossae and Laodicea are both important New Testament cities, it is evident that the gospel got an early start in this area. Colossae, which is sixteen miles from Hierapolis, was the location of a highly developed church during the lifetime of the apostle Paul and the location of the church to which Paul wrote his letter to the Colossians.

By the time John wrote the book of the Revelation, nearby Laodicea was the site of a church which doubtless had been founded by

Paul and which had, by John's time, matured to a position of great wealth and influence. If the tradition of Philip's preaching in Scythia (south Russia) is true, it certainly is not unreasonable to believe that he may have eventually returned to Asia Minor, where he would have been in proximity to his old friend, John, who was located in Ephesus. Since John, in the book of Revelation refers to the church of the Laodicians, which was just six miles from Philip's place of ministry in Hierapolis, there can be no historical reason to doubt that Philip indeed ministered and died in Hierapolis. It is in the stories of Philip that history and tradition come so close together as to validate and illuminate each other.

There are some strong later traditions also that Philip visited France. Before we look at the documentation, we should understand that the Gauls of France first emigrated from Galatia in Turkey. Since the ministry of Philip most definitely took him to Galatia, where the city of Hierapolis was located, we are on rather firm ground in supposing that this was the area of most of his ministry. Traditions regarding a visit of Philip to France (Gaul) seem to be based upon a mistake which confuses *Gaul* with *Galatia*, since the two names are related.

> The only apostle whom tradition associates with France is Philip.

But it would seem the argument would work the other way as well. If the Gauls of France are to be traced to an emigration from Galatia, why would it not be completely reasonable for Philip, as a missionary to the Galatians, to also have traveled to France to be a missionary to their kinsmen, the Gauls? The burden of proof is, of course, upon those who contend that this is what happened. But as to its reasonableness and possibility, there can be little doubt.

As every school boy knows, Gaul was conquered by Julius Caesar who killed more than a million men in the process. In Caesar's time, Gaul had large cities and was evidently civilized enough for Caesar to enjoy living there for almost ten years. This conquest took place about 80 years before Philip's ministry. During that time, Roman civilization and culture were fully established. It was from Gaul that Caesar attempted to conquer England twice, and it was from Gaul that Claudius did accomplish this task. It would have been incredible if the Gospel had not penetrated Gaul rather thoroughly by the climax of the Apostolic Age.

The only apostle whom tradition associates with France is Philip, although there are sub-apostolic figures such as Mary Magdalene, the sisters Mary and Martha, and Lazarus their brother, who are identified with Marseilles in France. In fact, their tombs are shown there to this day.

With the realization, therefore, that the confusion between *Gaul* and *Galatia* may have led some early church writers astray, let us look at the traditions of Philip in France.

Isidore, Archbishop of Seville, AD 600–636, whom Dr. William Smith, author of *A Dictionary of Christian Biography* calls "undoubtedly the greatest man of his time in the Church of Spain . . . a voluminous writer of great learning . . . He had also a trained and cultivated mind" wrote:

> Philip of the city Bethsaida, whence also came Peter, preached Christ to the Gauls, and brought barbarous and neighbouring nations, seated in darkness and close to the swelling ocean, to the light of knowledge and port of faith. Afterwards he was stoned and crucified, and died in Hierapolis, a city of Phrygia, and having been buried with his corpse upright along with his daughters rests there.[4]

Cardinal Baronius narrates: "Philip the fifth in order is said to have adorned Upper Asia with the Gospel, and at length at Hierapolis at the age of 87 to have undergone martyrdom, which was also John Chrysostom hands down, and they say that the same man traveled over part of Scythia, and for some time preached the Gospel along with Bartholomew. In Isidore one reads that Philip even imbued the Gauls with the Christian faith, which also in the Breviary of Toledo of the School of Isidore is read. But we have said in our notes to the

Roman Martyrology that 'to the Galatians' must be corrected in the place of 'to the Gauls.'"[5]

But the learned Archbishop Ussher says, 'I am not at all satisfied here with the conjecture of Baronius in transferring the statements of Isidore from our Gauls to the Galatians of Asia; much less with the temerity of a recent Editor of the works of Isidore, Jacobus Breulius, in substituting Galatians for the Gauls in the text itself, without any reference to the ancient reading."[6]

Archbishop Ussher also says that Bede (or whoever was the author of *Collections and Flowers*), born about AD 673, "also assigned Gaul to Philip at the foot of the 3rd tome of his works."[7]

Freculphus, Bishop of Lisieux in France (AD 825–851), wrote:

> Philip of the City of Bethsaida whence also came Peter, of whom in the Gospels and Acts of the Apostles praiseworthy mention is often made, whose daughters also were outstanding prophetesses, and of wonderful sanctity and perpetual virginity, as ecclesiastical history narrates, preached Christ to the Gauls.[8]

St. Epiphanius, AD 315–407, Bishop of Salamins, who, according to William Smith's *A Dictionary of Christian Biographies* is "one of the most zealous champions of orthodox faith and monastic piety" wrote:

The ministry of the divine word having been entrusted to St. Luke, he exercised it by passing into Dalmatia, into Gaul, into Italy, into Macedonia, but principally into Gaul, so that St. Paul assures him in his epistles about some of his disciples—"Crescens," said he, "is in Gaul." In it must not be read, "In Galatia" as some have falsely thought, but "in Gaul."[9]

Pere Longueval remarks in Lionel Lewis's book *St. Joseph of Arimathea at Glastonbury* that this sentiment was so general in the East, that Theodoret who read "in Galatia" did not fail to understand "Gaul" because as a matter of fact the Greeks gave this name to Gaul, and the Galatians had only thus been named because they were a colony of Gauls.[10] Lewis is incorrect in supposing Galatia to have been colonized by the Gauls. It was the other way around.

Polycrates (194 A.D.) wrote, as we have said, a synodical letter against Victor Bishop of Rome in which he says that he "follows the authority of the Apostle John and of the ancients." Also he adds, "Philip, one of the twelve Apostles, sleeps at Hierapolis."[11] Thus we may look with confidence upon Hierapolis as the place of the death and original entombment of Philip.

Whether Philip visited France and returned to Galatia where he died or whether he never went to France at all cannot, of course, be absolutely proven in the light of the late date of the writers we have quoted above.

However, we know that Pope John the Third (560–572) acquired the body of St. Philip from Hierapolis and interred it in a church in Rome. He named it The Church of the Holy Apostles Philip and James. A guide book[12] written by Emma Zocca and published by that church traces the history of the church building back to the sixth century. The church is now known as The Church of the Holy Apostles, but that name is traced only to the tenth century. The longer-named The Church of the Holy Apostles Philip and James was the earlier title. Today one can see the bones of the apostles in a large marble sarcophagus under the altar and in a reliquary room behind it. The fragments of bones of other apostles can be seen in the same room.

LUKE WRITES

Philip went to the city of Samaria and told the people there about the Messiah. Crowds listened intently to Philip because they were eager to hear his message and see the miraculous signs he did. Acts 8:5-6

CHAPTER EIGHT

BARTHOLOMEW (NATHANAEL)

[Upon meeting Nathanael], Jesus said, "Now here is a genuine son of Israel—a man of complete integrity." John 1:47

This name literally means "son of Tolmai." He is mentioned as one of the twelve apostles (Matthew 10:3; Mark 3:18; Luke 6:14; Acts 1:13). There is no further reference to him in the New Testament. According to the *Genealogies of the Twelve Apostles*, he was of the house of Naphtali. Elias of Damascus, a Nestorian of the ninth century was the first man to identify Bartholomew with Nathanael. In the lists of the Twelve in the first three Gospels and in Acts, the names of Philip and Bartholomew always occur together. In the fourth Gospel we learn that it was Philip who brought Nathanael to Jesus (John 1:45). This has led many to believe that Bartholomew and Nathanael are the same person.

In the apocryphal *Gospel of Bartholomew* is recorded the tradition that he preached the gospel in India, and that he brought a copy of Matthew's Gospel in Hebrew with him. In the *Preaching of St. Bartholomew in the Oasis* he is said to have preached in the oasis of Al Bahnasa. According to *The Preaching of St. Andrew and St. Bartholomew* he labored among the Parthians. Another tradition has him preaching in Phrygia in Asia Minor.

The *Acts of Philip* tells how Philip and Bartholomew preached in Hierapolis, and how Philip was martyred by being pierced through the thighs and hung upside down. Bartholomew, however, escaped martyrdom at that place. He is further said to have preached in Armenia, and the Armenian Church claims him as its founder. Another tradition has him martyred at Albana, which now is modern Derbend, in the Soviet Union. However, this is near or in ancient Armenia, so there is no contradiction involved in these traditions.

The apocryphal *Gospel of Bartholomew* records the tradition that he preached the gospel in India, bringing with him a copy of Matthew's Gospel.

The Martyrdom of St. Bartholomew states that he was placed in a sack and cast into the sea. There is, however, a contrary account of his martyrdom in the city of Albana. This tradition is found in the *Apostolic History* of Abdias. Bartholomew is described as having healed the king's daughter, and exposed the emptiness of the king's idol. The king and many others were baptized, but the priests and the king's brother, Astyages, remained hostile. They arrested Bartholomew, beat him, and eventually crucified him.

The Historical and Traditional Accounts of Bartholomew

Apparently the traditions of Bartholomew have been long and widely known, as the following accounts prove.

In 1685, Dorman Newman tells an astonishingly complete story:

> Bartholomew for the Enlargement of the Christian Church, went as far as *India* for this purpose; he there found a *Hebrew* Gospel of St. *Matthew*, amongst some who still retained the Knowledge of Christ, who assured him from the Tradition of the Ancestors, that it had been left them by St. *Bartholomew*, when he preached the Gospel in those Parts.

> For a farther account of our Apostle, 'tis said, that he returned from *India* to the North-West Parts of *Africa*. At *Hierapolis* in *Phrygia* we find him in company with St. *Philip*, (as was observed before in his Life) at whose Martyrdom he was likewise fastened

to a Cross, in order to have suffered at the same time; but for some special reason the Magistrates caused him to be taken down again, and dismissed. Hence, probably, he went into *Lycaonia*, where *Chrysostom* affirms, *Serm, in SS. XII. Apost.* that he instructed the People in the Christian Religion. His last Remove was to *Alban-ople* in *Armenia* the Great, (the same no doubt which *Nicephorus* calls *Vrbanople*, a City of *Cilicia*) a place miserably overrun with Idolatry; from which, while he sought to reclaim the People, he was by the Governour of the place condemned to be crucified. Some add, that he was crucified with his Head downwards; others that he was flead alive, which might well enough consist with his Crucifixion; this Punishment being in use, not only in *Egypt*, but amongst the *Persians*, next Neighbours to these *Armenians*, from whom they might easily borrow this piece of barbarous and brutish Cruelty. *Theodorus Lector* 1.2. assures us, that the Emperor *Anastasius* having built the City *Daras* in *Mesopotamia*, A.D. 508, removed St. *Bartholomew's* Body thither; which *Gregory* of *Tours* seems to contradict, saying, that the People of *Liparis*, near *Sicily*, translated it from the place where he suffered into their Isle, and built a stately Church over it. By what means it was removed from hence to *Beneventum* in *Italy*, and afterwards to the Isle of *Tiber* at *Rome*, where another Church was built to the Honour of this Apostle, is hard to account for.

The Hereticks (according to their Custom) have forged a Gospel under St. *Bartholomew's* Name, which *Gelasius* Bishop of *Rome* justly branded as *Apocryphal*, altogether unworthy the Name and Patronage of an Apostle. And perhaps of no better Authority is the Sentence which *Dionysius*, the pretended Areopagite, ascribes to him, *That Theology is both copious, and yet very small; and the Gospel diffuse and large, and yet withal concise and short.*[1]

In modern Iran, Christian leaders agree as to the first-century ministry of Bartholomew:

By commonly accepted tradition the honour of sowing the first seeds of Christianity in Armenia, and of watering them with their blood, rests with St. Thaddeus and St. Bartholomew, who are consequently revered as the First Illuminators of Armenia.

St. Bartholomew's labours and martyrdom in Armenia are generally acknowledged by all Christian Churches. It is said that after preaching in Arabia, the South of Persia and the borders of India, he proceeded to Armenia, where he suffered martyrdom by being flayed alive and then crucified, head downward, at Albac or Albanopolis, near Bashkale.

The mission of St. Bartholomew in Armenia lasted sixteen years.[2]

In *A History of Eastern Christianity*, Aziz Atiya writes:

The first illuminators of Armenia were St. Thaddaeus, and St. Bartholomew whose very shrines still stand at Artaz (Macoo) and Alpac (Bashkale) in southeast Armenia and have always been venerated by Armenians. A popular tradition amongst them ascribes the first evangelization of Armenia to the Apostles Judas Thaddaeus who, according to their chronology, spent the years 43 to 66 A.D. in that country and was joined by St. Bartholomew in the year 60 A.D. the latter was martyred in 68 A.D. at Albanus (Derbend). Furthermore, the annals of Armenian martyrology refer to a host of martyrs in the Apostolic age. A roll of a thousand victims, including men and women of noble descent, lost their lives with St. Thaddaeus, while others perished with St. Bartholomew. On two occasions Eusebius (VI, xlvi) refers to the Armenians in his *Ecclesiastical History*. First, he states that Dionysius of Alexandria, pupil of Origen, wrote an Epistle "On Repentance," "to those in Armenia . . . whose bishop was Meruzanes."[3]

Dr. Edgar Goodspeed touches on the location of the ministry of Bartholomew:

We must also remember that "India" was a term very loosely used by the ancients, as the statement that Bartholomew went there as a missionary and found "the Gospel of Matthew in Hebrew" shows. Eusebius declares, in his *Church History*, (v:10:12), that about the time of the accession of Commodus, A.D. 180, Pantanus, the leading teacher in the church at Alexandria, was sent as missionary as far as India. He goes on to say that Bartholomew had preached to them, and left with them the Gospel of Matthew "in the Hebrew language," a very perplexing statement! Indeed, it is sometimes said that "India" in the first century was very loosely used, being understood to begin on the Bosporus. Alexander's march to India had done much, three and a half centuries before the Christian mission began, toward opening the great Parthian hinterland to the western mind. He had reached the easternmost of the tributaries of the Indus River before he turned south to the Indian Ocean, and then west again. His great march and the seventy cities he had built or founded had in a measure opened the way to India.[4]

JOHN WRITES

Philip went to look for Nathanael and told him, "We have found the very person Moses and the prophets wrote about! His name is Jesus, the son of Joseph from Nazareth."

"Nazareth!" exclaimed Nathanael. "Can anything good come from Nazareth?"
John 1:45-46

The story of Bartholomew in Persia was known very early:

Pantaenus, a philosopher of the Stoic school, according to some old Alexandrian custom, where, from the time of Mark the evangelist the ecclesiastics were always doctors, was of so great prudence and erudition both in Scripture and secular literature that, on the request of the legates of that nation, he was sent to India by Demetrius, bishop of Alexandria, where he found that Bartholomew, one of the twelve Apostles, had preached the advent of the Lord Jesus according to the gospel of Matthew. On his return to Alexandria he brought this with him written in Hebrew characters.[5]

William Barclay mentions two legends crediting St. Jerome with the following:

> By far the most interesting conjecture comes from Jerome. Jerome passes on the suggestion that Bartholomew was the only one of the twelve to be of noble birth. As we have seen, his name means son of Tolmai, or possibly son of *Talmai*. Now in 2 Samuel 3:3 there is mention of a Talmai who was king of Geshur; this Talmai had a daughter called Maacah; and this Maacah became the mother of Absalom, whom she bore to David. The suggestion is that it was from this Talmai that Bartholomew was descended, and that, therefore, he was of nothing less than royal lineage. Later still another story arose. The second part of Bartholomew's name was connected with *Ptolemy*, and he was said to be called *son of Ptolemy*. The Ptolemies were the kings of Egypt, and it was said that Bartholomew was connected with the royal house of Egypt. It cannot be said that these suggestions are really likely; but it would be of the greatest interest, if in the Apostolic band one who was of royal lineage lived in perfect fellowship with the humble fishermen of Galilee.
>
> He is said to have preached in Armenia, and the Armenian Church claims him as its founder; and he is said to have been martyred at Albana, which is the modern Derbend. There is an account of the martyrdom of Bartholomew in *The Apostolic History* of Abdias, although there the death of Bartholomew seems to be located in India. The story runs as follows. Bartholomew preached with such success that the heathen gods were rendered powerless. A very interesting personal description of him is given. "He has black, curly hair, white skin, large

eyes, straight nose, his hair covers his ears, his beard long and grizzled, middle height. He wears a white robe with a purple stripe, and a white cloak with four purple gems at the corners. For twenty-six years he has worn these, and they never grow old. His shoes have lasted twenty-six years. He prays a hundred times a day and a hundred times a night. His voice is like a trumpet; angels wait upon him; he is always cheerful, and knows all languages."

Bartholomew did many wonderful things there, including the healing of the lunatic daughter of the king, and the exposing of the emptiness of the king's idol, and the banishing of the demon who inhabited it. The demon was visibly banished from the idol by an angel and there is an interesting description of him—"black, sharp-faced, with a long beard, hair to the feet, fiery eyes, breathing flame, and spiky wings like a hedge-hog."

The king and many others were baptized; but the priests remained hostile. The priests went to the king's brother Astyages. The king's brother had Bartholomew arrested, beaten with clubs, flayed alive and crucified in agony. And so Bartholomew died a martyr for his Lord.

There is still extant an apocryphal *Gospel of Bartholomew* which Jerome knew. It describes a series of questions which Bartholomew addressed to Jesus and to Mary in the time between the Resurrection and the Ascension.[6]

The Armenian tradition concerning Bartholomew is a source of pride to the Armenian Patriarchate:

> The indestructible and everlasting love and veneration of Armenians for the Holy Land has its beginning in the first century of the Christian Era when Christianity was brought to Armenia directly from the Holy Land by two of the Apostles of Christ, St. Thaddeus and St. Bartholomew. The Church that they founded converted a greater part of the people during the

second and third centuries. At the beginning of the fourth century, in 301, through the efforts of St. Gregory the Illuminator, the King of Armenia Tiridates the Great and all the members of his family and the nobility were converted and baptized.

The early connection with Jerusalem was naturally due to the early conversion of Armenia. Even before the discovery of the Holy Places, Armenians, like other Christians of the neighbouring countries, came to the Holy Land over the Roman roads and the older roads to venerate the places that God had sanctified. In Jerusalem they lived and worshipped on the Mount of Olives.

After the declaration of Constantine's will, known as Edict of Milan, the discovery of the Holy Places, Armenian pilgrims poured into Palestine in a constant stream throughout the year. The number and importance of Armenian churches and monasteries increased year by year.

Bishop Marcarius of Jerusalem who presided over the discovery and construction of the Holy Places in and around Jerusalem, was in communication with the head of the Armenian Church, Bishop Vertanes. One of the epistles which he wrote to him between the years 325 and 335 A.D. deals with certain ecclesiastical questions and conveys greetings to the bishops, priests and people of Armenia.[7]

Another tradition, believed universally by the Armenians, is that "The traditional founders of the Armenian Church were the apostles Thaddeus and Bartholomew, whose tombs are shown and venerated in Armenia as sacred shrines."[8]

The Roman Catholic tradition tells of the disposition of the remains of the apostle:

A written account says that after the Emperor Anastasius built the city of Duras in Mesopotamia in 508, he caused the relics to be taken there. St. Gregory of Tours assures us that, before the end of the sixth century, they were carried to the Lipari Islands near Sicily; and Anastasius, the Librarian, tells us that in 809 they were taken to Benevento and then transported to Rome in 983 by the Emperor Otto III. They now lie in the church of St. Bartholomew-on-Tiber in a porphryr shrine under the high altar. An arm was sent by the Bishop of Benevento to St. Edward the Confessor, who gave it to Canterbury Cathedral.[9]

The above quotation represents the Roman Catholic tradition in part; however, there is also a Greek Orthodox tradition which cannot be ignored. John Julius Norwich in his monumental book *Mount Athos*, tells the story of his travels to the remote Greek Orthodox monasteries located in Mt. Athos, Greece.

As the sun began to sink over the mountain we reached our goal for the night, *the cenobitic abbey of Karakallou*, favoured retreat of Albanians and Epirote.

The sacristan appeared, suitably invested, and exposed the relics on a trestle table in front of the iconostasis: the skulls of the Apostle Bartholomew and St. Dionysius the Areopagite, the remains of a neomartyr, St. Gideon, a converted Turk.[10]

It is obvious from the above account that the bones (relics) of Bartholomew, like those of most of the other apostles, are widely scattered today.

Otto Hophan adds a few more details. "An Armenian tradition maintained that his body was buried in Albanopolis—also written Urbanopolis—a city of Armenia where the Apostle is said to have suffered martyrdom. Then his remains were taken to Nephergerd-Mijafarkin, and later to Daras, in Mesopotamia."[11]

Nevertheless the larger parts of the body of Bartholomew are probably in Rome. It is as Hugo Hoever writes: "The relics of the saint are preserved in the church of St. Bartholomew on the island in the Tiber River near Rome."[12]

In the book *El Escorial: The Wonders of Man*, Mary Cable says, "Saint Martin, the apostle Bartholomew, and Mary Magdalene were represented in the arm collection—and as for such relics as fingers, toes, and small joints, this category was so extensive that only three well-known saints were not represented: Saint Joseph, Saint John the Baptist, and Saint James (the last being preserved entire at Santiago de Compostela in northwestern Spain). Philip's successors added to the collection and there are now more than 7,000 relics at the Escorial, including 10 bodies, 144 heads, and 306 limbs."[13]

> It is said that after preaching in Arabia, Persia and India, Bartholomew proceeded to Armenia, where he [was] flayed alive and then crucified, head downward.

A Suggested Biography of Bartholomew

Bartholomew seems to have been the "son of Tolmai." The suggestion that there was a political movement called the "sons of Tolmai" seems to be without wide support. Even if such a group did exist, there is no reason to suppose that Bartholomew was connected with it. The greater probability is that he was a patronymic, that is, a person bearing the name of his father. (Thus, John's son becomes Johnson, etc.)

He was led to Christ in the region of Galilee, possibly by Philip, and is listed as an apostle in the final list in Acts 1:9. He would naturally have been present in the company of the other apostles during the early years of the Jerusalem church. His ministry belongs more to the tradition of the Eastern churches than to the Western churches. It is, however, evident that he went to Asia Minor (Turkey), in the company of Philip, where he labored in Hierapolis (near Laodicea and Colosse in Turkey).

The wife of the Roman proconsul had been healed by the apostles and had become a Christian. Her husband ordered Philip and Bartholomew to be put to death by crucifixion. Philip was indeed crucified, but Bartholomew escaped and went eastward to Armenia. Bartholomew carried with him a copy of Matthew's Gospel, (which copy was later found by a converted Stoic philosopher, Pantaenus, who later brought it to Alexandria). Bartholomew labored in the area around the south end of the Caspian Sea, in the section that was then called Armenia, but which today is divided between Iran and the [former] Soviet Union.

The modern name of the district where he died is Azerbaijan and the place of his death, called in New Testament times Albanopolis, is now Derbend. Derbend is the sea gate through which the wild horsemen of the Steppes (Scythians, Alans, Huns, and Khazars) later rode down upon civilized communities. The city of Tabriz, which was the chief mart of Iranian Azerbaijan, was also located in this area. It was visited by Marco Polo in 1294. The statement that Bartholomew was skinned alive before being beheaded, is contained in the *Breberium Apostolorum*, prefixed to certain ancient manuscripts.

In Butler's *Lives of the Saints*, which is a notable Roman Catholic summary of the biographies of saints, the following account appears with reference:

> The popular traditions concerning St. Bartholomew are summed up in the Roman Martyrology, which says he "preached the gospel of Christ in India; thence he went into Greater Armenia, and when he had converted many people there to the faith he was flayed alive by the barbarians, and by command of King Astyages fulfilled his martyrdom by beheading. . . ." The place is said to have been Albanopolis (Derbend, on the west coast of the Caspian Sea), and he is represented to have preached also in Mesopotamia, Persia, Egypt and elsewhere. The earliest reference to India is given by Eusebius in the early fourth century, where he relates that St. Pantaenus, about a hundred years earlier, going into India (St. Jerome adds "to preach to the Brahmins"), found there some who still retained the knowledge of Christ and showed him a copy of St. Matthew's Gospel in Hebrew characters, which they assured him that St. Bartholomew had brought into those parts when he planted the faith among them. But "India" was a name applied

indifferently by Greek and Latin writers to Arabia, Ethiopia, Libya, Parthia, Persia and the lands of the Medes, and it is most probable that the India visited by Pantaenus was Ethiopia or Arabia Felix, or perhaps both. Another eastern legend says the apostle met St.Philip at Hierapolis in Phrygia, and travelled into Lycaonia, where St. John Chrysostom affirms that he instructed the people in the Christian faith. That he preached and died in Armenia is possible, and is a unanimous tradition among the later historians of that country; but earlier Armenian writers make little or no reference to him as connected with their nation. The journeys attributed to the relics of St. Bartholomew are even more bewildering than those of his living body; alleged relics are venerated at present chiefly at Benevento and in the church of St. Bartholomew-in-the-Tiber at Rome.

Although, in comparison with such other apostles as St. Andrew, St. Thomas and St. John, the name of St. Bartholomew is not conspicuous in the apocryphal literature of the early centuries, still we have what professes to be an account of his preaching and 'passion', preserved to us in Greek and several Latin copies. Max Bonnet (*Analecta Bollandiana*, vol. xiv, 1895, pp. 353-366) thinks the Latin was the original; Lipsius less probably argues for the priority of the Greek; but it may be that both derive from a lost Syriac archetype. The texts are in the *Acta Sanctorum*, August, vol v; in Tischendorf, *Acta Apostolorum Apocrypha*, pp. 243-260; and also in Bonnet, *Act. Apocryph.*, vol. ii, pt. 1, pp. 128 *seq.* There are also considerable fragments of an apocryphal Gospel of Bartholomew (on which see the *Revue Biblique* for 1913, 1921 and 1922), and traces of Coptic 'Acts of Andrew and Bartholomew.' The gospel which bears the name of Bartholomew is one of the apocryphal writings condemned in the decree of Pseudo-Gelasius. The statement that St. Bartholomew was flayed alive before being beheaded, though this is not mentioned in the *passio*, is contained in the so-called 'Breviarium Apostolorum' prefixed to certain manuscripts of the 'Hieronymianum.' It is the flaying which has probably suggested the knife, often associated as an emblem with picture of the saint; but on St. Bartholomew in art see Künstle, *Ikonographie*, vol. ii, pp. 116-120. The Indian question is examined in some detail by Fr. A. C. Perumalil in *The Apostles in India* (Patna, 1953).[14]

CHAPTER NINE

THOMAS

Then [Jesus] said to Thomas, "Put your finger here, and look at my hands. Put your hand into the wound in my side. Don't be faithless any longer. Believe!" "My Lord and my God!" Thomas exclaimed. John 20:27-28

Thomas was also known as Didymas. The word means "twin," but we do not know anything about the brother or sister who was his twin. He was a native of Galilee and by trade, a fisherman. The few biblical references which single him out from among the Twelve for special attention seem to indicate that he was a questioner or doubter. Even to this day he is known as "doubting Thomas."

Thomas possessed a nature which contained within it certain conflicting elements: He had exceeding difficulty in reconciliation, possessed little natural buoyancy of spirit, and was inclined to look at life often with icy coolness or despondency. Yet Thomas was a man of indomitable courage and entire unselfishness. He combined a perpetual faith in the teaching of Jesus mingled with a sincere love for Jesus the teacher. He is referred to in detail by the Gospel of John alone, though his election to the Twelve is recorded in Matthew 10:3, Mark 3:18, Luke 6:15, and Acts 1:13.

John records that when Jesus, despite imminent danger at the hands of hostile Jews, declared his intention of going to Bethany to help Lazarus, Thomas alone opposed the other disciples who sought to dissuade him, and protested, "Let's go too—and die with Jesus"

(John 11:16). Was this courage or a fatalistic pessimism? Perhaps, in a strange way, it was both.

On the eve of the Passion, Thomas put the question to Jesus, "We have no idea where you are going, so how can we know the way?" (John 14:5). In this question he revealed an insensitivity to what Jesus had taught which came from an unwillingness to believe.

After the Crucifixion, Thomas was not present when the risen Christ first appeared to the disciples. Later he arrived and upon hearing of the Resurrection was stubbornly unconvinced. Said Thomas, "I won't believe it unless I see the nail wounds" (John 20:25).

Paradoxically, for one who did not believe in the Resurrection, Thomas remained in the company of the other apostles until eight days later when Jesus suddenly appeared in their midst. Addressing Thomas, Jesus invited him to come and examine his wounds and "Don't be faithless any longer. Believe!"

Whereupon Thomas prostrated himself and uttered the expression, "My Lord and my God!" He was reproved by Jesus for his previous unbelief: "You believe because you have seen me. Blessed are those who believe without seeing me" (John 20:24-29).

> Thomas was a man who struggled against his doubts and was ready to abandon them when he could.

John, who has given us the greatest amount of detail about Thomas and who had probably known him from boyhood, since they were of the same craft and city, mentions that Thomas was present when Jesus manifested himself to the disciples who were fishing on the Sea of Tiberias.

The constant picture of Thomas is that of a personality intent on gloom and doubt, yet a believer just the same. He never had a wicked heart of unbelief. Instead he was a man who struggled against his doubts and was ready to abandon them when he could.

It is good that we have the picture of doubting Thomas in the biblical record for, as has been commonly noted by the commentators, "Thomas doubted that we might have no doubts."

The Missionary Activities of Thomas

A great many legends have grown around the far-reaching ministry of this apostle. However, in the light of traditions, which have a great deal of history to back them up, we need not worry about the myths, but may rather confidently reconstruct the actual missionary journeys of Thomas. In fact, we really know more about Thomas than we do about almost any other apostle with the exception of John and Peter.

It is evident that Thomas visited Babylon. Because the tradition of the Western churches revolved around Constantinople and Rome, it is astonishing how little is known, even by many church historians, about the many other vital Christian movements which began during apostolic times. These movements quickly spread eastward, and therefore owed nothing to western Christianity.

Some of the Eastern churches boast that their hierarchial organizations date prior to those established in Constantinople and Rome. This may be more of a presumption than a historical fact since the hierarchy was a late development everywhere. But the traditions are clear: There was an apostolic movement eastward and Thomas was a central figure.

The Tradition of the Church of the East

The official name of the Church of the East is the Holy Apostolic and Catholic Church of the East. Its publications claim:

> It was founded by the Apostles, St. Peter, St. Thomas, St. Thaddeus and St. Mari of the Seventy. In the early centuries of Christianity there was only one Church. The affairs of the Church were managed by Bishops in their respective areas. There were also chief Bishops known as Patriarchs. Writes Mar Yacob Manna, a Uniate Bishop of the Roman Church, in his book *Margy Peghyany*, "Places where Patriarchates were organized by the holy Apostles are the following mothers of all cities; the first, Babylon. It is the metropolis, yea, the mother of all cities,

and therefore was the Head of the Assyrian Kingdom. Then Alexandria, Antioch, Rome, and Constantiople." Of these only Babylon was at that time outside the Roman Empire of the West. . . . The Church of the East is variously called by various historians. Some of the popular appellations are Assyrian Church, Nestorian Church, Chaldean Syrian Church, etc. . . . The Church of the East traces its origin directly back to the original Apostles. One of its chapels founded by the Three Wise Men on their return from Bethlehem, is still in use today in the town of Resaieh, in Northern Iran. The Patriarch attended that chapel as a boy.[1]

This special volume, published to commemorate the visit to India of the Patriarch of the Church of the East, contains many references to the apostolic tradition of that church body and St. Thomas.

More than one thousand and nine hundred years ago, the holy Apostle St. Thomas, after establishing the first Christian Church among his own people in ancient Babylon, turned to India, led by the Holy Spirit, and with an evangelical zeal traversed this subcontinent preaching the good news and baptizing those who believed in Him. His words 'had fallen into good ground, bearing fruit bringing forth a hundredfold' and spreading to countries all over Asia. But by the vicissitudes of history, through the centuries, this Church, founded on the blood of martyrs, has become almost extinct, leaving a scattered remnant.

After establishing churches and ordaining clergy in the Middle East, St. Thomas came to this country as deputed by his Lord. Here, too, he instructed thousands and thousands of people in the true faith of our Lord, baptized them in the name of the Father, Son and Holy Ghost, set up churches for their worship and ordained the necessary clergy to cater to their spiritual needs. Afterwards he endured various persecutions and consequently martyrdom for the belief and justice of our Lord, by a lance thrust by miscreants deputed by King Mizdi.[2]

Traditions of the Syrian Indian Church

Dr. Edgar J. Goodspeed bears witness to the tradition of the Syrian Indian Church. "It is a striking fact that the so-called Acts of Thomas relate the mission of Thomas to India, and they were written early in the third century, as modern authorities (Harnack, M. R. James) agree. This goes far to confirm the legend of the Syrian Indian church, that Thomas did indeed not only cross Parthia with his message but actually penetrated India with it! These Acts have some links with the first-century Indian history, also."[3]

Traditions of the Nestorian Church

When I visited Iran in 1971, I held conferences with a number of noted Christian authorities. Among them was His Excellency Yohannan S. Issayi, the archivist of the Chaldean Catholic Library at Teheran. He had a book written by a church historian, John Stewart, PhD. (Narsai Press, Trichur, Kerala, India, 1928, 1961). In the introduction Stewart writes, "The message must have been carried to the furtherest confines of the Asiatic continent with almost the rapidity of a prairie fire. It is evident St. Thomas arrived in India no later than 49 A.D."[4]

Speaking of the Nestorians and their apostolic origins Stewart says, "The center of this marvelous church was first in Edessa and then in the Persian province of Abiabene. There was a large and widespread Christian community throughout the whole of central Asia in the first centuries of the present era. Countries such as Afganistan, and Tibet were centers of Christian activity."[5]

Historical Confirmation of First Century Travel to India

A news item from the *Los Angeles Times* confirms the fact that many traveled from the Roman Empire to India in the first century. The story was headlined, "Ancient Jewish Colony in India Disappearing."

Cochin, India—The Synagogue here celebrated its 400th anniversary in 1968 and visitors included Prime Minister Indira Gandhi and Jews from as far away as the United States. Now there is no rabbi.

The white Jews along the Malabar Coast once numbered tens of thousands. Now there are only 80.

The Jews of Cochin came to India in AD 72, driven from Jerusalem by Roman legions. Now many—a critical number— are returning to Israel.

The Cochin synagogue—others closed when the congregations returned to Israel—contains many historic treasures. Among them are the copper plates given by the local ruler in AD 379 to the Jewish community, conveying a large land grant.[6]

Several details of the story confirm the likelihood of the historicity of the traditions of early Christianity in India. The fact that a colony of Jews came there in AD 72 proves that the Jews of the first century *knew* about this part of the world and that *travel* of even large groups was possible. There was no question of an exploration of an unknown continent. Further, the continuity of the Jewish community demonstrates how a Christian community could also continually exist from the first century until the present in the same area. The references to the copper plates is similar to several stories about this means of granting and certifying political and property rights in ancient times.

Modern Scholarship

There is one great work of scholarship which reveals a very thorough study of the St. Thomas tradition in India, which seems to confirm its historicity. We are greatly indebted to the Roman Catholic scholar, A. M. Mundadan, who wrote his doctoral dissertation on St. Thomas at a German University in 1960, and later expanded it into a book *The Sixteenth Century Traditions of the St. Thomas Christians*. It presents a truly enormous amount of documentation, some of which is in the following excerpt:

The Portuguese arrived in India at the end of the fifteenth century. When they came they certainly possessed some vague information concerning the apostolate of St. Thomas in India. Not long after their arrival they began to hear reports about the existence of what was described as the "house" and "tomb" of St. Thomas in Mylapore on the Choromandel Coast. But it was only in the early twenties of the sixteenth century that they made earnest efforts to explore Choromandel and Mylapore and the "house" of St. Thomas.

The earliest written record about St. Thomas' preaching in India is the romantic apocryphal *Acts of St. Thomas*, written in Syriac towards the end of the second century or by the beginning of the third century. From the third century onwards we find frequent allusions to the Parthian or Indian apostolate of St. Thomas in the writings of the Church-Fathers and other ecclesiastical writers.

The contents of the western tradition, whether it is single or combined, may be summarised thus: Thomas the Apostle preached the Gospel in Parthia and India, converted many, including members of some royal family, suffered martyrdom there, and was first buried in India itself; later his mortal remains were transferred to the West (to Edessa) where they were honourably deposited and venerated. The main source for this tradition is, no doubt, the *Acts of St. Thomas* in which India is named the field of St. Thomas' activity.

> Thomas preached in Parthia and India, converted many, including royal family members. He suffered martyrdom there, and was first buried in India.

The Indian tradition is not so clearly uniform; it varies, as we go from source to source and from place to place. The general trend may be summarised: St. Thomas, one of the twelve Apostles of our Lord came direct from the Near-East and landed in Cranganore about 52 A.D.; he converted high caste Hindu families in Cranganore, Palayur, Quilon etc.; consecrated priests from some of these families; built some seven churches, erected crosses; then passed over to the eastern coast and suffered martyrdom there; his tomb is in Mylapore on the coast.

The entire relics are known to have been removed from India to Edessa and later to Ortona in Italy where now they rest.

Thome Lopes, who accompanied V[asco] da Gama on his second journey to India in 1503 says that, among other events reported by them, the Christians who came to meet Gama told the Portuguese how they were conducting a big pilgrimage to the tomb of St. Thomas who was buried near their country, and who worked many miracles.

Apostolate
Mundalan explains how Thomas's ministry was far-reaching:

> St. Thomas preached the gospel and baptized people in all the places he went and founded churches. According to a stone inscription which the Christians of St. Thomas read and interpreted for Roz, the Apostle converted three principal kings of India: that of Bisnaga called by them Xoren Porumal, that of Pandi called Pandi Perumal and that of all Malabar called Xaran Perumal. Fr. Guerreiro found in a Chaldean book that the Apostle had converted six kings and three emperors: the emperors correspond to Roz's three principal kings. The Pandi kingdom, according to Guerreiro, corresponded to the then existing kingdom of Cape Comorin.

The Chaldean Abuna told the inquirers of 1533 that the Apostle was murdered with a lance by a low caste. Barros has the following version. The Apostle was murdered while preaching to the people near a tank. At the instigation of the Brahmins he was stoned by some people and he fell down. As he lay there almost dead a Brahmin struck him with a lance and the saint breathed the last. According to Dionysio the Apostle was martyred with a lance while praying on a mountain.

As to the possibility of St. Thomas preaching in India, whether in North or South India, nobody can have any serious doubt. It is repugnant to think that Christianity was preached from the beginning only in the Roman empire and all the twelve Apostles went westwards to the parts of the Roman empire. At the dawn of Christianity there were trade routes connecting the West and the East, routes very well frequented. The land routes reached parts of N. India while the sea routes reached the coasts of Malabar and other parts of South India. Hence no one can sensibly deny the possibility of one or another of the twelve Apostles having reached India and preached Christianity there.

As for the relics, it is very probable, as has been suggested earlier, that the early Portuguese explorers did not know anything about the alleged translation of the relics to Edessa and later to Ortona and hence they believed that they discovered the whole body of the Apostle in the tomb. But it is very clear that they did not actually discover the whole body from their own testimony. However, their belief persisted.[7]

Comments by Various Scholars on the Life of St. Thomas
Asbury Smith reports an interesting insight from the *Acts of St. Thomas the Apostle to India*:

There is an ancient tradition that Thomas carried the Gospel to India. The *Acts of Saint Thomas the Apostle to India*, a manuscript that goes back to the second or third century, is the oldest written record in support of this tradition.

In the *Acts of Saint Thomas* the apostles are shown as dividing the world among themselves for evangelistic activity. When Thomas was assigned India, he protested, "I cannot go there because of the fatigue of the body on the journey, for I am a Hebrew." Jesus then appeared to Thomas, urging him to go to

India, but he continued to resist, saying, "I would that Thou wouldst send me into another country, for unto the country of India I cannot go."

It was then that our Lord showed himself to Abbanes, a merchant from India, and sold Thomas to him as a slave. Thomas recognizing himself as Jesus' slave, yields, and thus came to India as a slave of Abbanes.

Until a few decades ago no record existed of a king named Gondaforus and this story was considered entirely legendary. But recent excavations have established that a king by the name of Gondaforus did reign in North India during the time Thomas might have lived there. Coins and inscriptions have been unearthed bearing Gondaforus' name. This leaves to be explained the presence of Thomas in North India when the Christians who bear his name seem always to have centered in South India. Dr. J. N. Farquhar explains this by saying that Thomas remained in North India until war destroyed Gondaforus and his kingdom, and then he went to South India. Hazel E. Foster thinks that "this reconstruction of what may have happened has a good historical underpinnings as have the various stories regarding the origin of other ancient churches."

In 1952 the Syrian Christians celebrated the 1900th anniversary of the arrival of Thomas in their country. In connection with this celebration the World Council of Churches held three important meetings. The Study Committee and the Central Committee met at Lucknow and the World Council of Christian Youth met at Kottayam.

Aside from the tradition that Thomas founded the Church in India little is known of the early history of this ancient Syrian Church. Unfortunately when the Portuguese arrived in India they destroyed the church records, hoping thereby to destroy what they considered a heretical brand of Christianity.

Thomas, tradition says, died a martyr's death on a mountain now called Mount Thomas in Mylopur, a suburb of Madras.

His death was accomplished by piercing with a lance. A shrine erected by the Portuguese marks the sacred site.

A hymn of praise recorded in the *Acts of Thomas* expresses the great honor given the church by the Syrian Christians. "The church is she in whom is the splendor of royalty. She is pleasant of aspect and lovely. Beautiful is she to him that looketh upon her. Her garments are like unto flowers of every kind, and the odor thereof cometh forth and anointeth the head. . . . Truth is upon her head, and joy with her feet."

The *Acts of Thomas* gives a description of the all-night service used by Thomas to receive Gondaforus into the Christian Church:

They brought oil and lighted many lamps, for it was night. Then the Apostle rose up, and prayed over them with his voice, saying, "Peace be unto you, O my brethren." Now they heard the voice only, but they did not see his form, for as yet they had not received baptism, and the Apostle took the oil and poured it over their heads, and recited prayers over them, and he answered and said,

"Let the name of Christ, which is over all things, come!
Let the name which is holy, and exalted, and perfect in
mercy, come!
Let thy mercy come!
Let that which is a hidden mystery come!
Let the mother of the seven mansions come, and let thy
rest be in the eighth habitation."[8]

Mundadan, already quoted, describes the recent history of the tomb of St. Thomas:

In the four hundred years between 1523 and 1903 the tomb in Mylapore was broken open three times for one reason or other: in 1523 the first Portuguese excavation took place; in 1893–1896 the present Gothic cathedral was built; in 1903 the tomb was widened westward when the present crypt was built in commemoration of the tri-centenary of the erection of the Mylapore diocese.[9]

The Burial Place of St. Thomas

It has been well established that Thomas was buried in Mylapore, India, now a suburb of Madras. In her interesting devotional book *By Post to The Apostles*, Helen Homan refers to the history of the treatment of the remains of St. Thomas, which she evidently obtained from the *Catholic Encyclopedia*. She says it is accepted as fact that some of the bones of St. Thomas were transported to Edessa in Mesopotamia. She describes how the Crusaders evidently carried them to the island of Chios and tells how later Manfred, Prince of Taranto carried them by ship to Ortona in Italy, where they were placed in a great Cathedral. After this the Turks sacked Ortona and rifled the tomb for suspected treasure.[10]

Mary Sharp in *A Traveller's Guide to Saints in Europe*, reports the results of her research concerning the relics of St. Thomas. "They are," she says, "reputed to be at Goa and Meliapore in India, and at Ortona, Italy. The finger is in the church of Santa Croce in Gerusalemme, Rome." She adds, "In the church of Mylapore (now Meliapore) is a stone cross—The Thomas Cross of the sixth to eighth century, which is said to mark the place where his body was buried until taken to Edessa in the fourth century." She concludes, "However wild the stories about St. Thomas in his *Acts*, the names of Gundaphor and Gad, the Indian rulers he is said to have encountered, have recently been shown to exist, as they issued coins which have survived."[11]

A guide book published by the Church of the Holy Cross (Santa Croce) entitled *The Sessorian Relics of the Passion of Our Lord* by Bedini, claims that in this church:

> . . . is preserved the index finger of St. Thomas. Some say that this relic has been in Santa Croce from the time of St. Helen. In the basilica there is an altar dedicated to St. Thomas. The reli-

quary, which was remade after the French revolution, is shaped like a chalice at the bottom. Above the knob two palms, the symbol of the martyrdom of the apostle, entwine in the shape of a crown surmounted by a cross with rays. In the centre of the crown is inserted an oval case with both sides of crystal. In the middle of the case arises a holder in the shape of a finger with two openings in the side. Through the openings the phalanges of the venerated Finger can be clearly seen.[12]

It is evident that Thomas, who as a disciple was pessimistic and filled with doubt, became a vigorous missionary. The weight of scholarship has grown so great, concerning his mission to Babylon, Persia and India, that it must be accepted as probable. The stories of Thomas, like those of several others of the apostles, provide a record which throws much light on the world of the first century beyond the borders of the Roman Empire. In turn, as the history of the first century in that area is revealed by contemporary scholars, it throws much light on the life of Thomas.

The one great insight about Thomas himself, which comes to us from the history of Thomas in Babylonia and India, is that he was a fearless evangelist and a great builder of churches. Those people in the modern world who would accept Christianity but who would reject the *church* (i.e., assembly or local congregation) as the central human instrument in the strategy of God have divorced themselves from the apostolic tradition. Were the apostles to return to earth today, they would have little time for those who imagine there can be a churchless Christianity. Such "Christianity," if we even dare call it that, is incapable of survival.

If we would have Christianity survive, our first loyalty must be to the One whom Thomas called "My Lord and my God," and secondly to the only divinely ordained institution on earth, the local assembly or congregation of His people. No one can estimate how many millions of Christians came to believe in Christ because of Thomas. They are beyond counting. The churches which Thomas founded in India have kept Christianity alive and extended the faith which survives there to this day.

Both the churches and the apostolic faith with which Thomas identified himself were, of course, subjected to change, decay and even corruption. Human beings inevitably produce these effects. But to this day missionaries in India report that the pure message of the New Testament is still welcome, and is still effective among the St. Thomas Christians there.

CHAPTER TEN

MATTHEW

As Jesus was walking along, he saw a man named Matthew sitting at his tax collector's booth. "Follow me and be my disciple," Jesus said to him. So Matthew got up and followed him. Matthew 9:9

Matthew was a brother of James the Less and both were the sons of Alphaeus (Mark 2:14). Matthew's other name was Levi. He was a tax collector (Matthew 10:3) in Capernaum, in the territory ruled by Herod Antipas. He belonged to the class of bureaucrats called *portitores* serving under the *publicani*, the officers who were concessionaires for taxes according to the Roman custom of that day. As such he would have had some education and have been acquainted with the Aramaic, Greek, and Latin languages. The tax collectors of whom he was one, although scorned by the Jews, seemed as a group to hear the message of Jesus gladly (Matthew 11:19; Luke 15:1).

By the time Matthew was called, Peter, James, and John, who also came from Capernaum, were already disciples of Jesus (Mark 5:37). Unlike some of the other apostles Matthew did not enter the group from the followers of John the Baptist.

Significantly, among the events recorded in his Gospel is the notation that the first thing Matthew did after his call was to invite Jesus to his home for a feast. Matthew filled the place with the only people who would set foot in his house, his fellow "tax gatherers and sinners." The term was an epithet, not a description. When Jesus was criticized for keeping company with them He responded, "Healthy people don't need a doctor—sick people do." And in a paraphrase of the words of Micah 6:6-8 Jesus added, "Now go and learn the meaning of this Scripture: 'I want you to show mercy, not offer sacrifices.' For I have come to call not those who think they are righteous, but those who know they are sinners" (Matthew 9:11-13).

Like most of the apostles, Matthew seemed to have evangelized in a number of countries. Irenaeus says that he preached the gospel among the Hebrews. Does this mean in Palestine or to the Jews abroad? Probably both. Clement of Alexandria stated that Matthew spent fifteen years in this work. Clement also said that Matthew went to the Ethiopians, the Greeks of Macedonia (northern Greece), the Syrians, and Persians.[1] An early Christian writer named Heracleon declared that Matthew did not suffer martyrdom. But most authorities affirm that he was painfully put to death.

The Writing of the Gospel

Jerome tells the story of the authorship of the Gospel by Matthew:

> Matthew, also called Levi, Apostle and aforetimes publican, composed a gospel of Christ at first published in Judea in Hebrew for the sake of those of the circumcision who believed, but this was afterwards translated into Greek though by what author is uncertain. The Hebrew itself has been preserved until the present day in the library at Caesarea which Pamphilus so diligently gathered. I have also had the opportunity of having the volume described to me by the Nazarenes of Beroea, a city of Syria, who use it. In this it is to be noted that wherever the Evangelist, whether on his own account or on the person of our Lord the Saviour, quotes the testimony of the Old Testament he does not follow the authority of the translators of the Septuagint, but the Hebrew. Wherefore these two forms exist, "Out of Egypt have I called my son," and "for he shall be called a Nazarene."[2]

Eusebius quotes Papias, who lived 100 A.D., as saying that Matthew had composed in Aramaic the Oracles of the Lord which were translated into Greek by each man as he was able. Irenaeus, about a century and a half earlier than Eusebius had stated that "Matthew also issued a written Gospel among the Hebrews in their own dialect."[3] St. Augustine also said Matthew had written only in Hebrew while the other Gospel writers wrote in Greek.

Matthew understood the way in which Jesus fulfilled the prophecies of the Old Testament. More references appear in his Gospel to this fact than in any of the other three Gospels.

> Matthew understood the way in which Jesus fulfilled the prophecies of the Old Testament. More of these references appear in his Gospel than in the other three.

We are in Matthew's debt for the only version of the story about the man who found a treasure hid in a field and sold all he had to purchase it. Matthew knew from personal experience what that meant. He, too, had forsaken his profitable and lucrative career and had followed Jesus.

Various Traditions of Matthew's Ministry and Death

There are so many traditions which seem to be mutually contradictory that one can but list them all and try to make a synthesis of them as Barclay has done:

> Socrates said that Matthew was allotted Ethiopia in the apostolic comity agreement (The E.H., 1, 19; cf. Rubinus, 1, 9). Ambrose connects him with Persia, Paulinus of Nola with Parthia, Isidore with Macedonia.
>
> Clement of Alexandria indicates that he died a natural death (*The Miscellanies*, 4, 9). Clement says he was a vegetarian eating seeds, nuts, and vegetables without flesh. The *Talmud* says that Matthew was condemned to death by the Jewish Sanhedrin.

The apocryphal *Acts of Andrew and Matthew* which later was put into Anglo-Saxon verse, claims that he was sent to the cannibalistic *Anthropophagi* who attempted to put his eyes out and put him in prison for 30 days before eating him. On the 27th day he was rescued by Andrew who came by sea miraculously escaping a storm and thus rescued Matthew. Matthew returned to the *Anthropophagi* working miracles among them and the king became jealous of him. They bound Matthew, covered him with papyrus soaked in dolphin oil, poured brimstone, asphalt and pitch upon him, heaped up tow and wood and surrounded him with the golden images of the 12 gods of the people. But the fire turned to dew and the flames flew out and melted the metal of the images. Finally the fire took the form of a dragon, chased the king into his palace and curled around about him so that he could not move. Then Matthew rebuked the fire and prayed and gave up the ghost. The King was converted and became a priest and with two angels Matthew departed to heaven.[4]

According to Edgar Goodspeed in his book *Matthew, Apostle and Evangelist*, there was confusion in the early stories between Matthias and Matthew. The tradition of the *Babylonian Talmud* (Sanhedrin 43 a.) tells of the trial and execution of one "Matthai." Matthew probably did not die in the same country as Matthias.

The difficulty in knowing for certain the countries which Matthew probably visited lies in the identification of the country called "Ethiopia." The Ethiopia in Africa is well known to us, but there was also an Asiatic Ethiopia which was south of the Caspian Sea in Persia. It was in the kingdom of the Parthians, but from all accounts was off the well-traveled trade routes.

As we have seen, Ambrose links Matthew with Persia. The associations of Thomas with a "Gospel of Matthew" which was reputedly found in India are well known. This would seem to indicate at least a tradition of the apostle Matthew as having been near the Asiatic

Ethiopia. It would be natural for a copy of Matthew's Gospel to have found its way to India if Matthew himself had been in Persia, which he probably indeed did visit, for Persia was on the direct trade route from Antioch to India.

The Present Burial Place of Matthew's Body

Next door to the cathedral in Salerno, Italy, that contains the body of Matthew, there is an archeological museum which publishes a guide book for those who make pilgrimages to the church. It is written by Arturo Carucci and offers the following information about the tomb of the apostle:

> A fresco on the side of the center balcony shows John, Bishop of Paestum receiving Athanasias the monk who found the body of Matthew. Another shows Gisolfo I ordering the Abbott John to get the body of the evangelist Matthew at Capaccio to bring it to Salerno. Above the seats of the chorus (choir) there is a reminder of the moving of the body of St. Matthew. It shows a procession with the body of the Apostle being brought into the church.
>
> In the center of the crypt there is the tomb of Saint Matthew located at about 2 meters of depth and surmounted by a two-fronted altar, rich of marble and dominated by an ample "umbrella canopy," finely embroidered, which covers two bronze statues representing the Evangelist: one for each front of the altar. They were made in 1606 by Michelangelo Naccarino (1622); the Saint is in the traditional position. The sculptor knew how to give the bronze a great expression of power. The tomb and the altars are adorned in an elegant marble base which has enormous candelabras at each corner. They were a gift from the School of Medicine.
>
> In 1969 the floor at the north side was opened and the altar was erected at the tomb of the Evangelist, altering the harmony and the original design of the two-fronted altar.[5]

Carucci also gives us the date of the building of the cathedral and the interment of the body of the apostle Matthew:

> Inside is the "holy seat" [special chair, ed.] said to be that of Saint Gregory VII; because, from the 11th century the Holy Pontiff ascended during the consecration of the temple in 1084. The seven circular steps, instead, are new like the chairs of the "bema." The inscription celebrates the millennium (1954) of the translation of the relics of Saint Matthew.

> Dedicated to the Virgin Mary the church was elevated over the tomb of St. Matthew by the Norman Duke, Robert Guiscardo right after the conquest of Salerno in 1076.

> Not everybody knows that the body [of St. Matthew] is entrusted to and honored in Salerno. It is enclosed in a magnificent crypt deserving of the veneration of the people of Salerno and deserving of St. Matthew.[6]

Legends about Matthew

It is evident from the legends and traditions of the apostles that the confusion in the records in the Middle Ages about place names have made it impossible to be sure which "Ethiopia" is associated with Matthew. For example, did the following story arise out of imagination or does it correctly associate Matthew with the Ethiopia in Africa?

> It is related in the *Perfetto Legendario*, that, after the dispersion of the Apostles, he travelled into Egypt and Ethiopia, preaching the Gospel; and having arrived in the capital of Ethiopia, he lodged in the house of the eunuch who had been baptized by Philip, and who entertained him with great honor. There were two terrible magicians at that time in Ethiopia, who by their diabolical spells and incantations kept all the people in subjection, afflicting them at the same time with strange and terrible diseases; but St. Matthew overcame them, and having baptized the people, they were delivered forever from the malignant influence of these enchanters. And further, it is related that St. Matthew raised the son of

the King of Egypt from the dead, and healed his daughter of the leprosy. The princess, whose name was Iphigenia, he placed at the head of a community of virgins dedicated to the service of God. A certain wicked heathen king, having threatened to tear her from her asylum, was struck by leprosy, and his palace destroyed by fire. St. Matthew remained twenty-three years in Egypt and Ethiopia, and it is said that he perished in the ninetieth year of our era, under Domitian; but the manner of his death is uncertain; according to the Greek legend he died in peace, but according to the tradition of the Western Church he suffered martyrdom either by the sword or the spear.[7]

The Roman Catholic tradition of the life and death of Matthew is given us by Mary Sharp in *A Traveller's Guide to Saints in Europe*:

Matthew's body is reputed to be enshrined in the Cathedral of San Matteo at Salerno, Italy, and other relics in many churches, including Santa Maria Maggiore, Rome.

After the Ascension, St. Matthew is said to have traveled to Ethiopia where he was entertained by the eunuch whom St. Philip had baptised. He performed several miracles, including the healing of the King of Egypt's daughter of leprosy. Accounts differ as regards his death. Some say that he was beheaded, others that he died a peaceful death.[8]

A Suggested Biography of Matthew

Matthew, also called Levi, was the son of Alphaeus and the brother of James the Less. It is apparent that Alphaeus was a godly man, but though Matthew was given the priestly name of Levi, he was probably far from godly in his early life. It required a great deal of ambition and greed for a Jew to willingly be known as an associate of the House of Herod Antipas and a servant of the hated Romans by becoming a tax gatherer for them. The way this term (publican) is used in the Bible indicates that to be a tax gatherer was to obtain a position in which graft and corruption were not only possible, but likely. Also there was the embarrassment of being known as a collaborator with Rome. The Roman occupation troops were hated with the same kind of scorn that the Jews in the twentieth century felt toward the Nazis.

Nevertheless, Jesus sought to reconcile James, who may well have been a nationalistic Zealot, with his brother, Matthew, the collaborator with Rome. Both became in time ardent disciples of Jesus.

Matthew probably remained in the Holy Land, as tradition says, for fifteen years. After this, encouraged by the reports of the success of other Christian leaders among the Jews of the Diaspora, and also among the Gentiles, he went forth on several missionary journeys.

It is possible that he wrote his Gospel first in the Aramaic language which was well understood by the people of northern Palestine. Later he may have made copies in Hebrew and distributed them in several places where he went. This is most likely as it is evident that Matthew directed more of his appeal to potential converts among the Jews than to the Gentiles. The Gospel of Matthew is filled with many references to Old Testament prophecies about the Messiah as being fulfilled in Jesus. Those quotations would have been of only passing interest to Gentiles. But, like other apostles, Matthew eventually incurred the wrath of the Jewish establishment and was forced to turn to the Gentiles who gave him a more ready hearing.

> It required a great deal of ambition and greed for a Jew to willingly be a servant of the hated Romans as a tax gatherer for them.

There are too many references in the traditions and legends of Matthew's ministry to kings and other high government officials for us to ignore the possibility that his evident literacy and his former experience as a bureaucrat may well have fitted him to understand just how to present the gospel to people in high places. It is certain that he did indeed go to Persia and to the mysterious area there known as "Ethiopia." And it is possible that he was in grave danger of his life there.

It is not impossible that he may also have journeyed to the Ethiopia in Africa as Roman Catholic tradition indicates. We do not know just how or when his body was eventually discovered. But it is evident that the monk Athanasias appeared before the Norman Duke of Salerno and confidently announced that the body had indeed been found, and he advised the Duke to bring it to Salerno as an apostolic relic deserving of the great cathedral which was built there. Probably a few of the same bones were later transferred to Rome. (There is no good reason to deny, however, that the majority of the bones remain in Salerno to this day.)

> Matthew was a gifted writer, an ardent disciple, and perhaps the best educated of any of the Twelve.

There are too many stories of Matthew's death to be certain just where he died. It is likely that it was not in Ethiopia in Africa, but rather in Egypt. The connection of the legends of Matthew with the Sanhedrin is significant. The Sanhedrin was a body of important Jews in Alexandria, Egypt. This would hint as to an historical relationship of Matthew to Egypt. It is perhaps possible that Matthew was martyred in Egypt upon his return from Ethiopia in Africa, but this conclusion is not certain.

What is certain is that Matthew was a gifted writer, an ardent disciple, and perhaps the best educated of any of the Twelve. Thus he was well equipped to witness to people in places of authority, and was a vessel well chosen to write the great Gospel which bears his name.

CHAPTER ELEVEN

JAMES, SON OF ALPHAEUS

Jesus went up on a mountain to pray, and he prayed to God all night. At daybreak he called together all of his disciples and chose twelve of them to be apostles [including]. . . . James (son of Alphaeus). Luke 6:12-13, 15

James, the son of Alphaeus, who is also called the "Less" or perhaps "Younger," was a brother of Matthew Levi and the son of Mary. Which Mary is not altogether certain, though she appears to be the wife of one Clopas [Cleophas], which may have been another or second name for Alphaeus.

As with Matthew, James was a native of Capernaum, a city on the northwestern shores of the Sea of Galilee. Here in the early part of his ministry Jesus also moved into his own house. He preached in the local synagogues, in private homes, as well as at the seashore where large numbers of people often gathered. We do not know how or where Jesus first met James and Matthew. Probably they had heard Jesus preach. It is quite likely that when Jesus called Matthew to follow Him, He was not (so much) giving a call to a first acquaintance, but a final call to decision to one who had already shown a keen interest. If James and Matthew were brothers, and were cousins of Jesus, that fact would of course shed light on their previous acquaintance.

Matthew, no doubt, suffered in his conscience because, as a tax-gatherer for the house of Herod Antipas, the satrap of Rome, he must necessarily have incurred the displeasure of the Jews who hated

Herod and Rome alike. In any case, it would seem quite evident that Matthew had made his peace with Herod's administration if not with the Romans. But to obtain this uneasy peace would have caused him to deny his conscience. After Jesus called him, Matthew immediately threw a great feast for his friends, who included a number of other tax-gatherers and their mutual friends, none of whom could have been in very good repute with the Jewish community.

Jesus was the guest of honor at this feast. We get a picture of the enmity of the Jewish community toward the tax collectors when Jesus was bitterly criticized by the local Pharisees for eating with those they called, "tax collectors and sinners." In Israel at the time this phrase "tax collectors and sinners" seems to have been a colloquialism for those who were hopelessly corrupt and outside the mercy or interest of God. Having defiled themselves they would necessarily defile anyone whom they contacted.

We have no indication that James was among those who gathered for the feast. Every indication is that he was not. Temperamentally and perhaps ideologically, he differed from his brother Matthew.

James and Matthew Levi Bar Alphaeus were said to have been of the tribe of Gad, one of the ten tribes of the northern confederacy which was taken captive in the eighth century BC as a result of the Assyrian invasion by Tiglath Pileser. However, bearing the name Levi more probably indicates that both Matthew and James were of the tribe of Levi, the priestly tribe. The tribe of Levi, unlike the tribe of Gad, had fled from northern Israel before the Assyrian invasion and had joined with Judah. It would have been most unlikely in biblical days for a child not from the priestly tribe of Levi to have been named Levi.

> Temperamentally and perhaps ideologically, James differed from his brother Matthew.

But Matthew had betrayed his priestly heritage and had become a collaborator with Herod and Rome. It would be natural to suppose that his brother James was in total disagreement with Matthew Levi's choice of secular matters. A later tradition about James indicates that James himself was at first a "Zealot" (the revolutionary group seeking to throw off the yoke of both Herod Antipas and Rome). But his patriotic and nationalistic idealism was rudely dashed by the policy of bloodshed which characterized the Zealots. Therefore, James probably became an ascetic, who sought refuge in his own piety from the bloodshed of the Zealots. But was he an ascetic? This opens the question which must be settled about the identity of James himself.

The Distinction between the Men Called "James"

With the identity of James, the brother of John, the son of Zebedee, known otherwise as James the Elder and James the Great, we have no trouble. His story is the most complete of any of the original twelve disciples, except for Judas Iscariot. This James was beheaded at the command of Herod Antipas to please the Jewish leaders who always suspected Herod's devotion to Judaism was mere lip service.

James the Less or Younger, son of Alphaeus and Mary, discussed here, is a man of whom we know comparatively little except that his brother Matthew was also an apostle, and his other siblings were Joseph, an early Christian, and Salome, an unknown woman.

There is also a James who was the father of the apostle named Judas or Thaddeaus, now commonly called Jude, who is carefully distinguished in Scripture from Judas Iscariot. James, the father of Jude, is probably the same as James, the son of Zebedee and brother of John.

James, the brother of Jesus, is the best known of all the early apostles except for Peter, John, and Paul. He was not one of the Twelve, however.

It is the confusion of identity between James the Less and James the brother of Jesus which makes it practically impossible to know who each was, and what each did distinctly from the other.

Most of the ancient denominations, such as the Roman Catholic or Armenian Orthodox, identify James the Less and James the brother of Jesus as one and the same. Their reasoning is complicated, contradictory, and not defensible by the Scriptural record. Essentially though, it is an attempt to assert that, contrary to what Paul wrote in Galatians about "James the *brother* of the Lord," James the Just was a *cousin* of Jesus. The reason for this tortured attempt to explain Paul's plain statement away is to protect the doctrine of the perpetual virginity of Mary by implying that when Paul wrote "brother" he really meant cousin. Obscure references in Greek literature are used by some to show that this was possible.

The early heresy of Docetism attempted to convince Christians that all sexual intercourse was evil. The later elevation of Mary to the stature of a demigoddess, forced some of those who took this view to invent out of whole cloth the notion that the brothers and sisters of Jesus were perhaps children of Joseph by a previous marriage. Thus James the brother of the Lord becomes James the half brother. However, at this point a further contradiction inserts itself. How could James the Less be the son of Joseph and also be the son of Alphaeus?

The answer which has apparently satisfied most of the scholars of the oldest branches of organized Christianity is to make Mary, the mother of James the Less, a sister of Mary, the mother of Jesus! This reduces James the Less to the status of a cousin of Jesus rather than a half brother.

> James the brother of Jesus was indeed just that. James did not believe in Jesus before the Resurrection. Jesus made a special post-resurrection appearance to a "James."

One cannot but sympathize with the defenders of this point of view under the pressure they were under to preserve the doctrine of the perpetual virginity of Mary, the mother of Jesus. But their solution is simply impossible. The purpose of names is to distinguish between children. With the great number of names available to the ancients it would be unlikely that there were two Marys in the same family.

We may be safe, therefore, in assuming that James the brother of Jesus was indeed just that. There is little doubt that this James did not believe in Jesus before the Resurrection, for the New Testament is careful to tell us that Jesus made a special post-resurrection appearance to a "James." This was probably the brother of Jesus. We are not told when this happened, or why it was necessary, but we do have two facts. Jesus' brothers in the flesh did not believe in Him before the Resurrection, yet in the book of Acts, James the brother of Jesus, is described as the chairman of the church of Jerusalem, exceeding Peter and John in rank. Paul certainly mentions him as having been the first and only apostle with whom he personally conferred three years after his conversion, except for Peter.

When Paul went to Jerusalem again before his final imprisonment there, James appears again as the spokesman of the Twelve, urging Paul to demonstrate his fidelity to the Mosaic Law in order not to offend the Jews in Jerusalem. Paul purposely refers to this James as one of the "pillars" of the church along with John.

A careful reading reveals that it is James, the brother of Jesus, whom Paul meant rather than James the Great, since by this time James the Great was dead. It is not an utter impossibility that James the Less is meant, but the whole thrust of Paul's historic references to James seemed to be, according to the context of Paul's writing, the James who is the brother of the Lord.

James the brother of Jesus undoubtedly wrote the Epistle that bears that name.

There is also a great deal of traditional information about the life and death of James the brother of Jesus, which has been wrongly attributed to James the Less.

Over two hundred years ago, the English scholar Dorman Newman summed up this tradition:

> Prayer was [James's] constant business and delight. He seemed to live upon it and to trade in nothing but the frequent returns of converse with heaven.
>
> In the procuratorship of Alvinus the successor to Festus, the enemies of James decided to dispatch him. A council was

hastily summoned. They plotted to set the scribes and Pharisees to insnare him. They told him they had a mighty confidence in him and that they would that he might correct the error and false opinion the people had of Jesus. To that end he was invited to go to the top of the temple where he might be seen and heard by all. There they demanded, "Tell us, what is the institution of the crucified Jesus?" The people below, hearing it, glorified the blessed Jesus.

The Scribes and Pharisees perceiving now that they had overshot themselves and that instead of reclaiming the people had confirmed them in their (supposed) error, thought there was no way left but presently to dispatch him, that by his sad fate others might be warmed not to believe him. Wherefore, suddenly crying out that James the Just himself was seduced and had become an imposter, they threw him down from the place where he stood. Though bruised, he was not killed by the fall, but recovered so much strength, as to get upon his knees and pray to heaven from them.

They began to load him with a shower of stones until one more mercifully cruel than the rest with a fuller's club beat out his brains. Thus dyed [sic] that good man in the 90th year of his life [this of course, impossible—ED] and about 24 years after Christ's ascension. He was buried upon the Mt. of Olives in a tomb which he had built for himself.[1]

Newman based his narration on fairly good early traditions.

James the brother of Jesus is, therefore, the James who was prominent in the Jerusalem church and was martyred by being thrown from the pinnacle of the temple and then buried on the Mt. of Olives.

This is the James whom the Armenians and others confuse with James the Less. According to Armenian tradition, after the destruction of the monastery in which the body of the martyred apostle was originally buried, his bones were removed to the Cathedral of St. James in Jerusalem on Mt. Zion. They were placed beneath the principal altar.

This cathedral is also believed to be the site in which the head of the apostle James the Great, brother of John, was buried.

The Armenian Monastery of St. James covers the entire summit of Mt. Zion totaling three hundred acres, or one-sixth of the entire old city of Jerusalem. The remains of James the brother of Jesus were transferred from the Kedron Valley in the fourth century and buried in his home, the ruins of which were later incorporated into the cathedral.

In the Treasury of the Armenian Patriarchate of Jerusalem are listed a reliquary containing the "arm of James the Less" and another containing "the fingers of James the brother of the Lord."

It is more likely that the reliquaries contain bones of the same man, James the brother of the Lord.

The tomb in the Valley of the Kedron, now called the Grotto of St. James, was originally the burial place of a Herodian priestly family of the sons of Hezir. In the fourth century, monks living in the grotto found a skeleton which was held to be that of an apostolic James though they incorrectly identified this skeleton as that of James the Less. There is nothing to mitigate against it being the genuine skeleton of James the brother of Jesus, merely because it was found in the family tomb of the sons of Hezir. From the treatment of the body of Jesus by Joseph of Arimathea, who welcomed Jesus' body in his own family tomb, it is quite conceivable to infer that the family of Hezir might have extended compassionate burial to the body of James. This is the skeleton which now lies under the altar in the Cathedral of St. James.

An unbroken tradition among the Armenians traces this body back to its discovery in the fourth century.

The tomb of the sons of Hezir is located immediately across from the pinnacle of the temple area to this day. Of James, Theodorus said, "He was thrown from the pinnacle of the temple and [it] did not hurt him, for a fuller slew him with a club he carried and he was buried on the Mt. of Olives."[2]

It is interesting and perhaps significant that recent excavations of the exterior southwest wall of the Old City have uncovered fullers' vats. Fullers were the laundrymen of the first century, and fullers' "earth" was a kind of soap in wide use until comparatively modern times. The water that comes from the pool of Siloam, which is not far from the pinnacle of the temple, would have been a necessity for the public laundries of Jerusalem.

One can easily get the picture: the crowd gathers on the pinnacle of the temple to throw James to his doom in the valley below. Not far away, the fullers rush up from their laundry with clubs in their hands which they had used for beating their garments. Caught up in the fury of the mob, they smashed the skull of the aged apostle after he fell. The compassionate members of the sons of Hezir, a family of priests, offer a niche in their extensive tomb. Not far from where he was slain the battered body of the brother of Jesus is laid to rest. Standing in the doorway of this tomb, while on the steep western rock wall of the lower slopes of the Mt. of Olives, the visitor of today can easily reenact the entire dreadful scene of martyrdom and burial.

It would be helpful to a critical study such as this if this James the brother of Jesus could indeed be successfully and firmly identified as also James the Less, but this is simply not possible to honest scholarship.

But what then of James the Less?

The linking together of James, the son of Alphaeus in the various lists of the apostles gives the impression of more than an arbitrary or accidental grouping. James is listed with Simon the Zealot. Jude, the son of James the Great, is also referred to as a Zealot in the *Apostolic Constitutions*. The quotation in two of the ancient manuscripts of that work describes him thus: "Thaddeus was called Lebbaeus who was surnamed Judas the Zealot."[3]

The fourth figure in the apostolic listing is Judas Iscariot. He, too, may have been a Zealot according to Barclay.[4]

James's mother was a faithful follower of Jesus, in company with Mary, the mother of Jesus, all the way to the Cross.

However, it is quite evident that this is only speculation as far as James the son of Alphaeus is concerned. His mother was a faithful follower of Jesus, in company with Mary, the mother of Jesus, all the way to the Cross. Was it his mother, Mary, who won him to Christ, or was it James who won his mother? We do not know. But certainly one thing is evident. If James the son of Alphaeus was during his idealistic youth a Zealot, he soon forsook the movement and became an ardent Christian.

One of the earliest church historians Heggesippus, who is quoted by Eusebius, wrote in AD 169 that James lived the life of a Nazarite before and after becoming an apostle of Jesus Christ. As a member of this order he drank no wine and ate no meat except the Paschal Lamb, never shaved or cut his hair and never took a bath. James wore no clothes except a single linen garment which (he) also carefully avoided cleaning (with) water. He spent so much time in prayer his knees became hardened like the hooves of a camel. [These legends (which lack probability and which echo the sounds of the early days of the monastics more than those of the first century) earned for James the title "James the Just."] So righteous was his life that he alone of the Christians was allowed to go into the Holiest of Holies, and Jews as well as Christians strove to touch the hem of his garments as he passed in the street.

This tradition of Heggesippus simply does not ring true. First, the description more nearly fits James the brother of Jesus who is the more likely bearer of the title "James the Just." Second, it is almost certain that no one but the Jewish high priest was permitted to go into the Holiest of Holies. Whether he was a Jew or a Jewish Christian, there is no reason to believe that anyone else, however holy his life, was ever permitted into the Holy of Holies. Third, none of the other apostles are recorded to have held scruples against eating of meat and washing. This would have been contrary to the traditions of the Jews and the early Christians alike. We feel there is nothing whatsoever in this description to fit James, the son of Alphaeus.

A more interesting and perhaps more likely tradition is preserved in the *Golden Legend,* a seven-volume compilation of the lives of the saints arranged by Jacobus de Voragine, Archbishop of Genoa in AD 1275, which relates that James resembled Jesus Christ so much in body, visage, and manner that it was difficult to distinguish one from the other. The kiss of Judas in the garden of Gethsemane, according to this tradition, was necessary to make sure that Jesus and not James was taken prisoner.[5]

If Mary, the mother of Jesus, was a cousin of Mary, the mother of James, this could account for the family resemblance between the two. Certainly there was no closer relationship between the two Marys than that of cousins. But then, bearded young men of the same race often have a resemblance. Yet we must point out that it is not certain that Jesus even wore a beard. Even so, a facial resemblance *could* have existed. On the basis of this tradition, James is usually pictured in Christian art as beautiful of countenance. His handsome features—full of spiritual and intellectual beauty—make him easily recognizable in early pictures of the Twelve.

> One tradition says that James resembled Jesus so much that it was difficult to distinguish one from the other.

Again, we must challenge the generally held concept of Jesus as being a handsome man. There is no indication whatsoever in the New Testament that this was true. The only reference at all to the appearance of Jesus is found in Isaiah 53:2 where we read the prophetic prediction that the Messiah would have "nothing beautiful or majestic about his appearance, nothing to attract us to him."

Yet, in all of this, perhaps we can detect a small kernel of truth. James the son of Alphaeus may indeed have had a facial resemblance to Jesus. Such traditions as are preserved often contain at least a grain of truth.

Though confusing James the Less with the James who was the brother of Jesus, the authoritative writer Aziz S. Atiya in his *History of Eastern Christianity* relates the one historical tradition that has a ring of probability. He says, "The seeds of Syrian Christianity had been sown in Jerusalem during the Apostolic age, and the contention has been made that the first bishop of the Syrian church was none other than St. James of the Twelve Apostles, identified as 'St. James the Less.' "[6]

According to the study made by E. A. Wallis Budge, James was stoned by the Jews for preaching Christ, and was buried by the Sanctuary in Jerusalem.[7] We must speculate at this point how and when the body of James the Less was discovered in Jerusalem and taken to Constantinople for interment in the Church of the Holy Apostles. This could have happened during the reign of Justinian. According to Gibbon, Justinian rehabilitated the Church of the Holy Apostles which was built by Constantine the Great in the year 332 in Constantinople.[8] Justinian had a keen awareness of biblical history and compared his building of Santa Sophia with the temple of Solomon.[9]

Since this was the age of the frantic search for the relics of the early Christians, especially those of the apostles, it is entirely possible that the body identified as that of James the Less was brought from Palestine to Constantinople to add apostolic association to the Eastern Orthodox Church and empire. This cannot be proven but it is highly likely since Justinian's word was law in the entire Middle East, and the churchmen were eager to please him.

The Armenian Church in Jerusalem had, by the time of Justinian, established its claim to the body of James the brother of Jesus, whom they mistakenly supposed to be identical with James the Less.

Justinian would probably have honored this conviction and left the body of James, the brother of Jesus, in place in Jerusalem while disagreeing with the identification of it as the body of James the Less. Why he later forwarded the body or parts of it to Rome can only be guessed. Perhaps it was a part of some political agreement to keep his political alliance with Rome intact.

The body of James the son of Alphaeus, was brought from Constantinople to Rome about the year 572[10] and was interred by Pope John III in a church which was first known as the Church of the Apostles Philip and James the Less. Only in the tenth century was this title shortened in common speech to the Church of the Holy Apostles.

Archaeologists who have examined the lower part of the present day structure of the church in Rome affirm that the structure is the work of the sixth century and beyond doubt that which was constructed by Pope John III. The original church was dedicated the first of May AD 560. The bones of Philip were probably interred on that date, and later the bones of James were added. Still later, skeletal remains of other apostles were added. They may be seen there to this day.

CHAPTER TWELVE

JUDE THADDAEUS

During the forty days after his crucifixion, [Jesus] appeared to the apostles from time to time, and he proved to them in many ways that he was actually alive. And he talked to them about the Kingdom of God. Acts 1:3

There are a number of men named Judas mentioned in the New Testament for Judas is simply the Greek form of "Judah," probably the most common name among the Jews. Jude is the Latin form of Judah.

Jerome called this Judas, "Trionius," which means, the man with three names. In the Gospel of Matthew he is called "Lebbaeus" whose surname was "Thaddaeus" (Matthew 10:3). In the Gospel of Mark, he is called "Thaddaeus" (Mark 3:18). In Luke 6:16 and in Acts 1:13, he is referred to as "Judas (son of James)."

The correct identification of this Judas is extremely complicated, not only because of the three names which are used for him in the Scriptural record but also because of the enigmatic reference to him as the "son of James." We could tell considerably more about him if we were certain exactly who this James was.

The Roman Catholic versions of Scripture choose to translate the reference in Luke 6:16 as "brother of James." But the revised versions generally agree that he was the son of the man named James. In the Greek, it merely says, "Judas of James" but the common meaning of this is "son of."

Further complicating the identification of this apostle is the fact that there are two other prominent New Testament characters by the name of Judas. There is Judas Iscariot who betrayed Jesus, and Judas the half brother of Jesus who was probably the author of the Epistle of Jude. In that epistle, the writer spoke of himself as the "brother of James." It is believed that modesty forbade him to claim Jesus as his brother after the flesh, but it is quite certain that he was a younger son of Joseph and of Mary.

However, the "Judas, son of James" we are looking at here was probably the son of James the Great, the son of Zebedee. This identification is based upon the following argument. (1) This Judas was the son of James. (2) He could hardly have been the son of James the brother of Jesus, since that James was probably younger than Jesus and it would have been impossible for him to have a son old enough to have been an apostle. Besides, all early tradition describes James the brother of Jesus as a holy man who was probably an ascetic, and therefore, probably unmarried. (3) James the Less was the son of Alphaeus, the brother of Matthew, Joseph, and Salome.

The name Thaddeaus may be a diminutive of *Theudas* or *Theodore*, meaning "dear" or "beloved," one close to the heart of the one who named him.

If his title, James the Less, actually means "James the Younger," we must ask, younger than whom? Obviously, younger than James the Great. Would, therefore, a man who is plainly declared to be the younger of the two James have a son old enough to be an apostle? This leaves us with James the Great, sometimes called James the Elder, as the father of Judas. If this is so, then we can clearly identify Judas Thaddeaus Lebbaeus as the grandson of Zebedee and the nephew of the apostle John.

The name Thaddeaus may be a diminuative from *Theudas* or *Theodore*, derived from the Aramaic noun *tad* which means "breast" and which would mean "dear" or "beloved," that is, one close to the heart of the one who named him.

The other name, Lebbaeus, may be a derivation of the Hebrew noun *leb*, which means heart, and in that case it would bear the same meaning as Thaddaeus.[1]

Early Christian Traditions about St. Jude

The *Gospel of the Ebionites* mentioned by Origen narrates that Jude was also among those who received their call to follow Jesus at the Sea of Tiberius. In the *Genealogies of the Twelve Apostles* Jude was declared to be of the house of Joseph. According to the *Book of the Bee*, he was of the tribe of Judah. (It is, however, more probable that if Jude is the son of James the Great, he was of the tribe of Judah—ed.)

Another apocryphal document called *The Belief of the Blessed Judas the Brother of Our Lord Who Was Surnamed Thaddaeus* describes his mission in Syria and Dacia and indicates him as one of the Twelve. The apocryphal book *The Acts of St. Peter* describes that apostle as appointing Jude "over the island of Syria and Edessa." It is obviously at this point that we are suffering from a corrupted translation since there can hardly be any such place as "the *island* of Syria." Syria is an inland country, the capital of which is Damascus.

A solution suggests itself. Damascus is an "island" of green, that is to say an oasis, in a "sea" of sand and wilderness. Further, when the apostle Paul was baptized it was in Damascus, at the hands of a Christian named Ananias. Paul (then Saul) was staying in the "house of Judas," a person about whom we know nothing except this once reference (Acts 9:11). Admittedly, this is flimsy evidence indeed for an apocryphal writer to build a legend upon, to the effect that Peter appointed Jude to be a missionary to "the island of Syria." But this obscure Scripture reference to a Judas in Damascus, and the fact that the word "oasis" could mean an "island" of fertility in a barren wilderness, might actually be enough for the birth of the legend. The Jude of Damascus is not St. Jude, but the reference might well have assisted the association of St. Jude with Syria.

When it comes to a reference to a city called Edessa we are, of course, on firmer ground, since there is an abundance of tradition associating Jude with that part of Armenia of which Edessa was the leading city.

The *Acta Thaddaei* mentioned by Tischendorf[2] refers to Thaddaeus as one of the Twelve and also as one of the Seventy; Eusebius does the same. Jerome, however, identifies this same Thaddaeus with Lebbaeus and "Judas of James."

A book published by the Church of the East in India contains a statement which confirms the movement of Jude from Jerusalem eastward. This church makes a claim that the leaven which they use in their Communion bread is made from "the Holy Leaven. . . . a portion of the original bread used by Christ at the Last Supper brought to the East by the Apostle Thaddaeus. And in every Holy Communion since the bread used is made from meal continuous with that used in the first Lord's Supper." The same book continues, "The Apostolic liturgy of St. James of Jerusalem, brother of our Lord who celebrated the first Qurbana or Holy Communion, is still in use in the Church of the East, without variation or change. It is known among us by the name of saints 'Addai' [St. Jude Thaddaeus—ed.] and Mari who brought the Liturgy from Jerusalem to Edessa."[3]

Despite the charm of this tradition it presents at least one difficulty. The bread of the Lord's Supper could not have been made with leaven, since the first Lord's Supper was the celebration of the Passover, in which Mosaic Law commanded that unleavened bread be used (Exodus 12:15). Thus we cannot accept the tradition that Thaddaeus (Jude) brought the leaven or sourdough from the original Lord's Supper. Nevertheless, the name of the city of Edessa appears in connection with Thaddaeus (Jude), and this at least demonstrates the historical continuity of that association.

An early church historian Nicephorus Callistus (*His. Eccl.*, 240) tells how Thaddaeus (Jude) preached in Syria, Arabia, Mesopotamia and Persia. He adds that Thaddaeus (Jude) suffered martyrdom in Syria.

St. Jude and the Armenian Church

The association of the Armenian Church with the apostles is one of the firmest facts in all post-biblical Christian historical tradition. Jude is consistently associated as one of five of the apostles who visited Armenia and evangelized there. Armenia became the first Christian nation in the world. Christianity was officially proclaimed in AD 301 as the national religion of Armenia. King Tiridates, together with the nobility of his country, were baptized by St. Gregory the Illuminator. Writing about the history of the Armenian Church, Assadour Antreassian states:

> Thus all Christian Churches accept the tradition that Christianity was preached in Armenia by the Apostles Thaddeus and Bartholomew in the first half of the first century, when the Apostles of Christ were fulfilling their duty in preaching the Gospel—In Jerusalem and all Judea and in Samaria, and unto the uttermost parts of the earth—(*Acts* 1:8). Armenia was among the first to respond to the call of Christ so early. Thus, the above mentioned Apostles became the first illuminators of Armenia. The generally accepted chronology gives a period of eight years to the mission of St. Thaddeus (35-43 A.D.) and sixteen years to that of St. Bartholomew (44-60 A.D.), both of whom suffered martyrdom in Armenia (Thaddeus at Ardaze in 50 A.D. and Bartholomew at [Derbend] in 68 A.D.).[4]

Jude is consistently associated as one of five of the apostles who evangelized Armenia. Armenia became the first Christian nation in the world.

Antreassian, writing about the organization of the Armenian Church, makes the following claim. "As head of the Armenian Church, the Catholicos of all Armenians at Etchmiadzin is regarded as the successor of the Apostles Thaddaeus and Bartholomew."

In his authoritative *History of Eastern Christianity*, Aziz S. Atiya deals with the origins and development of Armenian Christianity with restraint but with a clear reflection of this tradition:

It is conceivable that Armenia, because of its close proximity to Palestine, the fountain head of the faith of Jesus, may have been visited by the early propagators of Christianity, although it is difficult to define the extent of the spread of this new religion among its inhabitants. Orthodox Armenian historians, such as Ormanian, labour to make a case for the continuity of Apostolic succession in their church. To him the 'First Illuminators of Armenia' were Saints Thaddaeus and Bartholomew whose very shrines still stand in the churches of Artaz (Macoo) and Alpac (Bashkale) in south-east Armenia and have always been venerated by Armenians. A popular tradition amongst them ascribes the first evangelization of Armenia to the Apostle Judas Thaddaeus who, according to their chronology spent the years 43–66 A.D. at 'Derbend.' According to Armenian tradition, therefore, Thaddaeus became the first patriarch of the Armenian Church, thus rendering it both Apostolic and autocephalous. Another tradition ascribes to the See of Artaz a line of seven bishops whose names are known and the periods of whose episcopates bring the succession to the second century. Furthermore, the annals of Armenian martyrology refer to a host of martyrs in the Apostolic age. A roll of a thousand victims including men and women of noble descent lost their lives with St. Thaddaeus, while others perished with St. Bartholomew.

It is interesting to note that the apocryphal story of King Abgar and Our Lord was reiterated by some native writers as having occurred in Armenia in order to heighten the antiquity of that religion amongst their forefathers.

Though it is hard to confirm or confute the historicity of these legends so dear to the hearts of Armenians, it may be deduced from contemporary writers that there were Christians in Armenia before the advent of St. Gregory Illuminator, the fourth-century apostle of Armenian Christianity. Eusebius of Caesarea (ca. 260–340 A.D.) refers to the Armenians in his *Ecclesiastical History* on two occasions. First, he states that Dionysius of Alexandria (d. ca. 264), pupil of Origen, wrote an Epistle "On Repentance," "to those in Armenia. . . . whose bishop was Meruzanes." On a second occasion, speaking of Emperor Maximin's persecution of 311–313, he says that "the tyrant had the further trouble of the war against the Armenians, men who from ancient times had been friends and allies of the Romans; but as they were Christians and exceedingly earnest in their piety towards the Deity, this hater of God [i.e., Maximin], by attempting to compel them to sacrifice to idols and demons, made of them foes instead of friends, and enemies instead of allies." Although this second episode must have occurred in the lifetime of Gregory the Illuminator, there is no doubt as to the antiquity of the first reference to the Armenians.

Further, if we believe the argument advanced by Ormanian and other native Armenian historians about a second-century quotation from Tertullian, it must be admitted that Christianity was not unknown in that region at that early date.[5]

In a book published by the Armenian Christians in Jerusalem called *The Armenian Patriarchate of Jerusalem*, the Armenian tradition of St. Jude is described as natural from the early relationship of Armenia to the Holy Land:

> The indestructible and everlasting love and veneration of Armenians for the Holy Land has its beginning in the first century of the Christian Era when Christianity was brought to Armenia directly from the Holy Land by two of the Apostles of Christ, St. Thaddeus and St. Bartholomeus.
>
> The early connection with Jerusalem was naturally due to the early conversion of Armenia. Even before the discovery of the Holy Places, Armenians, like other Christians of

the neighbouring countries, came to the Holy Land over the Roman roads and the older roads to venerate the places that God had sanctified. In Jerusalem they lived and worshipped on the Mount of Olives.

After the declaration of Constantine's will, known as Edict of Milan, and the discovery of the Holy Places, Armenian pilgrims poured into Palestine in a constant stream throughout the year. The number and importance of Armenian churches and monasteries increased year by year.[6]

One of the most unusual side references to the association of Jude (Thaddaeus) with Armenia is found in the *Treasures of the Armenian Patriarchate of Jerusalem*. "The traditional founders of the Armenian Church were the apostles Thaddeus and Bartholomew, whose tombs are shown and venerated in Armenia as sacred shrines. During the period between the Apostolic origins of the Armenian Church and the beginning of the 4th century, when the country as a whole formally adopted Christianity, there have been Armenian bishops whose names are mentioned by ancient historians."[7]

The association of Jude with Persia, where part of ancient Armenia is found today (the other parts being within Turkey and the [former] Soviet Union) is acknowledged by Roman Catholic tradition as follows: "St. Jude preached throughout Samaria, Edessa and Mesopotamia and penetrated as far as Persia where he was martyred with a javelin or with arrows or by being tied to a cross. He is pictured as a young or middle aged man in sacred art. His relics are widely distributed. Some are in St. Peter's, Rome, and others in the Church of St. Saturninus in Tolosa, Spain."[8]

We have a mixture of traditions about the death and burial places associated with Jude. In *The International Standard Bible Encyclopaedia*, C.M. Kerr says that the burial place of Thaddaeus is variously placed in Beirut and in Egypt.[9] However, in 1971 I carefully investigated these claims and found no evidence of an Egyptian tradition for the tomb of St. Jude, and no knowledge whatever in Beirut of any such association. When I consulted with both Catholic and Syrian Orthodox Church leaders in Lebanon, there was no indication that such a tradition exists there today.

On the other hand the Assyrian Church leaders, as well as a major general of the Iranian Army, informed me during a visit on October 16, 1971, to Teheran that the original tomb of Jude (Thaddaeus) was in a small village called Kara Kelisa near the Caspian Sea, about forty miles from Tabriz. This is in Iran, near the [former] Soviet border. This could well be the site of the original tomb of Jude even though it is likely that to keep the relics safe from the invasion of Genghis Khan, the relics themselves may have been moved westward and scattered from Rome to Spain. The tremendous tomb which is built for these relics in St. Peter's Basilica in Rome, which is located directly south of the main altar in a side area, attests to the firm belief among the Catholic authorities that some of the genuine relics of Jude are indeed to be found there in Rome to this day.

The Biography of Jude

Subject to the corrections of further discoveries, the following biographical sketch can be deduced from the traditions and discoveries which are at hand.

Jude was the son of James the Elder and the grandson of Zebedee. He was of the tribe of Judah as befits a man whose name is the Greek form of Judah. He probably followed his father into the ranks of the apostles from the place near Capernaum where they were engaged in fishing. He may have had a close alliance with the seventy who were also disciples of Jesus. But he had, as well, a firm position as one of the Twelve.

Jude is mentioned in the Bible as asking a single question of Jesus. "Lord, why are you going to reveal yourself only to us and not to the world at large?" (John 14:22).

Many scholars believe this was the last question any disciple asked of Jesus before Jesus began his prayer vigil in Gethsemane, which concluded with Jesus being seized by the sergeants of the high priests.

Jude

Jesus answered Thaddaeus, "All who love me will do what I say. My Father will love them, and we will come and make our home with each of them" (John 14:23).

After the resurrection Thaddaeus is listed in the official roster of the apostles (Acts 1:13). He was present on the day of Pentecost. Doubtless he was one of the first apostles to leave Jerusalem for a foreign country. If there is even a grain of truth in the Abgar legend, Jude became one of the first apostles to witness directly to a foreign king, a Gentile. There is no serious reason to doubt that Jude did indeed evangelize that area of Armenia associated with the city of Edessa, in company perhaps with Bartholomew, and for a brief period with Thomas.

Jude's single question to Jesus—"Lord, why are you going to reveal yourself only to us and not to the world at large?"—is believed to be the last question any disciple asked Jesus.

One can also believe that he spent his years of evangelistic effort in Syria and northern Persia. It is likely that he died there and was originally buried at Kara Kelesia. It is also likely that later a part—or all of his body—was removed for safekeeping because of the threat of the Mongolian invasion. It is also not unreasonable to believe that important relics of St. Jude are now to be found in Rome and Tolosa, Spain.

Another apostle with whom he is frequently associated is Simon Zelotes. It is said that Jude's bones are mixed with those of Simon in the tomb at the Vatican. The Persian tradition is that the two were slain at about the same time, or possibly together.

CHAPTER THIRTEEN

SIMON THE CANAANITE

Simon the Zealot may have been a member of the Zealots, a radical political party working for the violent overthrow of Roman rule in Israel. —*The Life Application Study Bible*

Simon was also called *Canaanite*, or *Cananean*, or *Zealot* (Greek: *Kanaios*) in various New Testament references; "the Canaanite" (Matthew 10:4; Mark 3:18, AV) or "The Cananaean" (Matthew 10:4; Mark 3:18, RSV) or "Zelotes (Luke 6:15; Acts 1:13, AV) or "the Zealot" (Luke 6:15; Acts 1:13, RSV).

According to the *Gospel of the Ebionites* or *Gospel of the Twelve Apostles* (of the second century and mentioned in Origen), Simon received his call to the apostleship along with Andrew and Peter, the sons of Zebedee, Thaddaeus, and Judas Iscariot at the Sea of Tiberias (see also Henneke, *Neutestamentliche Apokryphen*, 24–27).

Writing in 1685, Dorman Newman gave the following account of Simon Zelotes:

> He is said to have diverted his journey towards Egypt, Cyrene, Africa, Martania, and Lybia. Nor could the coldness of the climate benumb his zeal or hinder him from shipping himself over into the Western Islands, yea, even to Britain itself. Here he is said to have preached and wrought many miracles, and after infinite troubles and difficulties which he underwent, suffered martyrdom for the faith of Christ, being crucified by the infidels and buried among them.

Others indeed affirm that after he had preached the gospel in Egypt he went to Mesopotamia, where he met with St. Jude the Apostle and together with him took his journey into Persia where, having gained a considerable harvest to the Christian Faith, they were both crowned with martyrdom: but this is granted by all learned men to be fabulous, wanting all clear foundation in Antiquity to stand on.[1]

The Coptic Church of Egypt affirms that Simon "went to Egypt, Africa, Britain and died in Persia."[2]

Otto Hophan in his book *The Apostles* says, "A third general opinion, which later Greek commentators in particular followed placed the scenes of Simon's Apostolic labors in N. W. Africa, Mauretania and even Britain."[3]

The Coptic Church of Egypt affirms that Simon "went to Egypt, Africa, Britain and died in Persia."

The exhaustive study of the Bollandistes records that "Alford in his annals of the British church accepts that an Apostle came to Britain because Eusebius says, "Surely later, Apostles preached in Britain."[4]

According to the Bollandistes, the arm of St. Simon was given by a Persian bishop to the Premonstrarians convent in Trier but preserved in the monastery church of St. Norbet, Cologne, Germany.[5] This monastery seems to have been destroyed in the saturation bombing of Cologne in World War II. When I investigated further in November of 1971, I turned up no trace of the monastery.

In his book, *The Christian Centuries*, Jean Danielou indicates that Christianity had indeed penetrated all along the coast of North Africa.

Christianity was probably planted in Carthage as early as the end of the first century, otherwise it is difficult to explain how the city had a large Christian population at the time of Tertullian. "We fill your squares, your markets, your amphitheaters," he writes in the *Apologeticum*. The Council of Carthage, in 216, was attended by seventy-one African bishops, but we know nothing about the conditions in which the Gospel was preached.[6]

The importance of the presence of Christianity in Carthage to our story of the journeys of Simon is that the historical record and traditions indicate Simon traveled westward from Jerusalem through Mauritania, which was the name of one of the countries of North Africa. It probably included Carthage. That tradition is mentioned in *The Popular and Critical Bible Encyclopaedia*:

> These traditions, however, assigned a different destiny to this Simon, alleging that he preached the Gospel through North Africa, from Egypt to Mauritania, and then he even proceeded to the remote isles of Britain.[7]

The Traditions of Simon in Britain

There is a long and widespread tradition which links several of the apostolic figures to Great Britain. Later we will show that this was by no means unreasonable. If Thomas could journey east to India, surely other apostles could have journeyed northwest to Britain. It would be more than strange if some of them did not. Dorman Newman in his book on the lives of the apostles gives us the following tradition:

> St. Simon continued in Worship and Communion with the other Apostles and Disciples of Christ at *Jerusalem*; and at the Feast of *Pentecost* received the same miraculous Gifts of the Holy Spirit; so that he was equally qualified with the rest of his Brethren for the Ministry of the Gospel. And we cannot doubt but that he exercised his Gifts with Zeal and Fidelity: But in what part of the World, is not very certain. Some say he went into *Egypt*, *Cyrene* and *Africa*, and all over *Mauritania*, preaching the Gospel to those remote and barbarous Countries. And, if we may believe our own Authors, he came into these Western Parts,

as far as our Island of *Great Britain*; where having converted great Multitudes, with manifold Hardships and Persecutions, he at last suffered Martyrdom by Crucifixion, as 'tis recorded in the *Greek* Menologies. But *Bede, Vsuardus,* and *Ado,* place his Martyrdom in Persia, at a city called *Suanir,* where they say the idolatrous Priests put him to Death; and for this they allege the Authority of *Eusebius* his Martyrology translated by St. *Jerome,* which, though it be not without many Faults, nor entirely either *Eusebius's* or St. *Jerome's* hath yet the advantage of Antiquity above any now extant. As to the city *Suanir* in *Persia,* it is not known to our Geographers. Possibly it might be the Country of the Suani or *Surani,* a People mentioned by *Pliny* and *Ptolemy,* in *Colchis,* or a little higher in *Sarmatia*; which may agree with a Passage in the spurious History of St. *Andrew,* That in the *Cimmerian Bosphorus* there is a Tomb in a Grot, with an Inscription, *That Simon the Zealot, or Canaanite, was interred there.* But this is but uncertain Tradition.[8]

Scholar Lionel S. Lewis lists the following historical tradition:

There is Eastern confirmation of the story that Simon came to Britain.

(1) Dorotheus, Bishop of Tyre (A.D. 303), or the writer who attributed the *Synopsis* to him, in his *Synopsis de Apostol.,* 9. Simon Zelotes says: "Simon Zelotes preached Christ through all Mauritania, and Africa the less. At length he was crucified at Brittania, slain and buried."

(2) Nicephorus, Patriarch of Constantinople and Byzantine historian, A.D. 758-829, wrote (Book II, c. 40): "Simon born in Cana of Galilee, who for his fervent affection for his Master and great zeal that he showed by all means to the Gospel, was surnamed Zelotes, having received the Holy Ghost from above, traveled through Egypt and Africa, then through Mauritania and all Lybia, preaching the Gospel. And the same doctrine he taught to the Occidental Sea, and the Isles called Britanniae."

(3) Greek Menology. The Menology of the Greek Church celebrates St. Simon's Day on May 10, and supports the statements of his having preached and been martyred in Britain (*Annales Ecclesiastici*, Baronius under A.D. 44. Sec. XXX-VIII).[9]

George F. Jowett draws the same conclusion:

In the year A.D. 60 special mention is made of Joseph going to Gaul and returning to Britain with another band of recruits, among whom is particularly mentioned Simon Zelotes, one of the original twelve disciples of Christ. This is the second time it is specially mentioned that Philip consecrated Joseph and his band of co-workers prior to embarking for Britain. Probably the inclusion of Simon Zelotes indicated an important missionary effort, hence the consecration. This was the second journey to Britain for Simon Zelotes and his last. According to Cardinal Baronius and Hippolytus, Simon's first arrival in Britain was in the year A.D. 44, during the Claudian war. Evidently his stay was short, as he returned to the continent.

Nicephorus, Patriarch of Constantinople, and Byzantine historian, A.D. 758–829, writes: "Simon born in Cana of Galilee who for his fervent affection for his Master and great zeal that he showed by all means to the Gospel, was surnamed Zelotes, having received the Holy Ghost from above, traveled through Egypt, and Africa, then through Mauretania and all Libya, preaching the Gospel. And the same doctrine he taught to the Occidental Sea, and the Isles called Britanniae."

Simon arrived in Britain during the first year of the Boadicean war, A.D. 60, when the whole Island was convulsed in a deep, burning anger against the Romans, which was never equaled before or after in the long years of conflict between the two nations. Tacitus states that from A.D. 59 to 62 the brutalities of war were at their worst. Atrocities occurred on both sides, but the Romans carried their vicious perpetrations to such an extent that even Rome was shocked. Bearing this in mind we can readily understand that any Christian evangelizing outside the British shield would be fraught with imminent danger. At all times the disciples of Christ were oblivious to danger, but when the pressure became too severe invariably they fled the land until matters quietened down. In the year A.D. 44 a Claudian Edict expelled the Christian leaders from Rome. Many of them sought sanctuary in Britain. Among those who fled to Britain from Rome was Peter.

The south of England was sparsely inhabited by the native Britons and consequently more heavily populated by the Romans. It was far beyond the strong protective shield of the Silurian arms in the south and the powerful northern Yorkshire Celts. In this dangerous territory Simon was definitely on his own. Undeterred, with infinite courage, he began preaching the Christian gospel right in the heart of the Roman domain. His fiery sermons brought him speedily to the attention of Catus Decianus, but not before he had sown the seed of Christ in the hearts of Britons and many Romans who, despite the unremitting hatred of Decianus for all that was Christian, held the secret of the truth locked in their hearts.

The evangelizing mission of Simon was short-lived. He was finally arrested under the orders of Catus Decianus. As usually his trial was a mockery. He was condemned to death and was crucified by the Romans at Caistor, Lincolnshire, and there buried, *circa* May 10th, A.D. 61.

The day of the martyrdom of Simon Zelotes, the devoted disciple of Christ, is officially celebrated by the eastern and western church on May 10th and so recorded in the Greek Menology. Cardinal Baronius, in his *Annales Ecclesiastici*, gives the same date in describing the martyrdom and burial of Simon Zelotes in Britain.[10]

We cannot agree with Jowett that Simon was killed in Great Britain. But there is no doubt that Simon could *also* have gone to Britain, preached for awhile, perhaps even in London, and then fled to the Middle East because of the destruction of London at the hands of anti-Roman revolutionaries led by Queen Boadicea.

Theodoret, the bishop of Cyrrhus, wrote in the fifth century:

> Know, O holiest Augustus, that this faith is the faith preached from everlasting, this is the faith that the Fathers assembled at Nicea confessed. With this faith all the churches throughout the world are in agreement, in Spain, in Britain, in Gaul, in all Italy and Campania, in Dalmatea and Mysia, in Macedonia, in all Hellas, in all the churches throughout Africa, Sardinia, Cyprus, Crete, Pamphylia and Isauria, and Lycia, those of all Egypt and Lybia, of Pontus, Cappadocia and all the neighboring districts and all the churches of the East except a few who have embraced Arianism.[11]

In his book *Roman Britain*, I. A. Richmond tells of the development and growth of British industry and trade with the continent of Europe:

> Much of the most famed of British metals in the days before the Roman occupation was tin. The vivid accounts by Diodorus Siculus, of overland pack-horse transport of Cornish tin from the Gallic coast to Narbo (Narbonne) in the first century B.C., and of the island emporium on the British coast, from which merchants obtained it, all speak of a brisk and flourishing early trade, monopolized in Caesar's day by the Beneti of Brittany.[12]

We must realize that Britain was first invaded by Julius Caesar long before the birth of Jesus. While this attempt at conquest did not last, it definitely demonstrates a Roman presence eighty years before the permanent takeover of Britain by the Romans under Claudius in AD 43. Anyone interested in the careers of the apostles will also be interested in Claudius, not the worst of the Caesars, and the one during whose reign much of the work by the apostles was undertaken.

Relating the lives of the apostles to the reign of the Caesars shows Paul was converted just after the death of Tiberius, (AD 37) perhaps during the brief reign of the mad Caligula (37–41). Claudius was forced to wear the purple after the assassination of Caligula in AD 41 and ruled until he was poisoned by his queen in AD 54. This was an intensive period of apostolic activity, as was also the time of Nero (AD 54–68). Paul's entire ministry thus was conducted during the time of Claudius and Nero, the latter outliving the great apostle by perhaps a year and a half after he ordered Paul's execution in AD 67.

What was true of Paul was also true of the other apostles, except that they also worked during the closing seven years of the reign of Tiberius and in some cases beyond Nero to the Flavian period (69–96). The apostle John alone is believed by church historians to have lived until the close of the first century.

As we have said, Simon was a Zealot. This movement was the extreme and violent Jewish nationalist party which sought to drive the hated Romans out of Palestine by revolution and guerrilla warfare. If Simon was a Zealot, he was also certainly an idealistic revolutionary. The fate of this party of the Zealots was bloody indeed. It was mainly responsible for the revolt of AD 68–70 which brought down the walls of Jerusalem, and the destruction of the Temple by Vespasian and Titus in AD 70. The last stand of the Zealots was at Masada in AD 71 where their final outpost of defiance saw the suicide of hundreds of Jews, after a long siege conducted by the Roman general Silva.

Masada, a remote "fortress in the sky" overlooks the Dead Sea in one of the most desolate spots in the Holy Land. Herod the Great fortified it as a place

> If Simon was a Zealot, he was also certainly an idealistic revolutionary. The Zealots' revolt brought about the destruction of the Temple by Vespasian and Titus in AD 70.

of refuge which could not be easily taken. Only by building a huge earthen ramp was the plateau finally assaulted by the Romans who found only three people alive. Masada is a synonym for heroism to the Jewish people somewhat like the Alamo is to Texans and for a similar reason, except that the defense of the Alamo was conducted to gain time for General Sam Houston's army, whereas the defense of Masada was simply an act of heroic and hopeless defiance, the decision on the part of the Zealots to die rather than to endure Roman slavery.

What led Simon to forsake the Zealots is not hard to guess. The Zealots were nationalist fanatics but many were also pure idealists. Simon apparently was more of an idealist than a nationalist and when the supreme idealism of Jesus Christ was presented to him, he forsook the lesser for the greater. However, there is no reason to doubt that Simon was first interested in the notion that Jesus as Messiah would restore the Kingdom to Israel and triumph over the Romans. Perhaps at Cana of Galilee the miracle of changing the water into wine might have fired Simon with the concept that the power of divine miracles was greater than that of the sword, and thus he might first have joined Jesus because of his interest in the fate of Israel.

Probably Simon gave up that concept only upon the announcement of Jesus, after the Resurrection, that the apostles were not to know the time and season of the restoration of the Kingdom to Israel. One among them had asked the question "Lord, has the time come for you to free Israel and restore our kingdom?" (Acts 1:6). Though the individual spokesman is not named, surely it could have been Simon who voiced it. Jesus firmly removed that issue from the consideration of the apostles and replaced it with the commandment to go into all the world and disciple all nations until the end of the age. Further, and more immediately, they were to tarry in Jerusalem until they had been endowed with power from on High.

Simon, with the others of the twelve, therefore, obediently went to the Upper Room, which was perhaps located in the house of John Mark's mother, Mary. There they remained until the day of Pentecost. Simon participated in the Pentecostal day of evangelism in which the task of international Christian evangelism was begun. On the day of Pentecost people from the entire Mediterranean world were visiting Jerusalem. After some three thousand of them were converted, many must have journeyed back to their homelands and there have become the first evangelists.

When eventually the apostles divided up the civilized world into areas of individual evangelism we can be sure they followed the same routes and arrived at the same destinations as those who had already heard the word in Jerusalem on the day of Pentecost. It is instructive to see that Jerusalem was an international city in the first century. Jews from all over the empire came there from time to time, as did others who were not Jews, such as the Ethiopian treasurer who was baptized by Philip on the way back to Ethiopia from a visit to Jerusalem.

> Jesus' miracle of changing the water into wine might have convinced Simon that the power of divine miracles was greater than the power of the sword.

Again and again in our search for the apostles we are impressed with the relative ease of travel in the first century which was made possible by the vast network of Roman roads all over the empire from Persia to Britain. Not only did the Romans force the local people in each area to build the roads but the Romans themselves also both built and protected the roads. It was not until the Roman Empire was invaded by the Goths, Huns, Visigoths, and others in the fifth century that the empire broke up, mostly because the Roman roads could neither be maintained nor kept secure.

While it lasted, the Roman conquest was not all bad. In fact, the average person perhaps felt more secure in the empire than out of it. When the Roman soldiers were pulled out of Britain in the fifth century (because their lines of communication with Rome were broken by the Goths) history reveals the Britons begged them to remain, trying unsuccessfully to keep them as their shield against the Danes and Saxons, who moved in as the Romans left.

Roman conquests were bloody and those who resisted were slain or enslaved. But those who surrendered were treated with surprising justice and before long were given the full benefits of Roman culture which surpassed anything the non-Roman world of northern Europe had known. Subsequently, so marvelous was the Roman Way (which lasted for about a thousand years—500 BC to AD 500) that the ruins of that time, in such places as Britain, reveal that the Romans and provincials alike were able to enjoy Roman civilization as fully as if they had been in Italy itself. Orderly cities, villas, and highways were everywhere, exactly as in Italy and France.

Britain was at first located on the extreme edge of the frontier of the empire. But the raw frontier conditions were soon overcome. There is much reason to believe that the Roman Way had penetrated everywhere even before the time of Claudius. England's wealth of minerals was surely imported by Rome before the time of Claudius—particularly the mineral, lead, which was used in the highly developed plumbing of the cities and villas of Italy. (Romans did not know they were slowly poisoning themselves with the lead, but then neither did other countries until modern times.) Lead and silver were also needed in vast quantities by Rome, two metals usually found together in the same mines. To insure the regular supplies of these commodities, the Romans used the ships of Spain to trade with Britain long before the time of Caesar.

The prophet Ezekiel makes a reference to the merchants of *Tarshish* (Ezekiel 38). Tarshish was a city on Spain's western coast, sometimes called Tartesus. It was the commercial point for trade by sea with the entire Atlantic seaboard of Europe, including Ireland and Britain. This city was known to Ezekiel in 550 BC while he was a captive in Babylon. Doubtless Rome, being nearer to Spain, knew of Britain long before the time of Caesar, who warred in Spain to achieve his ambition as the supreme consul in France, five hundred years after Ezekiel mentions Tarshish.

The point we cannot overlook is that Europe as a "barbarian" area was not as uncivilized as we have been led to believe. France had great cities by the time of Julius Caesar. So did Spain. Even England's barbarians were quite civilized, though not as highly as France's. England's people had developed mines, cities, and governments long before Julius Caesar. By the time of Claudius, the Roman Way was obviously quite attractive to the Britons, and Claudius found it suspiciously easy to conquer Britain. In fact, one wonders whether or not the British at that time put up much of a fight. Did they offer merely a token resistance to the Roman army? How else can one explain the fact that Claudius only spent sixteen days in England? It seems obvious the local kings generally wanted to be in the empire, for even the Romans could not have subdued the vast territory of southern England by force in a mere sixteen days! Apparently Claudius wanted—and got—a cheap "victory" for propaganda purposes back home immediately after becoming the emperor, and Britain was the place for it.

However that may have been, England soon became as Roman and as peaceful for a time as Italy, at least that part of England up to the land of the Picts. Londinium (London) became a Roman port city, laid out in the usual plan of a Roman town. Other cities also became Roman in style. Roads soon spread out all over southern England. Fortress cities were constructed to guard the roads. Roman soldiers retired to English farms when their enlistments expired.

The point for us is this: by the time of Simon the Canaanite's possible visit to Britain, say in AD 50, there was a general pacification and establishment of the Roman Way in large areas of Britain. Let us look at this in detail since it is most likely that Simon, if he came to Britain at all (which is certainly possible and even probable), must have ministered to people with whom he could converse. This would be the Greek- and Latin-speaking Roman troops and their fiefs and families. Probably the civilized Britons could speak Latin even

How did Christianity first come to Britain? Perhaps a Briton visiting Rome may have been converted and taken the gospel back to England.

before the Claudian conquest due to their commercial relations with the Romans.

Besides, the Roman armies were not altogether Italians since the Roman army habitually enlisted people from all the countries it conquered. It is entirely possible that the majority of the Roman army that occupied Britain was made up of Spaniards, Gauls, Swiss, and even Greeks from Asia Minor. All of these countries were by this time vital parts of the Roman Empire. In any case, people in these countries all spoke Greek and Latin and probably other languages as well. In all likelihood, so could Simon.

But how did Christianity first come to Britain? Perhaps a Briton visiting Rome may have been converted and taken the gospel back to England. Several of the people mentioned by the apostle in his prison epistles written in Rome had the same name as certain British royal hostages then dwelling in Rome. These hostages were treated kindly as guests though they stood as prisoners to insure the behavior of the kings of Britain. Perhaps upon release they carried the gospel home to England.

Or perhaps a Christian commercial traveler, or even a Christian Roman soldier, was the first bearer of the Christian faith to England.

Cottrell writes: "Undoubtedly there were Christians in these Romano-British towns. There is a small building at Silchester which may have been a Christian church, and at Caerleon, in 1954, Dr. Nash-Williams discovered a clay oil-lamp with a dotted pattern on the base which has been recognized as a secret symbol used by the early Christians to reveal their faith to their fellow-converts."[13]

Cottrell quotes from *The Journal of Roman Studies* concerning an excavation of a Christian church long before Augustine brought Catholicism to England:

> Among the churned mud and flooring-material filling the hollows was a group of Constantinian coins, to three of which still adhered the white mortar of the pavement, in which they had evidently once been embedded. The three coins in question are

a *follies* of AD 309–313, an *Urbis Roma* (Ad 330-335) and a *Fel. Temp. Reparatio* copy (AD 348–353), the last somewhat worn. This gives a *terminus post quem* of at least AD 360 for the laying of the pavement and the construction of the building.

. . . The combination of date and type of buildings strongly favours the notion of a Christian church, with a table of offerings at the north end of the vestibule and baptistery in an axial position in front of the church. The plan of the transeptal rooms echoes that of the famous large Constantinian churches, such as St. Peter's and the Lateran in Rome, and the Church of the Nativity in Bethlehem.

It now seems almost certain that some 250 years before St. Augustine landed in Kent to convert the pagan Saxon, Christ was being worshipped in a small building, the foundations of which now lie buried beneath a Hampshire meadow, and that humble structure bore distinct resemblances, in planning, to three of the holiest shrines in Christendom.[14]

The Venerable Bede, a British monk who is the best known early British Catholic historian, wrote (in about 730) that a second-century British king (Lucius) had written to Rome for direction on how to become a Christian. Obviously Bede was interested in tracing the history of the submission of Christian kings to the Roman Prelate, since he is almost silent in his *A History of the English Church and People* concerning Christianity before the time of St. Augustine (AD 579), from whom the medieval Catholic Church got its main impetus. Yet Bede recounts the frequent struggles within the Christian movement between the Catholics *and other Christians*. Who these other Christians were or how they got to be Christians Bede does not say. But the fact that they were there in England Bede does not challenge.

The Death of Simon
If Simon visited England it could not have been for long. Putting together the events of those days we would conclude that if the

apostle visited England he might have come to Glastonbury in company with Joseph of Arimathea. There certainly is no other tradition known concerning the history of Joseph of Arimathea and since the British tradition is vigorous we see no reason to challenge it, though admittedly, it stands only upon tradition and is not in proven history. Again, it must be observed that all of the early Christians had to go somewhere or else Christianity could not have spread throughout the Roman Empire as rapidly as it did. If in any country there is a strong tradition concerning some apostolic figures, and no counter-tradition elsewhere, then we at least stand on the ground of possibility and even probability. So it is with Simon and Joseph.

The Venerable Bede wrote that a second-century British king had written to Rome for direction on how to become a Christian.

The way we, therefore, postulate the story of Simon is this: he left Jerusalem and traveled first to Egypt and then through North Africa to Carthage, from there to Spain and north to Britain. Nothing in this theory is impossible or unreasonable. He may have then gone from Glastonbury to London, which was by that time the capital of the new Roman conquest. There he would have preached in Latin to members of the Roman community. He would not have been able to preach to the native Britons in their language, but Latin was already widely used by the Britons and it is possible that even some Britons could have heard the gospel from Simon.

If there were Jews in London, surely Simon would have gone to them. There is, however, no historical proof that a church was founded, and before long the revolutionaries led by the British Queen, Boadicea, came against the Roman occupation forces. The frightening rumors of her extermination of all Romans and her destruction of London would surely have caused Simon to flee to the south of England. There he would have embarked upon a ship to return to Palestine, because it was obvious that the disruption of the Roman peace made England at that time a doubtful field for the proclamation of the gospel. In other words, Simon witnessed and preached but because of unsettled conditions, was forced to retire.

The next strong tradition finds Simon in Persia in company with Jude with whom he was martyred. Mary Sharp writes, "They were thought to have preached together in Syria and Mesopotamia, traveling as far as Persia and to have been martyred, St. Simon being sawn asunder and St. Jude killed with a halberd."[15]

Sacred and Legendary Art affirms the same tradition of St. Jude and St. Simon, "They preached the Gospel together in Syria and Mesopotamia and suffered martyrdom in Persia."[16]

According to Roman Catholic tradition the bodies of Jude and Simon are buried together, the bones being intermixed, the major tomb being in St. Peter's in Rome, with fragments in the church of St. Saturninus, Tolosa, Spain, St. Sernin, Toulouse, France and until World War II in the monastery chapel of St. Norbet, Cologne, Germany.[17]

CHAPTER FOURTEEN

JUDAS ISCARIOT

[Jesus said], "But here at this table, sitting among us as a friend, is the man who will betray me. For it has been determined that the Son of Man must die. But what sorrow awaits the one who betrays him." Luke 22:21-22

On the night in which He was betrayed by Judas, Jesus offered a prayer which is recorded in John's Gospel: "During my time here, I protected them by the power of the name you gave me. I guarded them so that not one was lost, except the one headed for destruction, as the Scriptures foretold" (John 17:12).

Of all the characters who march across the stage of Bible history there is none so tragic nor so despicable as that of Judas Iscariot. A poet described him as

> The base Judean who flung a pearl away richer than
> all his tribe.

There is something horrible about the way he betrayed Christ with a kiss. One preacher has described it as, "The hiss of a kiss."

Not the least of all the darksome aspects of his life is the way he died. There is a mystery of horror about this character which makes him typical of all the dastardly traitors of all the ages. Even Jesus said of him, "It would be far better for that man if he had never been born" (Matthew 26:24).

Thomas De Quincey, in his essay on Judas Iscariot, has tried to picture Judas as merely a miscarried patriot. He describes him as one who actually *loved* Jesus and only hung himself because his scheme for forcing Jesus into political leadership against Rome misfired, and Jesus Himself was *accidentally* put to death. The only trouble with this and other recent attempts to whitewash the character of Judas is that Jesus Himself rejected his interpretation before Judas even betrayed Him. Jesus said, "I chose the twelve of you, but one is a devil" (John 6:70).

And again, "For the Son of Man must die, as the Scriptures declared long ago. But how terrible it will be for the one who betrays him. It would be far better for that man if he had never been born" (Matthew 26:24).

The name *Judas Iscariot* is a corruption of *Judas of Kerioth*. Kerioth was a small town some miles south of Hebron. Judas was the only one of the apostles who was not a Galilean, but a Judean. His father's name was Simon (John 13:2).

Today the name of Judas is a synonym of scorn and loathing. No mother ever names her child Judas. Yet when Judas bore the name, it was an honorable one. One of the greatest patriots of the Jewish nation was Judas Maccabeus. One of the brothers of Jesus Christ was named Judas, though today we call him Jude, which is a shortened form of the name Judas. Indeed, the name Judas is merely a form of Judah. Judas, then, was named for his tribe, the tribe of Judah.

We think of Judas as being the arch-traitor. Even today a goat used to lure sheep to their destruction in the slaughter house is known as a Judas goat. A plant which grows in the East which looks attractive but which is bitter to taste is called the Judas tree.

Yet the disciples did not originally think of him in this light. They were perfectly willing to trust him because apparently he *seemed* trustworthy. They freely elected him treasurer of their

> We think of Judas as being the arch-traitor. Yet the disciples did not originally think of him in this light because he *seemed* trustworthy.

band. Not only this, but they were astounded when the revelation of his treachery was made.

When Jesus affirmed that someone would betray Him, the disciples began to ask, "Is it I?" Not, "Is it Judas?"

Judas probably became a disciple of Christ when Jesus was on one of His preaching tours through Judea. At least it is probable that Judas first met Jesus at this time, though his call to become a disciple may have taken place at the Sea of Galilee.

From the time of his call to be a disciple until the Passion Week, we have no specific references to Judas which describe any activities of himself alone. John's Gospel records a few things, mostly in retrospect to show that the character of Judas was black from the beginning. (*It was almost a year before His crucifixion* when Jesus said that Judas was a devil. However long Judas may have deceived the apostles, he did not, of course, deceive Jesus.)

About the time of the Passion Week, we begin to read more of his sinister character. At the anointing of Jesus by Mary, Judas asked, "'That perfume was worth a year's wages. It should have been sold and the money given to the poor.' Not that he cared for the poor—he was a thief, and since he was in charge of the disciples' money, he often stole some for himself" (John 12:5-6).

Jesus also mentioned Judas's coming defection when He said, "The one who eats my food has turned against me" (John 13:18).

This is a quotation from Psalm 41:9. It seemed by these veiled references that Jesus was giving Judas as much opportunity as he could to repent, as if to inform him that He knew all along that Judas was going to betray Him, but still was announcing that the door of mercy was open.

There are many difficulties to reconcile in the life of Judas. First of all we must try to answer the question: "Why did Judas become a disciple?" Some have said that he intended to betray Jesus all along because he saw in Jesus a threat to the Jewish nation. Others suggest that he was sincere for a while, but then saw that Jesus was not going to fulfill His destiny as a political deliverer and therefore sought to get out, currying favor with the priests, as well as earning what pitiful funds he could as the price of his betrayal. Some have even suggested that Judas was ordained by God to be a traitor because of the prophetic references in the Old Testament. This, however, must be rejected, for surely God condemns no one in advance to be anything, for every man is free to be *what he will.*

Perhaps the most significant thing that can be said of Judas was that in feeling sorrow for his crime of betrayal, he did not seek to *atone* for his sin to the One whom he had wronged, but went to his accomplices in crime, the priests, and there sought to set himself aright. And because those whom he had served in his selfishness failed him at the end, he went out and hanged himself.

The life of Judas is one of unrelieved tragedy. In fact, there is no more tragic spirit in all the world's history. Judas is the greatest failure the world has ever known. *His* life is a lesson which points vividly to the pitfalls of *our* spiritual pilgrimage.

An excellent summary of the last days of Judas is given in the *International Standard Bible Encyclopedia*:

> After the betrayal, Mark, Luke and John are silent as regards Judas, and the accounts given in Matthew and Acts of his remorse and death vary in detail. According to Matthew, the actual condemnation of Jesus awakened Judas' sense of

MATTHEW WRITES

Judas, one of the twelve disciples, arrived with a crowd of men armed with swords and clubs. They had been sent by the leading priests and elders of the people. The traitor, Judas, had given them a prearranged signal: "You will know which one to arrest when I greet him with a kiss." So Judas came straight to Jesus. "Greetings, Rabbi!" he exclaimed and gave him the kiss.

Jesus said, "My friend, go ahead and do what you have come for." Matthew 26:47-50 guilt, and becoming still more despondent at his repulse by the chief priests and elders, "he cast down the pieces of silver into the sanctuary, and departed; and he went away and hanged himself." With the money the chief priests purchased the potter's field, afterward called "the field of blood," and in this way was fulfilled the prophecy of Zechariah (11:12-14) ascribed by Matthew to Jeremiah (Matthew 27:2-10). The account given in Acts 1:16-20 is much shorter. It mentions neither Judas' repentance nor the chief priests, but simply states that Judas "obtained a field with the reward of his iniquity; and falling headlong, he burst asunder in the midst, and all his bowels gushed out" (ver. 18). The author of Acts finds in this the fulfillment of the prophecy in Ps. 69:25. The Vulgate rendering, "When he had hanged himself, he burst asunder," suggests a means of reconciling the two accounts.

> Judas's life points to the pitfalls of *our* spiritual pilgrimage. When the people whom he had served in his selfishness failed him at the end, Judas hanged himself.

According to a legendary account mentioned by Papias, the death of Judas was due to elephantiasis (cf. Hennecke, *Neutestamentliche Apokryphen*, 5). A so-called "Gospel of Judas" was in use among the gnostic sect of the Cainites.

. . . It is significant that Judas alone among the disciples was of southern extraction; and the differences in temperament and social outlook, together with the petty prejudices to which these generally give rise, may explain in part though they do not justify, his after treachery—the lack of inner sympathy which existed between Judas and the rest of the Apostles. He undoubtedly possessed a certain business ability, and was therefore appointed keeper of the purse. But his heart could not have been clean, even from the first, as he administered even his primary charge dishonestly. The cancer of this greed spread from the material to the spiritual. To none of the disciples did the fading of the dream of an earthly kingdom of pomp and glory bring greater disappointment than to Judas.

The cords of love by which Jesus gradually drew the hearts of the other disciples to Himself, the teaching by which He uplifted their souls above all earthly things, were as chafing bonds to the selfishness of Judas. And from his fettered greed and disappointed ambition sprang jealousy and spite and hatred. It was the hatred, not of a strong, but of an essentially weak man. Instead of making an open breach with his Lord, he remained ostensibly one of His followers: and this continued contact with a goodness to which he would not yield (cf. Swete on Mark 14:10), and his brooding over the rebukes of his Master, gave ready entrance for "Satan into his soul." But if he "knew the good and did not do it" (cf. John 13:17), so also he was weak in the carrying out of his nefarious designs. It was this hesitancy, rather than a fiendish cunning, which induced him to remain till the last moment in the upper room, and which prompted the remark of Jesus "What thou doest, do quickly" (*John* 13:27). Of a piece with this weak-mindedness was his attempt to cast the blame upon the chief priests and elders (cf. Matthew 27:3, 4). He sought to set himself right, not with the innocent Jesus whom he had betrayed, but with the accomplices in his crime; and because that world which his selfishness had made his god failed him at the last, he went and hanged himself. It was the tragic end of one who espoused a great cause in the spirit of speculation and selfish ambition, and who weighed

> He sought to set himself right, not with the innocent Jesus whom he had betrayed, but with the accomplices in his crime; and because that world which his selfishness had made his god failed him at the last, he went and hanged himself.

not the dread consequences to which those impure motives might lead him (cf. also [A. B.] Bruce, *Training of the Twelve*; [Henry] Lathan, *Pastor Pastorum*; [James] Stalker, *Trial and Death of Jesus Christ*).[1]

There is little material about Judas in any of the common apocryphal sources. In a work *The Arabic Gospel of the Infancy*, it relates that Judas was demon-possessed even when he was a child. Men all through history have sought to psychoanalyze the mind of Judas. J. G. Tasked in *The Dictionary of Christ and the Gospels* quotes two verdicts on Judas. Lavater said of Judas, "Judas acted like Satan, but like a satan who had it in him to be an apostle." Pressense said of Judas, "No man could be more akin to a devil than a perverted apostle."

A Jerusalem guidebook states:

> Haceldama (Field of Blood) is a name given to the so called "potter's field" that was bought with the 30 pieces of silver that Judas had earned for betraying Jesus. Judas, repenting of his deed, flung the money at the feet of the priests who were unwilling to accept it because it was "blood money." After Judas had killed himself the money was used to buy a field to serve as a burial place for strangers (Matthew 27:3-10). Today the Greek Convent of St. Onipruis marks the site which is riddled with rock-hewn tombs full of the skulls and bones of pilgrims who, through the ages, have been buried in potter's field—the Field of Blood. The traditional hiding place of the Apostles during Jesus' trial is shown within the convent in a rock-hewn tomb that has been appropriately named the "Cave of the Apostles."[2]

CHAPTER FIFTEEN

MATTHIAS

They all prayed, "O Lord, you know every heart. Show us which of these men you have chosen as an apostle to replace Judas in this ministry. . . ." Then they cast lots, and Matthias was selected to become an apostle with the other eleven. Acts 1:24-26

This disciple remains a figure of mystery. Not one of the original Twelve, he was later chosen to take the place of Judas. Some scholars such as David Smith and G. Campbell Morgan have questioned the manner of his choosing. Because of the silence of the Scriptures about his later ministry they have concluded the Eleven were hasty in their election of Matthias. Their reasoning goes that Paul should have been chosen, and that the disciples were moving ahead of the leading of the Spirit. We must reject this idea as unrealistic.

During this time James the Great had also been killed by Herod, thus leaving another vacancy among the Twelve. Paul was never accepted as one of the original apostles; nor indeed could he have been since he did not know Christ in the flesh. The purpose of an apostle was stated on the occasion of the election of Matthias by Peter:

> *"So now we must choose a replacement for Judas from among the men who were with us the entire time we were traveling with the Lord Jesus—from the time he was baptized by John until the day he was taken from us. Whoever is chosen will join us as a witness of Jesus' resurrection."* . . . *Then they all prayed, "O Lord, you know every heart. Show us which of these men you have chosen."*

*. . . Then they cast lots, and Matthias was selected to become an
apostle with the other eleven.* (Acts 1:21-26)

Years later the apostle John referred to the New Jerusalem as a city
with a wall having "twelve foundation stones, and on them were written the names of the twelve apostles of the Lamb" (Revelation 21:14).
By implication, this clearly affirms the importance of Matthias.

Edgar Goodspeed says it was James, the brother of Jesus Christ,
who actually took Judas's place, being named by Paul (in Galatians
1:19; 2:9) as a leader and "pillar" of the church. But this is suspect
on two grounds. First, Goodspeed's identification of James as an
apostle does not meet the qualifications set forth (above) by Peter,
since James the brother of Jesus was not converted until after the
Resurrection, and therefore he could not have been a witness of
Jesus' teachings.

Second, Dr. Goodspeed's theories of the identity of the authorship of the book of James are at variance with most other equally
competent commentators, and therefore it is probable that his identification of Jesus' brother James as an apostle, in the sense that the
eleven others were, is open to question, though this James was also
an apostle in the sense that others, who were were not of the Eleven,
were apostles.

What Early Christian Writers Have Said about Matthias

Clement of Alexandria identifies Matthias with Zacchaeus. This is
impossible since Zacchaeus was never a disciple of Jesus in the sense
that the other apostles were. And furthermore, Zacchaeus could not
have witnessed the teachings of Jesus "from the time he was baptized by John" (Acts 1:22). In *The Lives of the Saints*, Hugo Hoever
notes that "Clement writes that Matthias was remarkable for teaching the necessity of mortifying the flesh with its irregular passions
and desires."[1]

Eusebius suggests that Matthias had been one of the seventy sent
out by Jesus (Luke 10:1). This is entirely possible. In this role Mat-

thias must have had the opportunity to show qualities of leadership which impressed the Eleven.

The *Traditions of Matthias* is quoted by Clement in AD 190–210. Dr. Goodspeed estimates this apocryphal work to have been written shortly before this period, but fully a century after the lifetime of Matthias. This would indicate only a traditional value in this apocryphal story, but it is interesting to know that it is comparatively early, and that it at least reveals Matthias to have been important in the thinking of some early Christians.

Matthias is one of the five apostles credited by Armenian tradition with evangelizing Armenia. These five were Thaddaeus, Bartholomew, Simon the Cananaean, Andrew, and Matthias.[2]

E. A. Wallis Budge in his *The Contendings of the Twelve* records an apocryphal tradition which tells of Matthias being imprisoned and blinded by the Ethiopian cannibals.[3] This story claims he was rescued by Andrew.

> Eusebius suggests that Matthias had been one of the seventy sent out by Jesus.

It is interesting to note that there must have been two countries called "Ethiopia" in biblical times. The one in Africa is the one that we know today. There, local traditions still affirm that the Ethiopian eunuch who was led to Christ and baptized by Philip was the founder of the church which survives to this day. Ethiopian churches are Coptic churches which bear a historical tradition in common with the Copts of Egypt.

The other Ethiopia where Matthias is said to have encountered cannibalism is not altogether identifiable today, but it seems to have been one of the provinces of Mesopotamia or Armenia. Little historic evidence exists that cannibalism was ever regularly practiced in this Ethiopia though there is no proof that in isolated instances it might not have indeed occurred. There are some indications that ritualistic cannibalism (eating human flesh for the sake of some supposed benefit to the eater, i.e., eating the heart of a captured warrior to gain the victim's bravery) was practiced in ancient Britain and among the Mexican and American Indians before the Spanish conquest. Even among starving American degenerates cannibalism has at times been known. Thus we cannot say cannibals did not exist in this Middle Eastern "Ethiopia."

According to the *Martyrdom of St. Matthias*, he was sent to Damascus, and died at Phaleaon which is a city of Judea.[4] Other sources mention Jerusalem as the place of Matthias's ministry and burial. That tradition is that he was stoned to death there by the Jews.[5]

Irenaeus refers to Matthias as being "ordained" in the place of Judas.

No trace is left of an apocryphal *Gospel According to Matthias*. It was a heretical work referred to by Origen (*Hom. on Luke* i) and Eusebius. (Eusebius *HE* iii 25, 6)

The gnostic Basilides (AD 133) and his son Isadore claimed to ground their doctrine in the *Gospel of Basilides* on the teaching Matthias received directly from Jesus (Hippol., 7.20) (cf. Hennecke, *Neutestamentlicke Apokryphen*, 167).

According to ancient church tradition as recorded in *Sacred and Legendary Art*, Matthias suffered martyrdom at the hands of the Jews either by lance or by the axe.[6] Roman Catholic tradition concerning the death and burial of Matthias indicates that he preached and suffered martyrdom in Judea, but these sources acknowledge that some early writers indicate that Matthias was martyred at Colchis, and still others at Sebastopol in AD 64. They also indicate that the body of Matthias was kept in Jerusalem and later taken to Rome by St. Helena from which some relics (bones) were afterward transported to Treves [now Trier] in Germany.[7]

Dorman Newman writing in 1685 acknowledges many of these traditions:

> According to ancient church tradition, Matthias suffered martyrdom at the hands of the Jews either by lance or axe.

In the 51 year of our Lord, he died at a place called Sebastopol and was buried near the temple of the Sun. The Greeks, recorded herein by many Antiquaries tell us that he was crucified and his body was said to have been kept a long time in Jerusalem, thence transported to Rome by Queen Helena, and there parts are venerated to this day (i.e. 1685) though others with great eagerness contend that his relics were brought to and are still preserved in Trier in Germany.[8]

The Present Burial Places of the Relics

The visitor to Trier may obtain an extremely well written local *Guide to the Monuments*. It records:

> When in 1127 relics of the Apostle Matthias were found, the veneration of St. Eucharius was soon transferred to St. Matthias. Increasing pilgrimages to the tomb of the Apostle demanded a new building which was begun in 1127 and consecrated in 1148 by Pope Eugen III.
>
> The Matthias-church is still a center of pilgrimage to the tombs of the first holy bishops, St. Eucharius and St. Valerius, and to the recently reinstalled sepulcher of the Apostle Matthias under the intersection of the nave and the transepts. Thus this church preserves traditions from antique times until our present days.[9]

The reliquary containing the bones of Matthias is a noted tourist attraction in Trier. When I visited this ancient Roman city, I found that this burial was spoken of in local museum publications as "the only body of an apostle to be buried north of the Alps." On my first visit to Trier I was shown the relics of Matthias which were then kept in a golden sarcophagus located in a side chapel attached to the monastery church of St. Matthias.

On a later visit, I found that a new sarcophagus of white and dark gray marble had been placed in front of the main altar in the larger church building. The white marble part of the new sarcophagus is carved into a life-sized image of the apostle recumbent upon the gray marble reliquary now containing the bones. Thus, as is also true in the case of the head of Andrew, apostolic relics have been moved within a space of ten years. The visitor to Europe can visit two burial sites for Matthias, both described as authentic by Roman Catholic authorities.

Knowing the penchant of various relic-seeking religious groups in the Middle Ages for fragmenting the bodies or relics of the apostles, there need be little doubt that both Rome and Trier contain parts of the body of Matthias, if in fact his body was preserved and transported as the records indicate. Admittedly there is a great deal of room for mistakes to have been made at several of the important steps of the transmission of these relics.

Queen Helena, who first moved them, was as eager a believer as any who have ever lived. She had unlimited power and wealth with a faith to match. One can hardly believe that she was as critical a collector of apostolic relics, and for that matter sacred places, as modern scholarship could wish. Her "discovery" of the Holy Sepulcher in Jerusalem, for example, was based upon a vision she was reputed to have had. One can admire her piety, determination, and her indefatigable zeal to recover as much as she could of original first century apostolic associations. But it is certain that she was at times mistaken.

A Brief Biography

A synthesis of information about Matthias would indicate the following biography.

As one of the earliest followers of Jesus, Matthias was prominent among the Seventy. He had apparently accompanied the twelve apostles on numerous occasions and very possibly may have been at first a disciple of John the Baptist like John and Andrew. Matthias was certainly elected to take the place of Judas immediately after the ascension of Jesus. Therefore, he was in Jerusalem on the day of Pentecost and had a prominent part in the turbulent and thrilling days of early Christianity's expansion. As a Jew he would naturally have gone forth from Jerusalem to minister to the portion of the far-flung diaspora of Israel. There were colonies of Jews and other Hebrews to be found in practically every population center throughout the Middle East. There is therefore no difficulty in accepting the tradition of his apostleship in regions of Armenia, and of the probability of great peril which befell him in the cities of Colchis, Sebastopol, and elsewhere. It is certainly possible that he may at one time have been aided by Andrew since apostles often went forth in pairs.

One can see him returning to Jerusalem, a battered witness of dangerous missionary experience. Perhaps upon his return he found a greater antagonism toward Christianity among the Jews than when he had left. In any case, the antagonism proved more dangerous than before and ultimately it was fatal to him. One can also accept the possibility that later Queen Helena transferred his remains to Rome, although she was much fonder of Constantinople than of Rome. In any case, she may have initiated the preservation and transference of the body of Matthias.

> Matthias was in Jerusalem on the day of Pentecost and had a prominent part in the turbulent and thrilling days of early Christianity's expansion.

There is a systematic tradition of the western movement of almost all apostolic relics. Three factors contribute to this: (1) The collecting zeal of Helena and others. (2) The imminent peril to the Christian churches and the apostolic relics by the invading Persians in the fifth and sixth centuries. (3) The values placed upon relics and the need to safeguard them which was universally shared by churchmen in the Middle Ages.

These three factors rescued relics that were believed to have been authentic, and transported them to areas which were considered safer than the original tombs or the secondary burial places, such as Constantinople itself. One cannot overlook the fact that the Eastern Roman Empire frequently sought to strengthen alliances with Rome and the Roman Catholic Church. Relics of apostles were considered as extremely valuable political chessmen, which is one reason they have been so well preserved to this day.

> Relics of apostles were considered as extremely valuable political chessmen— one reason they have been so well preserved to this day.

In any case, the relics of Matthias seem to have found their final resting places in both Rome and Trier where they can still be seen.

OTHER NOTABLE APOSTLES

Although these men and others like them were not part of the original group of Jesus' twelve apostles, they fit the definition of apostle—a messenger or authorized representative of Jesus and His gospel. After Jesus' ascension, His apostles were filled with the Holy Spirit and empowered to carry out special roles in the growth of the early church.

John Mark
Barnabas
Luke
Lazarus
Paul

CHAPTER SIXTEEN

JOHN MARK

[Paul writes] Aristarchus . . . sends you his greetings, and so does Mark, Barnabas's cousin. . . .(the one we call Justus) also sends his greetings. These are the only Jewish believers among my co-workers; they are working with me here for the Kingdom of God. And what a comfort they have been! Colossians 4:10-11

In 1972 Louis Cassels, long-time religion editor for United Press International, wrote a story that got the attention of biblical scholars:

> Professor Jose O'Callaghan, a Spanish scholar at the Pontifical Biblical Institute in Rome, has identified 19 tiny scraps of papyrus, found in 1947 among the Dead Sea Scrolls as fragments of a copy of St. Mark's gospel written around AD 50.
>
> The date is what matters. Biblical scholars have long assumed that Mark's gospel, based on recollections of the Apostle Peter, was set down in writing shortly before Peter's death in Rome, which would date it around AD 68.
>
> Since Jesus was crucified about AD 33, the previous dating of Mark's gospel—generally regarded to have been the first one written—left a hiatus of 35 years in which the historical details of the life of Jesus either were transmitted by word of mouth or by now-lost records (such as the famous "Q" document which scholars have long postulated but never found).
>
> O'Callaghan's papyrus fragments, established by scientific methods as having been in a Palestinian library in AD 50,

indicates that Mark's gospel may well have been in circulation within about a dozen years of the time of Jesus' death.

This is very important because it means Mark's record had to survive the acid test of any journalistic or historical writing—being published at a time when it could be read, criticized, and if unauthentic, denounced, by thousands of Jews, Christians, Romans and Greeks who were living in Palestine at the time of Jesus' ministry.[1]

The writer of the second Gospel, as it appears in the order of the Bible, was a figure of great importance in the apostolic age.

He was given a Roman name (Mark, *Marcus*) and a Jewish name (John, *Jonah*). Mark's home was in Jerusalem (Acts 12:12). His father is not mentioned, so it is possible that at the time he was living in comfortable surroundings in a large house with his mother, Mary, and his cousin Barnabas (Colossians 4:10), who was also a man of means (Acts 4:36-37).

It is believed that Mark's family, perhaps upon his father's death, had moved to Jerusalem from Cyrenaica, a Roman colony in North Africa. This would perhaps imply that Mark had a Roman father and certainly a Jewish mother.

In AD 44, at the first mention of John Mark in Acts, he, as well as his mother, Mary, are already believers. Probably he was led to Christ by Peter who affectionately referred to him as his spiritual "son" (1 Peter 5:13).

When John Mark is first mentioned in Acts, he, as well as his mother, Mary, are already believers. Probably he was led to Christ by Peter.

After notable experience in the company of many of the leaders of the Jerusalem church, which probably made its headquarters in his mother's house, Mark was chosen to accompany Paul and Barnabas to Antioch. He went with Paul and Barnabas on their first missionary journey from Antioch to Cyprus, the original home of Barnabas.

When they went on to Turkey, John Mark suddenly decided to return to Antioch. Sir William Ramsey speculates that the possible contagion of Paul's fever, which occurred at Perga before the missionary team was scheduled to go inland to Antioch, plus the dire tales of bandits in the desolate mountains which lay ahead of them, might have dissuaded Mark from going to that wild central area of Turkey.

Others have suggested that Mark did not then fully accept the Pauline doctrine of salvation by grace through faith alone. This idea is alluded to in Acts 13:5, 13 with Luke's use of Mark's Hebrew name—John Mark. It is thought that Mark was of the Jewish party mentioned by Luke. This might imply a serious doctrinal difference with Paul based upon the fact that he (Mark) was still a devout Jew, and at that time unable to accept the doctrine of faith for salvation. No failure at this doctrinal point was apparently acceptable to Paul. Even later than this event, Barnabas himself is said by Paul to have had misgivings about the doctrine of salvation by faith (Galatians 2:13). Barnabas obviously influenced Mark, at least at first.

Two years after the departure of John Mark from Perga, Paul and Barnabas decided to go on another missionary journey from Antioch. Barnabas wanted again to take Mark but Paul disagreed. So Paul chose Silas and went overland in Turkey to visit the churches he and Barnabas had organized on their first journey there. Barnabas took Mark and retraced the steps he and Paul had taken in Cyprus. Barnabas eventually died on Cyprus probably in AD 58.

Eleven years later in Rome the breach between Paul and Mark was healed. Mark was one of the faithful few among the Jewish Christians in Rome who stood by Paul. He is described by Paul in Colossians as an honored fellow worker and a "great comfort" to him. In that Epistle there is a hint that Mark might visit Colossae. It may be that this indeed happened. He went with Peter to Babylon. In 1 Peter 5:13 Peter sends Mark's greetings from Babylon.

Later Mark returned to Turkey. At the time of his second imprisonment in Rome, Paul asked Timothy to bring Mark to him in

Rome. In his last letter Paul paid tribute to Mark as being "helpful to me in my ministry" (2 Timothy 4:11).

While in Rome Mark must have written his Gospel at the request of Peter. *The Post-Nicene Fathers* records the tradition:

> Mark the disciple and interpreter of Peter wrote a short gospel at the request of the brethren at Rome, embodying what he had heard Peter tell. When Peter had heard this, he approved it and published it to the churches to be read by his authority as Clemens, in the sixth book of his *Hypotyposes* and Papias, bishop of Hierapolis, record. Peter also mentions this Mark in his first epistle, figuratively indicating Rome under the name of Babylon, "She who is in Babylon elect together with you saluteth you and so doth Mark my son."[2]

We must, of course, differ from the idea that Peter's first epistle was written in Rome. The traditions of the eastern most churches are unanimous that it was instead written in Babylon which is exactly what it says in the epistle. The idea that *Rome* was meant instead of Babylon is the only interpretation possible similar to the figurative and symbolic language that John used later in the Revelation. But there was no need to use Babylon if Rome was meant in Peter's first epistle.

> After the deaths of Peter and Paul in Rome there is a clear tradition that John Mark went to Alexandria.

After the deaths of Peter and Paul in Rome there is a clear tradition that John Mark went to Alexandria, a Greco-Roman city in Egypt with a large Jewish population. For a time he labored there. It is possible that during the years before he joined Paul and Peter in Rome at the end of their lives, he might have visited Alexandria and helped to organize a church there. The chronology is not certain, but two visits to Alexandria do not seem unreasonable.

Eusebius marks the tradition that Anianus, a convert of Mark, succeeded him as the pastor of the church at Alexandria "in the eighth year of Nero's reign." Since Nero outlived Paul by less than two years this fact does not agree with the idea that Mark was in Rome at or near the time of the deaths of Peter and Paul. Yet from 2 Timothy it is clear that a short while before Paul's death Mark was in Turkey, not Egypt.

In *A History of Eastern Christianity*, Aziz S. Atiya tells about the very detailed and firm traditions in Egypt among the Coptic churches regarding Mark:

> St. Mark brought his Gospel with him to Alexandria; and though the Greek version could have fulfilled his purpose in that city, the suggestion is made that another version in the Egyptian language was prepared for the benefit of native converts who were not conversant with Greek.
>
> Mark's real labour lay in Africa. First, he crossed the Mediterranean to Cyrenaica—the Pentapolis which had been his parents' residence in bygone days. This country was colonized by Greeks and many Jews who offered his zeal a ripe and hopeful harvest. After performing many miracles and sowing the seeds of his faith, he went to Alexandria by a circuitous route through the oases and Babylon, or Old Cairo. Alexandria was the Eastern counterpart of Rome, both in importance and in being a stronghold of paganism, and it was imperative that Christianity should win the two. The task was as worthy as it was hazardous.
>
> Here we face the important problem of dates. *The History of the Patriarchs* mentions explicitly that the revelation to Peter and Mark, that they should advance on Rome and Alexandria, came in the fifteenth year after the Ascension of Christ, that is, A.D. 48. Other sources put his entry into Alexandria in A.D. 55, 58 and 61. Whatever the right date of Mark's appearance in the city, the consensus is that he was martyred in A.D. 68. Between those two dates he was able to fulfill his mission and to win many converts.

The story runs that on entering the city by the eastern gate, he broke the strap of his shoe. So he went to a cobbler to mend it. When the cobbler took an awl to work on it, he accidentally pierced his hand and cried aloud: "Heis ho Theos" (God is one). Mark rejoiced at this utterance and, after miraculously healing the man's wound, took courage and gave the lesson to the hungry ears of his first convert. This happened to be Anianus, Mark's successor as the second patriarch of Alexandria. The spark was fired, and the cobbler took the Apostle home with him. He and his family were baptized, and many others followed. So successful was the movement that the word spread that a Galilean was in the city preparing to overthrow the idols. Popular feeling began to rise, and the men sought him everywhere. Sensing danger, the Apostle ordained Anianus bishop, with three priests and seven deacons to watch over the congregation in case anything befell him.

Afterwards, he seems to have undertaken two voyages. First he sailed into Rome where he met Peter and Paul, and he left the capital only after their martyrdom in A.D. 64. He then stayed at Aquilea, near Venice, before his return to Alexandria. On finding his flock firm in the faith, he decided to visit the Pentapolis, where he spent two years performing miracles, ordaining bishops and priests, and winning more converts. When at last he reached Alexandria, he was overjoyed to find that the brethren had so multiplied that they were able to build a considerable church in the suburban district of Baucalis, where cattle grazed by the seashore.

Spreading rumours that the Christians threatened to overthrow the pagan deities infuriated the idolatrous populace. The end was approaching, and the saint was unremittingly hunted by the enemy. In the year A.D. 68, Easter fell on the same day as the Serapis festival. The furious mob had gathered in the Serapion and then descended on the Christians while they were celebrating Easter at Baucalis. St. Mark was seized, dragged

with a rope around his neck in the streets, and then incarcer-
ated for the night. In the following morning the same ordeal
was repeated until he gave up the ghost. His flesh was torn
and bloody, and it was their intent to cremate his remains. But
the wind blew and the rain fell in torrents, and the populace
dispersed. Thus the Christians stealthily carried off his body
and secretly buried it in a grave which they had carved in the
rock under the altar of the church.[3]

Eusebius and other early church writers were not always accurate
as to dates. But the tradition of St. Mark's ministry and martyrdom
in Alexandria has much historical justification as Atiya shows:

> In subsequent centuries the body of St. Mark did not remain
> intact. During the later times of schism between the Copts and
> the Melkites, who were in authority, the church where the body
> was kept remained in the hands of the latter. At the time of
> the Arab storming of Alexandria in 642,
> the church was pillaged and the vest-
> ments and the head of the Apostle were
> stolen. With the establishment of peace
> in the city, that church, together with
> the body, remained in Melkite hands.
> But the head somehow was returned to
> the Arab governor, who ceded it to the
> Coptic Patriarch Benjamin, the only
> ecclesiastical leader left after the depar-
> ture of the Greeks. According to their
> own story, Venetian merchants stole the headless body of St.
> Mark in 828. They smuggled it [to Venice] in a tub of pickled
> pork to evade Muslim inspection. In this wise, Venice earned
> its other title of the Republic of St. Mark.[4]

Mark seems to have lived a life of great usefulness, was a remarkable traveler, and had known many of the early Christian giants of the faith.

E. M. Forster in *Alexandria: A History and a Guide* explains that
the smuggling of St. Mark's body by the Venetians was an attempt

to save it from Saracen desecration and mentions that the Church of Limours near Paris possesses one of St. Mark's arms while Soissons has his head.[5]

Mary Sharp confirms the story of what befell St. Mark's relics:

> His remains were buried in Alexandria, but in 828 Venetian merchants took the remains to Venice, where the church of St. Mark was built to receive them. Beneath the church of St. Pudentiana in Rome are the ruins of a first-century house where it is said that Mark may have written his Gospel.[6]

There is a final note. Pope Paul VI restored parts of the body of St. Mark which had been in Venice at St. Mark's Cathedral, to the Coptic church in Alexandria. Like his similar gesture to the Greek Orthodox Church in Patras, when he restored the head of their patron St. Andrew to that place, this act also was an act of reconciliation between two very old branches of organized Christianity.

Mark was perhaps younger than the apostles whom he served. He seems to have lived a life of great usefulness, was a remarkable traveler, and either had accompanied or known many of the early Christian giants of the faith. Among them were Peter, Paul, and Barnabas, not to mention others such as Timothy.

It is believed that the discovery of the actual foundations of the house of Mary, the mother of Mark, has recently been made in the basement of the church of St. Mark in Jerusalem. An ancient inscription discovered and displayed there tells that the original church was built on the site of the house of Mary and Mark, and that it was the place of the "upper room" which was the gathering place of the first Christians and was also the site of the Pentecostal baptism of the Holy Spirit. If this all be true, then the experience of Mark is one of the richest of all the New Testament characters! Of course, his authorship of the Gospel of Mark immortalizes him for all Christians.

BARNABAS

When Barnabas arrived [in Antioch] and saw this evidence of God's blessing, he was filled with joy, and he encouraged the believers to stay true to the Lord. Barnabas was a good man, full of the Holy Spirit and strong in faith. Acts 11:22-24

William Smith provides us with the following description in the *Dictionary of the Bible*:

His name signifies *son of prophecy*, or *exhortation* (or, but not so probably, *consolation*, as A.V.), given by the Apostles (Acts 4:36) to *Joseph* (or Joses), a Levite of the island of Cyprus, who was only a disciple of Christ. In Acts 9:27, we find him introducing the newly converted Saul to the Apostles in Jerusalem, in a way which seems to indicate a previous acquaintance between the two. On tidings coming to the church at Jerusalem that men of Cyprus and Cyrene had been preaching to Gentiles at Antioch, Barnabas was sent thither (Acts 11:19-26), and went to Tarsus to seek Saul, as one specially raised up to preach to the Gentiles (Acts 26:17). Having brought Saul to Antioch, he was sent with him to Jerusalem, with relief for the brethren in Judaea (Acts 11:30). On their return to Antioch they (Acts 13:2) were ordained by the Church for the missionary work, and sent forth (AD 45). From this time Barnabas and Paul enjoy the title and dignity of Apostles.

Their first missionary journey is related in Acts 13. It was confined to Cyprus and Asia Minor. Some time after their return to Antioch (AD 47 or 48), they were sent (AD 50), with some others, to Jerusalem, to determine with the Apostles and elders the difficult question respecting the necessity of circumcision for the Gentile converts. (Acts 15:1) On that occasion Paul and Barnabas were recognized as the Apostles of the Uncircumcision. After another stay in Antioch, on their return, a variance took place between Barnabas and Paul on the question of taking with them, on a second missionary journey, John Mark, sister's son to Barnabas (Acts 15:36). "The contention was so sharp that they parted asunder," and Barnabas took Mark, and sailed to Cyprus, his native island. Here the Scripture notices of him cease.

As to his further labors and death, traditions differ. Some say he went to Milan, and became first bishop of the church there. There is extant an apocryphal work, probably of the fifth century, *Acta et Passio Barnabae in Cypro*; and still later an *Encomium* of Barnabas, by a Cyprian man, Alexander. We have an Epistle in twenty-one chapters called by the name of Barnabas. Its authenticity has been defended by some great writers; but it is very generally given up now, and the Epistle is believed to have been written early in the second century.[1]

The Later Life of Barnabas

An apocryphal document, perhaps dating from the second century, called *The Recognitions of Clement* mentions that St. Clement (supposedly the same as the Clement mentioned by Paul in Philippians 4:3) claims his first acquaintance with Christianity was through the preaching of Barnabas in Rome. There is no further confirmation of this fact however. Based on this tradition the Church of Cyprus (Greek Orthodox) stoutly maintains that it was on the island of Cyprus that Barnabas lived and died. Robin Parker, in his excellent guidebook *Aphrodite's Realm*, records this rather well documented historical tradition:

The Church of Cyprus was founded by the Apostles Paul and Barnabas in A.D. 45. The latter suffered death in his native town of Salamis during his second mission to the island and was buried secretly outside the town by his kinsman and companion, St. Mark. His relics, with a copy of St. Matthew's Gospel in Barnabas' handwriting, were discovered by the Archbishop of Cyprus, Anthemios, during the reign of the Emperor Zeno (474-491).

This discovery helped to secure the independence of the Church of Cyprus from the assailings of the Church of Antioch which was then trying to bring it under its jurisdiction. At a specially convened meeting in Constantinople the Church of Cyprus was declared "autocephalous" (self-governing) on account of its Apostolic foundation, and certain privileges were bestowed on it by the Emperor himself, among which was the right of the Archbishop of Cyprus to sign in red ink.[2]

According to Roman Catholic tradition the relics of St. Barnabas have been widely scattered. His head is said to be in the church of St. Sernin in Toulouse, France as Mary Sharp notes in her travel guide. "His body is said to have been buried near the place of his martyrdom; but in the seventh century, during the Saracen invasion, his head was taken to Milan and later to Toulouse."[3]

Most scholars today agree that Paul was *not* the author of the book of Hebrews. The noted authorities, Conybeare and Howson, make a strong argument that Barnabas, in fact, did. Taking into account his background in Judaism, his long Christian ministry, and his association with Paul, this is a very respectable theory. If it is true, then for a time after Paul's death in Rome, Barnabas may have gone to Rome until Timothy's release. This would not preclude Barnabas from returning to Cyprus to die.[4]

CHAPTER EIGHTEEN

LUKE

As a medical doctor, Luke knew the importance of being thorough. He used his skills in observation and analysis to thoroughly investigate the stories about Jesus. His diagnosis? The gospel of Jesus Christ is true! —*The Life Application Study Bible*

We are indebted to the late Dr. A. T. Robertson for the following succinct biography of Luke.

The legend that Luke was one of the Seventy sent out by Jesus (Epiphanius, *Haer.*, ii. 51, 11) is pure conjecture, as is the story that Luke was one of the Greeks who came to Philip for an introduction to Jesus (John 12:20f), or the companion of Cleopas in the walk to Emmaus (Luke 24:13). The clear implication of Luke 1:2 is that Luke himself was not an eyewitness of the ministry of Jesus.

In Colossians 4:14 Luke is distinguished by Paul from those "of the circumcision" (Aristarchus, Mark, Jesus Justus); Epaphras, Luke, Demas from the Gentile group. He was believed by the early Christian writers to have come directly from heathendom to Christianity. He may or may not have been a Jewish proselyte. His first appearance with Paul at Troas (cf. the "we" sections, Acts 16:10-12) is in harmony with this idea. The classic introduction to the Gospel [of Luke] (1:1-4) shows that he was a man of culture (cf. Apollos and Paul). He was a man of the schools, and his Greek had a literary flavor only approached in the New Testament by Paul's writings and by the Epistle to the Hebrews.

His home is very uncertain. The text of D (Cordex Bezae) and several Latin authorities have a "we" passage in Acts 11:27. If this reading, the so-called B text of Blass, is the original, then Luke was at Antioch and may have been present at the great event recorded in Acts 12:1f. But it is possible that the Western text is an interpolation. At any rate, it is not likely that Luke is the same person as Lucius of Acts 13:1. Ramsay (*St. Paul the Traveller*, 389f) thinks that Eusebius (*HE*, III, iv, 6) does not mean to say that Luke was a native of Antioch, but only that he had Antiochian family connections. Jerome calls him *Lucas medicus Antichensis.* He certainly shows an interest in Antioch (cf Acts 11:19-27; 13:1; 14:26; 14:22.23.30.35; 18:22). Antioch, of course, played a great part in the early work of Paul. Other stories make Luke live in Alexandria and Achaia and narrate that he died in Achaia or Bithynia. But we know that he lived in Philippi for a considerable period.

He first meets Paul at Troas just before the vision of the Man from Macedonia (Acts 16:10-12), and a conversation with Paul about the work in Macedonia may well have been the human occasion of that vision and call. Luke remains in Philippi when Paul and Silas leave (Acts 16:40, "They . . . departed"). He is here when Paul comes back on his 3rd tour bound for Jerusalem (Acts 20:3-5). He shows also a natural pride in the claims of Philippi to the primacy in the province, as against Amphipolis and Thessalonica (Acts 16:12, 'the first of the district'). On the whole, then, we may consider Philippi as the home of Luke, though he was probably a man who had traveled a great deal, and may have been with Paul in Galatia before coming to Troas. He may have ministered to Paul in his sickness there. (Galatians 4:14). His later years were spent chiefly with Paul away from Philippi (cf. Acts 20:3–28.31, on the way to Jerusalem at Caesarea, the voyage to Rome and in Rome).

Paul (Colossians 4:14) expressly called him "the beloved physician." He was Paul's medical adviser, and doubtless prolonged his life and rescued him from many a serious illness. He was a medical missionary, and probably kept up his general practice of medicine in connection with his work in Rome. (cf Zahn, *Intro.*, III, 1). He probably practised medicine in Malta (Acts 28:9f). He naturally shows his fondness for medical terms in his books (cf. Hobart, *The Medical Language of St. Luke*; Harnack, *NT Studies: Luke the Physician*, 175–98).

Luke was Paul's medical adviser, who doubtless prolonged his life and rescued Paul from many a serious illness.

It is possible, even probable (see Souter's article in *DCG*), that in 2 Corinthians 8:18 "the brother" is equivalent to "the brother" of Titus just mentioned, that is, "his brother." If so we should know that Paul came into contact with Luke at Philippi on his way to Corinth during his 2nd tour (cf. also 2 Corinthians 12:18). It would thus be explained why in Acts the name of Titus does not occur, since he is the brother of Luke the author of the book.

If the reading of D in Acts 11:27f is correct, Luke met Paul at Antioch before the 1st missionary tour. Otherwise it may not have been till Troas on the 2d tour. But he is the more or less constant companion of Paul, from Philippi on the return to Jerusalem on the 3d tour till the 2 years in Rome at the close of the Acts. He apparently was not with Paul when Philippians (2:20) was written, though, as we have seen, he was with Paul in Rome when he wrote Colossians and Philemon. He was Paul's sole companion for a while during the 2d Rome imprisonment (2 Timothy 4:11). His devotion to Paul in this time of peril is beautiful.

One legend regarding Luke is that he was a painter. Plummer

(*Comm. on Luke*, xxif) thinks that the legend is older than is sometimes supposed and that it has a strong element of truth. It is true that he has drawn vivid scenes with his pen. The early artists were especially fond of painting scenes from the *Gospel of Luke*. The allegorical figure of the ox or calf in Ezekiel 1 and Revelation 4 has been applied to Luke's Gospel.

Literature.—Bible dicts., comms., lives of Paul, intros. See also Harnack, *"Lukas, der Arzt, der Verfasser"* (1906); *NT Studies: Luke the Physician* (1907); Ramsay, *Luke the Physician* (1908); Selwyn, *St. Luke the Prophet* (1901); Hobart, *The Medical Language of St. Luke* (1882); Ramsay, *Was Christ Born at Bethlehem? A Study in the Credibility of St. Luke* (1898); Maclachlan, *St. John, Evangelist and Historian* (1912).[1]

The Catholic scholar, Rev. J. A. Fitzmyer illuminates the style of the writings of St. Luke:

A tradition that can be traced back to Irenaeus (c. 185) regards Luke as the author of the third Gospel. This attribution was probably also known to Justin in the middle of the 2nd century. The Muratorian canon ascribes both the third Gospel and Acts to Luke. The Lucian authorship of both books is generally (though not universally) accepted by modern scholars.

Luke belonged to cultivated Hellenistic circles, where he learned to write with ease good idiomatic Greek. His writings betray an acquaintance with the historical method of his day, and the "Semitisms" that shine through his Greek style of the latter is at times surprising. He was a perceptive, sensitive writer with a knack for telling a story and depicting a scene, and his Gospel has been described as "the most beautiful book" ever written. His two books constitute the earliest history of the Christian church.

> He was a perceptive, sensitive writer with a knack for telling a story. Luke's two books constitute the earliest history of the Christian church.

The Anti-Marcionite Prologue records that Luke wrote his Gospel in Greece, was not married and died in Boeotia (or Bithynia?) at the age of 84. But further details about his life come from either later traditions or legends.[2]

The Death and Burial of Luke

Catholic tradition is summarized by Mary Sharp. "Accounts differ as to the manner of his death; some say that he died peacefully in Boeotia and others that he was crucified with St. Andrew at Patras or at Elaea in Peloponnesus. In 356-357 Constantius II had his relics taken from Thebes in Boeotia to Constantinople and placed in the Church of the Apostles which was built soon afterwards. Later his head is said to have been taken to Rome where it is interred in St. Peter's Basilica."[3]

In 1685 Dorman Newman spoke with assurance in his *Lives and Deaths of the Holy Apostles* that "Luke is buried in Constantinople in that great and famous church dedicated to the memory of the Apostles." Jerome confirms this, writing that Luke "was buried at Constantinople to which city, in the twentieth year of Constantius, his bones, together with the remains of Andrew, the Apostle, were transferred."[4]

I have visited Thebes in central Greece where, inside a cemetery church, one can still see the original grave of Luke. It is a typical Roman sarcophagus carved in white pentellic marble from the not too distant marble quarries which are still being used today. In the church where this sarcophagus is found there are many signs,

> ### LUKE WRITES
>
> *Many people have set out to write accounts about the events that have been fulfilled among us. They used the eyewitness reports circulating among us from the early disciples. Having carefully investigated everything from the beginning, I also have decided to write a careful account for you . . . so you can be certain of the truth of everything you were taught. Luke 1:1-4*

inscriptions, and mementoes confirming that it was indeed in this ancient Greek cemetery that Luke was first buried. However, those in charge of the church do not seem to know about the fact that the body was transported to Constantinople in the fourth century.

In Rome the head of Luke is interred in a high altar facing the central altar which stands over the grave of Peter. Little attention is paid to it since its eminence is dimmed by the more widely publicized remains of Peter and other apostles resting nearby.

CHAPTER NINETEEN

LAZARUS

Jesus shouted, "Lazarus, come out!" And the dead man came out, his hands and feet bound in graveclothes, his face wrapped in a headcloth. Jesus told them, "Unwrap him and let him go." John 11:43-44

A thorough biography of Lazarus up to the time following his being raised from the dead has been written by G. H. Trever in the *Internationl Standard Bible Encyclopaedia*:

> Lazarus, laz'a-rus (Lázaros, an abridged form of the Hebrew name Eleazar, with a Greek termination): Means "God has helped." In the *Septuagint* and Josephus are found the forms *Eleazár*, and *Eleázaros*. The name was common among the Jews, and is given to two men in the New Testament who have nothing to do with each other.
>
> The home of the Lazarus mentioned in John 11:1 was Bethany. He was the brother of Martha and Mary (John 11:1, 2; see also Luke 10:38-41). All three were especially beloved by Jesus (John 11:5), and at their home He more than once, and probably often, was entertained (Luke 10:38-41; John 11).
>
> As intimated by the number of condoling friends from the city, and perhaps from the costly ointment used by Mary, the family was probably well-to-do. In the absence of Jesus, Lazarus was taken sick, died and was buried, but, after having lain in the grave four days, was brought back to life by the Saviour

(John 11:3.14.17.43.44). As a result many Jews believed on Jesus, but others went and told the Pharisees, and a council was therefore called to hasten the decree of the Master's death (John 11:45-53).

Later, six days before the Passover, at a feast in some home in Bethany where Martha served, Lazarus sat at a table as one of the guests, when his sister Mary anointed the feet of Jesus (John 12:1-3). Many of the common people came thither, not only to see Jesus, but also the risen Lazarus, believed in Jesus, and were enthusiastic in witnessing for Him during the triumphal entry, and attracted others from the city to meet Him (John 12:9.11.17.18).[1]

The Later Life of Lazarus

On the island of Cyprus there is a very firm and ancient tradition that Lazarus fled from Jerusalem about the year AD 60. It would seem that this is an unnecessarily late date although we have little more than tradition to go on in determining it.

A pamphlet published by The Church of St. Lazarus in Larnaca, Cyprus, records the local tradition:

> We do not know the names of his parents, because the *Holy Scriptures* mention nothing on this point. The only thing we know from them is that Lazarus had two sisters, Martha and Mary. Our Lord visited many times their home in Bethany and it is known that true friendship existed between him and his family. The feelings of Christ towards Lazarus are described in the Gospel of John, where we learn that, when our Lord was informed about his illness and the death of his friend, He hastened to Bethany and raised Lazarus from death, giving by this action joy to the unfortunate sisters, who received such a severe blow by the death of their brother.
>
> On account of this incident the Jews searched for Lazarus in order to kill him, because many people believed in Christ.

Lazarus, to avoid their revenge, was compelled to visit Cyprus and Citium about A.D. 60 or 63, according to an old tradition, which can be relied upon.

In Citium, Lazarus became the spiritual leader of the town, where he was bishop for thirty years. According to the same tradition Lazarus died in Citium, where his tomb is preserved up to the present day.

When Leo the Wise was emperor of Byzantine, the dead body of St. Lazarus was found and carried to Constantinople (A.D. 890).[2]

Robin Parker's guidebook about Cyprus, that is both well-written and comprehensive, affirms that "According to tradition St. Lazarus, after he was raised from the dead by Christ, came to Cyprus where he became the first bishop of the See of Kitium. The empty tomb, in which the relics of the saint were discovered, has been preserved and may be seen in the floor of the *bema*."[3]

When I visited the tomb of Lazarus in Cyprus, the Greek priest there explained that the body of Lazarus had sometime in the past been moved to Marseilles in France. He did not seem to know the details or the date. It is probable, as Patsides said, that the bones of Lazarus were indeed removed from Constantinople in the ninth century and taken to Marseilles. The relics have since disappeared from Marseilles, but there is some documentation that at one time they were there.

> The Jews searched for Lazarus in order to kill him, because many people believed in Christ [who raised Lazarus from the dead].

So firm indeed is the tradition that it opens a question: Might Lazarus have traveled from Cyprus to Marseilles and ministered there? This is not to say he could not also have eventually returned to Cyprus and died there, but there is more than a little indication that Lazarus spent some time preaching in Marseilles. Knowing the typical moving about of those who lived in the apostolic age, one can scarcely raise a serious objection to Lazarus having ministered in Cyprus, as did Paul and Barnabas, and then having gone on to Marseilles. But it is also not impossible that he may have returned to Cyprus to retirement and death.

Later his bones were most surely removed to Constantinople, and still later returned, not to Cyprus but to Marseilles, with which he had an early association. J. W. Taylor, who is a fascinating writer, describes the story of Lazarus in Marseilles as follows:

> If you land at Marseilles and go by the Quai de la Joliette to the bottom of the Rue de la Cannabiere, and then take any of the lower turnings on the right, you will find that you are skirting the older quay of Marseilles, and that as you bear again to the right and follow the Rue Sainte at some little height above the sea, directly in front of you, on an eminence, is the old church of St. Victor.
>
> It has rather the appearance of some old dungeon or fortress than that of a church, but the church you enter is only of secondary importance. It conceals something far more interesting underneath it. A door on the south side of the nave leads down to a subterranean church, large and lofty, which dates from the fourth century. This was built by the Cassianite monks, and from its position has been untouched and could not well be destroyed through all the centuries since.
>
> All this vast fourth-century church has been visibly built around a still older natural cave or grotto known as the original first-century church or refuge of St. Lazarus.
>
> Near the entrance to this is a carving of vine-leaves dating from the fourth century, and grouped near are old chapels dedicated to St. Cassian, St. Victor and other saints. The bodies of the saints, however, have been removed. Two sarcophagi stones, said to date from the second century, were too solid to be rifled of their contents and still remain.
>
> The great height of this underground abbey church, its

darkness, its stillness, the few scattered but perfect round pillars supporting the roof, and the 'first-century chapel' which is enshrined by it, all combine to produce a picture of early Christian life and architecture, striking and irresistible.

No explanation that I know of has been, or can be, offered other than that offered by tradition—that here was the place where Lazarus of Bethany lived and preached and ministered and died, and that therefore within some two hundred or three hundred years afterwards this church was built in honour of his memory and to enshrine his body which was then present here.

And all through the ages ever since this faith has been firmly held, and lives as strong today as ever. If we come back from the crypt or subterranean church into the (upper) church of St. Victor, at the west end of the nave, under the organ-loft, we find a life-sized statue of St. Lazarus, his left hand holding the crosier, his face upturned to heaven, and underneath the statue two pieces of stone removed from the old sepulcher at Bethany out of which our Saviour raised him.[4]

These appear to have been taken from a *Life* which was written by the monks of the Abbey at Bethany, a church and monastery having been erected at Bethany before the ravages of the Saracens, to guard the tomb from which our Lord was said to have raised St. Lazarus.

The extracts, according to Faillon (*Monuments In-edits*, vol. ii, p. 114, etc.), read

"Tradition states that St. Lazarus, after the ascension of Jesus Christ, remained for a time in the company of the Apostles, with whom he took charge of the Church which was at Jerusalem. After this he went to the Island of Cyprus in order to escape from the persecution which arose about Stephen. [This would indicate an earlier date for Lazarus having come to Cyprus than AD 60—ed.]

Having filled there for several years the office of a missionary priest, he entered into a ship, and traversing the sea, by the grace of God arrived at Marseilles, the most celebrated town of Provence. Here, exercising the functions of his priesthood, he served God, to whom he had entirely consecrated his life, in righteousness and true holiness. He preached the work of Life to those who had not yet received it, and gained many converts to Jesus Christ . . . We, who occupy his old house at Bethany—that is to say, his former tomb—and perform our religious duties at the place of his first internment, humbly pray to Jesus Christ, by the merit of St. Lazarus, our patron and His own especial friend, that He would deign to lead us by His goodness, so that we may rejoice in His help during this present life and be associated with Him in the joys of eternal life hereafter."[5]

There is no doubt that this tradition, much as it is given in the life of Rabanus, was accepted by the whole Latin Church for over a thousand years. For proof of this we have only to turn to the Breviary of St. Martha's Day, July 29th. There we find a lection for the second nocturne which tells how Mary, Martha and Lazarus, with their servant Marcella, and Maximin, one of the seventy-two disciples, were seized by the Jews, placed in a boat without sails or oars, and carried safely to the port of Marseilles. Moved by this remarkable fact, the people of the neighbouring lands were speedily converted to Christianity; Lazarus became bishop of Marseilles, Maximinus of Aix, Mary lived and died an anchoress on a high mountain of those

JOHN WRITES

Jesus told [Martha], "Your brother will rise again."

"Yes," Martha said, "he will rise when everyone else rises, at the last day."

Jesus told her, "I am the resurrection and the life. Anyone who believes in me will live, even after dying. Everyone who lives in me and believes in me will never ever die." John 11:23-26

parts, while Martha founded a convent of women, died on the fourth day before the kalends of August, and was buried with great honour at Tarascon. [The date of this tradition is not the first or second century since a reference to an elder as a "priest," or to Mary as an "Anchoress" is, at the earliest, third century.—ed.]

The oratory and cathedral at Arles (1152), which commemorates St. Trophimus—the Church of St. Martha at Tarascon (1187-1192), and the crypt of the old Abbey of St. Victor at Marseilles, dating from the fourth century, which forms a lasting memorial to St. Lazarus, all bear witness to the faith and devotion of those who built them.[6]

Roger de Hovedon in his third volume dealing with events which happened between 1170 and 1192, gives a good description of Marseilles, and writes: "Marseilles is an episcopal city under the dominion of the King of Arragon. Here are the relics of St. Lazarus, the brother of St. Mary Magdalene and Martha, who held the bishopric here for seven years after Jesus had restored him from the dead."[7]

Another is from old Church literature. In 1040, in the bull of Benedict IX (relative to the establishment of the Abbey of St. Victor, at Marseilles, after the expulsion of the Saracens), we find the history of the foundation of the Abbey of St. Victor in the time of the Emperor Antonine, of its building by St. Cassien, and of its enshrining the sufferings and relics of St. Victor, his companions, Hermes and Adrian, and "St. Lazarus, who was restored from the dead by Jesus Christ."[8]

George F. Jowett writes in *The Drama of the Lost Disciples*:

The ancient church records and Lyons confirm the same facts:
Lazarus returned to Gaul from Britain to Marseilles, taking with him Mary Magdalene and Martha. He was the first appointed Bishop. He died there seven years later.
He was the first Bishop of Marseilles and built the first

church on the site where the present cathedral stands. In the few years he lived to teach at Marseilles he founded other churches. His zealous preaching and kindly disposition left a deep impress in Gaul, to such an extent that he is better remembered in France than is Philip, regardless of the latter's long sojourn in Gaul. In many quarters he is regarded as the Apostle of Gaul and his relics are greatly treasured to this day. At Marseilles, Lyons, Aix, St. Maximin, La Sainte Baume and other places there still remain numerous monuments, liturgies, relics and traditions to his immortal memory. He was the first of the original Bethany band associated with Joseph to die. As the records state, he died a natural death seven years after returning to Marseilles . . . which would place the date of his death between A.D. 44 and 45.[9]

The dates suggested above are not compatible with the other traditions, which have greater acceptance among students of tradition.

The information furnished by Taylor and Jowett is not generally accepted by church historians but since it contains some valuable documentation not to be easily found elsewhere, the above is quoted for what it may be worth.

Whatever else may be true, the very least of what may be said about Lazarus is that he is firmly associated with both Cyprus and Marseilles, France.

PAUL

This letter is from Paul, an apostle. I was not appointed by any group of people or any human authority, but by Jesus Christ himself and by God the Father, who raised Jesus from the dead. Galatians 1:1

This noted apostle, while he was not one of the Twelve, nor could he possibly be described as a sub-apostle, is in a special class. Paul's conversion did not occur until a long time after the date of Matthias's election to replace Judas Iscariot. In addition, Paul had to endure years of obscurity in Tarsus after his conversion until he became a missionary. Almost all theological libraries have full and complete biographies of Paul. We shall, therefore, present only those traditions about Paul which are not commonly known, or which are not dealt with adequately in the standard biographies.

Paul in Petra

The fact that Paul went to Arabia after his escape from Damascus is attested to in Galatians 1:17. There is a very real possibility that the Arabia mentioned is that area far to the south of Amman, Jordan, that had as its chief city, Petra. This was the capitol city of King Aretus who significantly is mentioned by Paul in 2 Corinthians 11:32. It is difficult to imagine Paul spending time in Arabia Petrea (as it was known) without staying in the glorious city of Petra itself. It was the only city worthy of the name at that time in an otherwise barren desert area. Here he received from Jesus Christ, he said, those special revelations of the gospel of grace which gave such freedom and power to the churches he organized.

Paul in Spain

In his letter to the Romans, Paul indicated an intention to visit Rome "on my way to Spain" (Romans 15:28), but his first imprisonment prevented that. If he was released after his first trial, he may well have gone there and even farther. Why would he want to go to Spain? Because it was the westernmost portion of Europe and there were colonies of Jews there. Some were slaves, imprisoned as political prisoners by Herod Antipas. The *Epistle of Clement* and the *Muratori Fragment* both imply this possibility and assert that Paul visited Spain. Eusebius mentions, as Sir William Ramsey also points out, a gap in the life of Paul between AD 61 and 65. During this time he could have gone to Spain and elsewhere as well.

> Paul's conversion did not occur until long after Matthias's election to replace Judas Iscariot. Paul had to endure years of obscurity until he became a missionary.

"The *Acts*, however, of all the Apostles are written in one book, *Luke*, to the most excellent Theophilus, includes events because they were done in his own presence, as he also plainly shows by leaving out the passion of Peter, and also the departure of Paul from the City on his journey to Spain."[1]

One authoritative biography *The Life and Epistles of the Apostle Paul* by W. J. Conybeare and J. S. Howson, which is as widely accepted a biography of Paul as any, emphatically asserts that Paul did indeed go to Spain, spending at least two years there.[2]

Paul in Rome

The apostle's first imprisonment was really not a stay in a prison as such. Rather, Acts chapter 28 says that Paul lived two years in his own house, ministering to all who came to see him, of whom there must have been many. After his release, travels, and second arrest, he was placed in the Mamertine Prison, constructed for political prisoners a hundred years before Paul's incarceration there. It is a grim building that still exists in Rome.

"St. Paul was sent to Rome in the second year of Nero, [i.e. A.D. 56], in which date agree Bede, Ivo, Freculphus Platina, Scaliger, Capellus, Cave, Stillingfleet, Alford, Godwin *De Proesulibus*, Rapin, Bingham, Stanhope, Warner, Trapp. We believe this to be the true date."[3]

W. J. Conybeare and J. S. Howson concur:

> The evidence on this subject, though (as we have said) not copious, is yet conclusive so far as it goes; and it is *all one way*.
>
> The most important portion of it is supplied by Clement, the disciple of Paul mentioned in Philippians iv. 3, who was afterward bishop of Rome. This author, writing from Rome to Corinth, expressly asserts that Paul had preached the gospel "in the East and in the West," that he "had instructed *the whole world* [i.e. the *Roman empire*, which was commonly so called] in righteousness," and that he "had gone to the extremity of the West" before his martyrdom.
>
> Now, in a Roman author the extremity of the West could mean nothing short of Spain, and the expression is often used by Roman writers to denote Spain. Here, then, we have the express testimony of Paul's own disciple that he fulfilled his original intention (mentioned in Romans xv. 24-28) of visiting the Spanish peninsula, and consequently that he was liberated from his first imprisonment at Rome.
>
> The next piece of evidence which we possess on the subject is contained in the canon of the New Testament, compiled by an unknown Christian about the year AD 170, which is known as *Muratori's Canon*. In this document it is said in the account of the Acts of the Apostles that "Luke relates to Theophilus events of which he was an eye-witness, as also, in a separate place (semote) [viz. Luke xxii. 31-33], he evidently declares the martyrdom of Peter, but (omits) the journey of Paul from Rome to Spain."

In the next place, Eusebius tells us, "After defending himself successfully, it is currently reported that the Apostle again went forth to proclaim the gospel, and afterward came to Rome a second time, and was martyred under Nero."

Next we have the statement of Chrysostom, who mentions it as an undoubted historical fact that "Paul after his residence in Rome departed to Spain."

About the same time Jerome bears the same testimony, saying that "Paul was dismissed by Nero, that he might preach Christ's gospel in the West."

Against this unanimous testimony of the primitive Church there is no external evidence whatever to oppose. Those who doubt the liberation of Paul from his imprisonment are obliged to resort to a gratuitous hypothesis or to inconclusive arguments from probability.[4]

Jerome tells us about Paul and Nero:

It ought to be said that at the first defence, the power of Nero having not yet been confirmed, nor his wickedness broken forth to such a degree as the histories relate concerning him, Paul was dismissed by Nero, that the gospel of Christ might be preached also in the West. As he himself writes in the second epistle to Timothy, at the time when he was about to be put to death, dictating his epistle as he did while in chains; "At my first defence no one took my part, but all forsook me: may it not be laid to their account. But the Lord stood by me and strengthened me; that through me the message might be fully proclaimed and that all the Gentiles might hear, and I was delivered out of the mouth of the lion"—clearly indicating Nero as a lion on account of his cruelty. . . . [Paul] then, in the fourteenth year of Nero on the same day with Peter, was beheaded at Rome for Christ's sake and was buried in the Ostian Way, the twenty-seventh year after our Lord's passion.[5]

Some details regarding the place of residence of Paul in Rome during his first visit are included in R. W. Morgan's *St. Paul in Britain*:

> Baronius has the following note upon the Titulus:—"It is delivered to us by the firm tradition of our forefathers that the house of Pudens was the first that entertained St. Peter in Rome, and that there the Christians assembling formed the Church, and that of all our churches the oldest is that which is called after the name of Pudens."
>
> That the palace of Claudia was the home of the Apostles in Rome appears agreed upon by all ecclesiastical historians—even Robert Parsons, the Jesuit, admits. "Claudia was the first hostess or harbourer both of St. Peter and St. Paul at the time of their coming to Rome." See Parsons' *Three Conversions of England*, vol. I., p. 16.[6]

George F. Jowett broadens our knowledge of the historically based traditions of St. Paul in Rome when he notes:

> Yet we can still turn to the pages of the *Martyrologies of Rome, The Greek Menologies* and the *Martyrologies of Ado, Usuard and Esquilinus*, and therein read their glorious stories, noting the Natal Days of each, therein described. They are as follows:
>
> May 17. Natal Day of the Blessed Pudens, father of Praxedes and Pudentiana. He was clothed with Baptism by the Apostles, and watched and kept his robe pure and without wrinkle to the crown of a blameless life.
>
> May 17. Natal Day of St. Pudentiana, the virgin, of the most illustrious descent, daughter of Pudens, and Disciple of the Holy Apostle St. Paul.
>
> June 20. Natal Day of St. Novatus, son of the Blessed Pudens, brother of St. Timotheus the Elder and the Virgins of Christ, Pudentiana and Praxedes. All these were instructed in the faith by the Apostles.[7]
>
> The most authentic record of which can still be seen and read

is on the wall of the ancient former Palace of the British, the sanctified church of St. Pudentiana. The Memorial was carved on its walls following the execution of Praxedes in the second century, the last surviving member of the original Christian band and the youngest daughter of Claudia and Pudens.

Inscribed in these few words is told the noble, tragic story: "In this sacred and most ancient of churches, known as that of Pastor (Hermas), dedicated by Sanctus Pius Papa (St. Paul), formerly the house of Sanctus Pudens, the Senator, and the home of the holy Apostles, repose the remains of three thousand blessed martyrs which Pudentiana and Praxedes, virgins of Christ, with their own hands interred."[8]

The Martyrologies inform us that the Pudens, after retrieving the body of Paul, interred it on their estate on the Via Ostiensa road. We know from the historic records of the Emperor Constantine, first Christian Emperor of Rome, that he, knowing where the mutilated body of Paul lay, caused it to be excavated. He had it placed in a stone coffin, and over the spot built a church, still known as St. Paul's without—the—walls, meaning the church and his body are outside the city walls of Rome. The original church perished and a larger one was built on the site. Fire destroyed this in 1823. In the present church built after the fire, but still bearing its ancient name, a Benedictine priest is ever on guard before a grille on the floor of the High Altar. On occasion, for the benefit of special visitors, the priest moves the grille, lowering a light through the floor into a cell beneath, revealing to the eyes a crude slabstone on the floor bearing the name "Pauli."[9]

No other traditions suggest another place of martyrdom for Paul other than Rome. The book of Acts certainly leaves Paul in Rome. An interval between his first and final imprisonments there is clearly indicated and attested by the early Church fathers.

It is equally clear that Constantine erected a church building over the place where he reburied St. Paul, and the relics of the body of the apostle seem certainly to have been placed in the crypt under the altar of St. Paul's Outside-the-Walls on the Ostian Way, not too far from the place of his martyrdom at Tre Fontana.

According to tradition, St. Paul, who suffered martyrdom on a site known as the *Aquae Salviae*, now the Abbey of the Three Fountains, was buried in *praedio Lucinae*, that is to say, in a little cemetery beside the Ostian Way, about one thousand paces from the gate of the same name. A "cella memoriae" was probably erected over his tomb. Constantine transformed these "cellae memoriae" of the Apostles Peter and Paul into basilicas; the Liber Pontificalis, in fact, records that the emperor "fecit basilicam Sancto Paulo Apostolo cuius corpus recondidit et conclusit in arca sicut Sancti Petri."

Pope Sylvester I is said to have consecrated the church on the same day on which the basilica of St. Peter was consecrated, on November 18, 324. In the *Acts of St. Sylvester*, rich donations made to the church by Constantine are also recorded; the first church was probably quite small and faced on to the Ostian Way.

LUKE WRITES

Then Paul said, . . . "As I was approaching Damascus . . ., a very bright light from heaven shone down around me. I fell to the ground and heard a voice saying to me, 'Saul, Saul, why are you persecuting me?' . . . And the Lord told me, 'Get up and go into Damascus, and there you will be told everything you are to do.' "[In Damascus a man named Ananias] told me, 'You are to be [God's] witness, telling everyone what you have seen and heard.'" Acts 22:6-7, 10, 12, 15

In 386 an imperial edict of Valentinianus II, Theodosius and Arcadius to the prefect of Rome stated that the church was to be enlarged, in accordance with the sanctity of the site, the concourse of pilgrims and their devotion. It added that the new church "si placuerit tam populo quam Senatui" was to be extended towards the plain rather than towards the nearby slope. The construction was entrusted to a certain Ciriades known as the "mechanicus" or "Professor of mechanicus," who built a church with five aisles, eighty columns and a huge porch, probably similar to that of the ancient basilica of St. Peter. The church was consecrated by Pope Siricius in 390. It was finished, according to the inscription on the triumphal arch, whose mosaic ornament was commissioned and paid for by Galla Placidia, under Honorius in 395 and restored by Pope Leo the Great, after it had been severely damaged either by an earthquake or by fire. An inscription mentions the restorations carried out under Pope Leo the Great by the priest Felix and the deacon Adeodatus, and another records important works commissioned by a certain Eusebius.

The Confession has remained throughout the centuries on the spot where Constantine had the original basilica erected, over the tomb of St. Paul, which was visible until the IX century, when it was walled up and only came to light once more during works of restoration carried out in the XIX century. The sarcophagus containing the body of the Apostle of the Gentiles is covered with a marble slab bearing the inscription "Paulo-Apostolo Mart" which goes back, according to famous scholars who have studied the lettering, to the IV century.[10]

Mary Sharp presents the Catholic version of the death of St. Paul:

The history of St. Paul is fully recorded in the New Testament (except for his visit to Spain which is implied by the *Epistle of Clement* and asserted in the Muratori fragment and legend has added little to it). It is believed that he was martyred outside the Ostian Gate on the same day that St. Peter was crucified, and that when his head was struck off it bounced three times on the ground and at each place a fountain of water sprang up, the first hot, the second warm and the third cold. The spot is still venerated as the Tre Fontane, and the fountains remain, though there is little difference in temperature. He was originally buried on the Via Ostian where the basilica of St. Paul-outside-the-Walls now stands. When the Christian tombs were threatened with desecration in the Valerian persecution, it is said that the bodies of SS Paul and Peter were taken, on 29th June 258, to a place called Ad Catacumbas on the Appian Way. If this was so, the body of St. Paul was later returned to its original place, but his head, along with that of St. Peter, was taken to the basilica of St. John Lateran.[11]

Paul in England?

The idea that Paul and other apostles may have visited and ministered in England does not find much serious consideration or even interest among most church historians. They may be quite right, but there is too much evidence of at least the bare possibility of apostolic journeys there for serious scholars to dismiss the whole question out of hand.

The least a scholar with a searching mind can do is to examine what evidence, tradition, and legends do exist and determine how much—if any—validity they might have.

As has been noted in chapter thirteen, Britain was a relatively highly developed country by the time the first Phoenicians visited it more than a millennium before the Apostolic Age. Recent discoveries on the Greek mainland reveal British importance firmly dated at 1500 BC.[12]

By the Roman period Britain was a land of mines, cities, roads, schools, government, armies with advanced technology, etc. Seneca, the mentor of Nero, made large investments in Britain during the early apostolic age. Why should some of the apostles *not* have traveled there? They certainly went to many other equally distant and strange places, such as Russia, India, and the Balkan countries.

While visiting Bath, England, I purchased a silver coin of Nero found in the Roman baths there at Bath. The existence of such firm evidence by its coinage, had spread widely in Britain well before the climax of the age of apostolic labours. Such a find does not *prove* that the apostles, or even Christians, were in England at that time, but it is beyond the raising of trivial objections that such a thing was entirely *possible*. "From India to Britain," writes St. Jerome (AD 378), "all nations resound with the death and resurrection of Christ."[13]

R. W. Morgan says, "In A.D. 320, Eusebius, Bishop of Caesarea, speaks of Apostolic missions to Britain as a matter of notoriety: 'The Apostles passed beyond the ocean to the isles called the Brittanic Isles.' "[14]

Morgan continues:

> There are six years of St. Paul's life to be accounted for, between his liberation from his first imprisonment and his martyrdom at Aquae Salviae in the Ostian Road, near Rome. Part certainly, the greater part perhaps, of this period was spent in Britain, in Siluria or Cambria, beyond the bounds of the Roman Empire; and hence the silence of the Greek and Latin writers upon it.[15]

Perhaps the enthusiasts for this interpretation of history go too far. Their supporting quotations range from the early church fathers to the lesser-known modern writers in Christian history. These are examples of both:

> Eloquently St. Clement sums up the magnitude of the achievements of the Apostle to the Gentiles. Being one of the original Bethany band that dwelt at Avalon with Joseph, he knew St. Paul intimately, and long before he followed in the office of his beloved friend Linus, as Bishop of Rome. He writes:
> "To leave the examples of antiquity, and to come to the most recent, let us take the noble examples of our own times. Let us place before our eyes the good Apostle, Peter, through unjust odium, underwent not one or two, but many sufferings; and

having undergone his martyrdom, he went to the place of glory to which he was entitled. Paul, also, having seven times worn chains, and been hunted and stoned, received the prize of such endurance. For he was the herald of the Gospel in the West as well as in the East, and enjoyed the illustrious reputation of the faith in teaching the whole world to be righteous. And after he had been in the extremity of the West, he suffered martyrdom before the sovereigns of mankind; and thus delivered from this world, he went to this holy place, the most brilliant example of stedfastness that we possess."

"Extremity of the West" was the term used to indicate Britain.

Capellus, in *History of the Apostles*, writes that "I know scarcely of one author from the time of the Fathers downward who does not maintain that St. Paul, after his liberation, preached in every country of the West, in Europe, Britain included."[16]

However, there is more solid evidence for an early Christian tradition of apostolic evangelism in Britain—possibly that of Paul.

Tertullian (A.D. 155–222), the Early Father, the first great genius after the apostles among Christian writers, writing in A.D. 192, said: "The extremities of Spain, the various parts of Gaul, the regions of Britain, which have never been penetrated by the Roman Arms, have received the religion of Christ" (Tertullian, *Def. Fidei*, 179).[17]

In the same book, Lewis quotes Origen.

Origen, another Early Father (A.D. 185–254), wrote that "The divine goodness of Our Lord and Saviour is equally diffused among the Britons, the Africans, and other nations of the world."[18]

Gladys Taylor in *Our Neglected Heritage, The Early Church* points out:

St. Clement speaks of Paul going to "the extremity of the West, then returning to Rome and suffering martyrdom before the sovereigns of mankind."

Jerome and Chrysostom refer to Paul travelling to the extreme West and Theodore, the Syrian bishop of the fifth century, tells us that he "preached Christ's Gospel to the Britons and others in the West."

Even the Pope, wishing to please some important British visitors, in 1931, "Advanced the theory that it was St. Paul himself, and not Pope Gregory, who first introduced Christianity into Britain." We hailed that piece of news reported in *The Morning Post*, of March 27, with delight. We knew the truth, but here was the Pope voicing it too, an unprecedented event.[19]

What Did Paul Look Like?

There is absolutely no proof of how any biblical personalities looked except for a few Caesars whose coins and statues survive. However, a study of Paul has been made and some interesting concepts have developed. For example, Boyce W. Blackwelder has penned the following:

The apocryphal *Acts of Paul and Thecla*, written in the third century, has a portraiture of Paul which describes him as 'of a low stature, bald (or shaved on the head), crooked thighs, handsome legs, hollow eyed; had a crooked nose; full of grace; for sometimes he appeared as a man, sometimes he had the countenance of an angel. (1:7)

This is the earliest description of Paul's features which we have in Christian literature. Callan says, "In the fourth century Paul is ridiculed in the Philopatris of the Pseudo-Lucian as 'the bald-headed, hooknosed Galilean who trod the air into the third heaven and learned the most beautiful things' (Philopat. 12). Cone notes that John of Antioch, writing in the sixth century, preserves the tradition that Paul was 'round shouldered, with a sprinkling of gray on his head and beard, with an aquiline nose, grayish eyes, meeting eyebrows, with a mixture of pale and red in his complexion . . .'"

Scholars generally agree that the traditional view regarding Paul's personal appearance is correct. Holzner speaks of "the small,

Some biographers are sure that Paul must have been exceptionally robust or he could not have endured the rigors of missionary work.

emaciated figure of the man from Tarsus." Giordani describes Paul as "small of stature and all nerves;" a man "infirm in health" with "a miserable physique." He depicts "Paul with his sore eyes" as a sight "repulsive." Shaw, as quoted by Callan, speaks of Paul's "insignificant stature, his marred vision, his weak and often distorted frame." Stalker observes that Paul appears to have been small of stature, and that his bodily presence was weak. He says "This weakness seems to have been sometimes aggravated by disfiguring disease."

Callan writes, "St. Paul, according to the persistent tradition of the Church, was anything but commanding and beautiful in his physical appearance. Glimpses, doubtless, of the great soul within could be caught now and then, or frequently by his friends, as sunbeams are seen through openings in prison walls; but for all that the bodily make-up of the man was homely and poor."

The idea that Paul was of inferior stature may, in some respects, be confirmed in references gleaned from his own writings. In Second Corinthians 10:10, Paul quotes what his opponents said of him to the effect that "his letters . . . are weighty and powerful; but his bodily presence is weak, and his speech contemptible." Probably this was not a groundless statement, for even Paul's opponents would hardly dare to speak thus of him in one of his congregations without a basis in fact.

What about Paul's health? Scholars hold opposite opinions with regard to this question. Some biographers are sure that

Paul must have been exceptionally robust or he could not have endured the rigors of missionary work over a vast area for a period of approximately thirty years. Craig says, "A man who could trudge mountain and valley day after day, endure shipwreck and imprisonment, hardship and persecution, was no weakling."

Other authorities, on the contrary, are convinced that Paul was physically weak and frail throughout his life. Callan, following Hayes, thinks Paul was a chronic invalid, but that God's grace was upon the Apostle in such measure that physical deficiencies were overcome.

If Paul did not have a hardy appearance, this must have been a difficult problem for him when he worked among peoples of the Greek tradition which held that a vigorous body was essential to a normal personality.

There is no question but what the painful bodily sufferings which Paul endured (cf. 2 Corinthians 11:23-27) left lasting physical effects (Galatians 6:17; 2 Corinthians 4:10). There must have been terrible scarmarks remaining from the scourgings, and from the stoning at Lystra which was so severe that the perpetrators thought Paul had been killed (Acts 14:19).[20]

Paul and the Writings of Luke

Eusebius has an interesting observation about the relationship of these two great apostolic figures:

> . . . But at some he was present, and so he set them down.

The third book of the Gospel, that according to Luke, was compiled in his own name on Paul's authority by Luke the physician, when, after Christ's ascension, Paul had taken him to be with him like a legal expert. Yet neither did *he* see the Lord in the flesh; and he too, as he was able to ascertain events, begins his story from the birth of John.[21]

Apostles in the Bible

ANDREW
apostle Matthew 4:18; Mark 1:29; Mark 13:3; John 1:40, 6:8, 12:22; Acts 1:13.

BARNABAS (SON OF EXHORTATION)
Levite of Cyprus, sells his lands. Acts 4:36.
preaches at Antioch. Acts 11:22.
accompanies Paul. Acts 11:30, 12:25, 13:14; 1 Corinthians 5:6.
his contention. Acts 15:36
his error. Galatians 2:13.

BARTHOLOMEW (NATHANAEL)
son of Talmai. **apostle.** Matthew 10:3; Mark 3:18; Luke 6:14; Acts 1:13.

JAMES
son of Zebedee, called. Matthew 4:21; Mark 1:19; Luke 5:10.
apostle, *ordained one of the twelve.* Matthew 10:2; Mark 3:14-15; Luke 6:13.
witnessed Christ's transfiguration. Matthew 17:1-9; Mark 1:2; Luke 9:28.
present at the Passion. Matthew 26:36-37; Mark 14:33.
slain by Herod. Acts 12:1-2.

JAMES
apostle, *son of Alphaeus.* Matthew 10:3; Mark 3:18; 6:3; Luke 6:15; Acts 1:13, 12:17.
his judgment respecting ceremonial. Acts 15:13-29; Galatians 2:9.
his teaching. James 1–5
mentioned. Acts 21:18; 1 Corinthians 15:7; Galatians 1:19.

JOHN
apostle, *called.* Matthew 4:21; Mark 1:19-20; Luke 5:10.
ordained. Matthew 10:2; Mark 3:17.
enquires of Jesus. Mark 13:3.
reproved. Matthew 20:20-28; Mark 10:35-40; Luke 9:49-50.
sent to prepare the Passover. Luke 22:8.

declares the divinity and humanity of Jesus Christ. John 1; 1 John 1,
4, 5.
Christ's love for. John 13:23,19:26, 21:7, 20, 24.
his care for Mary the Lord's mother. John 19:25-27.
meets for prayer. Acts 1:13.
accompanies Peter before the council. Acts 3, 4.
exhorts to obedience and warns against false teachers. 1 John 1-5.
sees Christ's glory in heaven. Revelation 1:13.
writes the Revelation. Revelation 1:19.
forbidden to worship the angel. Revelation 19:10, 22:8.

JUDAS
the Lord's brother Matthew 13:55; Mark 6:3; Jude 1.
abbreviated from Judas. Jude 1.
enjoins perseverance. Jude 1:20-21.
denounces false disciples. Jude:" 4.

JUDAS ISCARIOT
apostle. Matthew 10:4; Mark 3:19; Luke 6:16; John 6:70.
betrays Jesus. Matthew 26:14-25, 47; Mark 14:10, 41-45;
    Luke 22:3-6, 47-48; John 13:21-30, 18:2-4.
hangs himself. Matthew 27:5 *(Acts 1:18).*

JUDE (THADDAEUS)
Jude, Lebbaeus Thaddaeus, **apostle,** *son of James.* Matthew 10:3;
    Mark 3:18; Luke 6:16; Acts 1:13.
his question to our Lord. John 14:22.

LAZARUS
brother of Mary and Martha
raised from the dead. John 11:1-44, 12:1.

LUKE
beloved physician, companion of Paul. Colossians 4:14, 2 Timothy
    4:11; Philemon 1:24 (included as "we" in Acts 16:12; 20:5).

MARK (JOHN MARK)
evangelist. Acts 12:12.
goes with Paul and Barnabas. Acts 12:25; 13:5.
leaves them at Perga. Acts 13:13.
contention about him. Acts 15:37-39.
approved by Paul. 2 Timothy 4:11.

MATTHEW (LEVI)
apostle *and evangelist, called.* Matthew 9:9; Mark 2:14;
Luke 5:27.
sent out. Matthew 10:3; Mark 3:18.

MATTHIAS
apostle. Acts 1:23, 26.

PAUL
a persecutor. Acts 7:58, 8:1, 9:1-2, 22:4-5, 26:9-11; 1 Corinthians
15:9; Galatians 1:13; Philippians 3:6; 1 Timothy 1:13.
a convert to the Gospel. Acts 9:3-18, 22:6-13, 26:12-19.
a preacher. Acts 9:3-18, 29; 13:1, 4, 14; 17:18.
stoned at Lystra. Acts 14:19.
contends with Barnabas. Acts 15:36.
is persecuted at Philippi. Acts 16:19-24.
the Holy Ghost given by his hands to John's disciples at Ephesus. Acts
19:6.
restores Eutychus. Acts 20:10.
his charge to the elders of Ephesus, at Miletus. Acts 20:17-36.
his return to Jerusalem, and persecution there. Acts 21.
his defense before the people and the council. Acts 22, 23.
before Felix, Acts 24; *Festus,* Acts 25; *and Agrippa,* Acts 26.
appeals to Caesar at Rome. Acts 25:10-12.
his voyage and shipwreck. Acts 27.
miracles by, at Malta. Acts 28:3-6, 8-9.
at Rome, reasons with the Jews. Acts 28:17.
his love to the churches. Romans 1:8-9; 15; 1 Corinthians 1:4; 4:14,
2 Corinthians 1, 2, 6, 7; Philippians 1; Colossians 1; 1 and
2 Thessalonians.
his sufferings. 1 Corinthians 4:9; 2 Corinthians 11:23; 12:7;
Philippians 1:12; 2 Timothy 3:11.
divine revelations to. 1 Corinthians 12:1.
defends his apostleship. 1 Corinthians 9; 2 Corinthians 11, 12.
commends Timothy, and others. 1 Corinthians 16:10-11; Philippians
2:19-23; 1 Thessalonians 3:2.
commends Titus. 2 Corinthians 7:13-15, 8:23.
blames Peter. Galatians 2:14-15.
pleads for Onesimus. Philemon.

his epistles mentioned by Peter. 2 Peter 3:15.

PETER (SIMON PETER)
apostle, *called.* Matthew 4:18-20; Mark 1:16-18; Luke 5:1-11;
    John 1:40-42.
sent forth. Matthew 10:2; Mark 3:16; Luke 6:14.
tries to walk to Jesus on the sea. Matthew 14:18.
confesses Jesus to be the Christ. Matthew 16:16; Mark 8:29;
    Luke 9:20.
witnesses the transfiguration. Matthew 17:1-13; Mark 9:2-12; Luke
    9:28-36; 2 Peter 1:16.
his self-confidence reproved. Luke 22:34; John 13:38.
denies Christ three times. Matthew 26:69-75; Luke 22:54-62; John
    18:17.
his repentance. Matthew 26:75; Mark 14:72; Luke 22:62.
addressing the assembled disciples. Acts 1:15.
preaching to the Jews. Acts 2:14; 3:12.
brought before the council. Acts 4.
condemns Ananias and Sapphira. Acts 5.
denounces Simon the sorcerer. Acts 8:18.
restores Aeneas and Tabitha. Acts 9:32, 40.
sent for by Cornelius. Acts 10.
instructed by a vision not to despise the Gentiles. Acts 10:9.
imprisoned, and liberated by an angel. Acts 12.
his decision about circumcision. Acts 15:7.
rebuked by Paul. Galatians 2:14.
bears witness to Paul's teaching. 2 Peter 3:15.
comforts the church, and exhorts the church to holy living in his epistles.
    1 and 2 Peter.
his martyrdom foretold by Christ. John 21:18; 2 Peter 1:14.

PHILIP
apostle, *called.* John 1:43.
sent forth. Matthew 10:3; Mark 3:18; Luke 6:14; John 12:22;
    Acts 1:13.
remonstrated by Christ. John 14:8.
deacon, elected. Acts 6:5.
preaches in Samaria. Acts 8:5.
baptizes the eunuch. Acts 8:27.

SIMON PETER (SEE PETER)

SIMON THE CANAANITE
brother of Christ. Matthew 13:55; Mark 6:3.
Zelotes (the Zealot), **apostle.** Matthew 10:4; Mark 3:18; Luke 6:15.

THADDAEUS (SEE JUDE)
Greek form of Theudas.
   apostle. Matthew 10:3.

THOMAS
apostle, Matthew 10:3; Mark 3:18; Luke 6:15; Acts 1:13.
his zeal. John 11:16.
his unbelief and confession. John 20:24.

TIMOTHY
accompanies Paul. Acts 16:3, 17:14-15; Romans 16:21;
   2 Corinthians 1:1, 19.
commended. 1 Corinthians 16:10; Philippians 2:19.
instructed in Paul's letters. 1 and 2 Timothy.

Endnotes

INTRODUCTION

1. Constantine celebrated the thirtieth anniversary of his accession in the summer of 335. Probably the most significant ceremonies at Rome that year were those accompanying the solemn translation of the bones venerated as relics of the Apostles St. Peter and St. Paul from the catacombs of St. Sebastian, where they had been venerated since 258, to the basilicas built to honour them at the traditional sites of their martyrdoms, at the Vatican and on the Ostian Way" (*Constantine the Great*, John Holland Smith, 286; also cf. *Liber Pontificalis*, ed. Duchesne, vol. 1, 172ff.).
2. J. Stevenson, *A New Eusebius*, (London: William Clowes and Sons, Ltd.. S.P.C.K., 1957, 1960), 395.
3. John Holland Smith, *Constantine the Great* (New York: Charles Scribner's and Sons, 1971), 301–302.
4. Robert M. Grant, *Augustus to Constantine: The Thrust of the Christian Movement into the Roman World* (London: William Collins Sons & Co., Ltd., 1971), 277.
5. Interchurch Centenary Committee, a lecture titled "The Armenian Christian Tradition in Iran," 1.

CHAPTER ONE: THE WORLD OF THE APOSTLES

1. *The Bible Research Handbook*, vol. II (London: Covenant Publishing Co., Ltd., second impression, 1969), pages unnumbered.

CHAPTER TWO: WHEN DID THE APOSTLES LEAVE JERUSALEM?

1. Jean Danielou and Henri Marrou, *The Christian Centuries* (London: Datton, Longman, and Todd, 1964), 39.

CHAPTER THREE: SIMON PETER

1. Baruch Sapir and Dov Neeman, *Capernaum*, vol. NI/9 (Tel-Aviv: The Historical Sites Library, 1967), 22.
2. Virgilio Corbo, *New Memoirs of Saint Peter by the Sea of Galilee* (Jerusalem: Franciscan Printing Press, 1969), 10–11.
3. Ibid., 21–22.
4. Baldi, O.F.M., *Enchiridion Locorum Sanctorum*, 293, 299 as quoted in Ibid., 53.
5. Virgilio Corbo, *The House of Saint Peter at Capharnaum* (Jerusalem: Franciscan Printing Press, 1969), 54, 70.
6. Ibid., 71.
7. Danielou and Marrou, *The Christian Centuries*, 51.
8. Eusebius, *Eusebius' Ecclesiastical History* (Grand Rapids: Baker Book House, 1962), 120.
9. Danielou and Marrou, *The Christian Centuries*, 50.

10. Hugo Hoever, *Lives of the Saints* (New York: Catholic Book Publishing Co., 1967), 82.
11. V. K. George, "The Holy See of Seleucia—Ctesiphon," *Souvenir of India, in Honour of the Visit to India of His Holiness Maran Mar Eshai Shimun XXIII*, (Editorial Board of the Publicity and Information Committee of H. H. The Patriarch Reception Committee, Ernakulam, Kerala State, India, 1962).
12. Aziz S. Atiya, *A History of Eastern Christianity* (London: Methuen & Co., Ltd., 1968), 172.
13. George F. Jowett, *The Drama of the Lost Disciples* (London: The Covenant Publishing Co., Ltd., 1970), 174–175.
14. J. W. Taylor, *The Coming of the Saints* (London: The Covenant Publishing Co. Ltd., 1969), 61.
15. Danielou and Marrou, *The Christian Centuries*, 28.
16. Ibid., 166.
17. Jowett, *The Drama of the Lost Disciples*, 176.
18. Anna Jameson, *Sacred and Legendary Art*, vol. I (Boston and New York: Houghton, Mifflin and Co., 1957, third edition), 209.
19. Ibid.
20. Ibid., 215.
21. Eusebius, *Ecclesiastical History*, 80.
22. Asbury Smith, *The Twelve Christ Chose* (New York: Harper and Brothers, 1958), 221–222.
23. Dorman Newman, *The Lives and Deaths of the Holy Apostles* (London: Kings Arms in the Poultry, 1685), 20.
24. Ibid., 21.
25. Robert M. Grant, *Augustus to Constantine, The Thrust of the Christian Movement into the Roman World* (London: William Collins Sons and Co., Ltd.), 166.
26. J. B. de Toth, *The Cathedral of the Pope*, (Rome: Tipografia Poliglotta Vaticana),18–19.
27. Aubrey Menen, "St. Peter's," *National Geographic*, vol. 140, no. 6 (December 1971), 872–73.
28. Edgar J. Goodspeed, *The Twelve* (Philadelphia: The John C. Winston Company, 1967), 157.

CHAPTER FOUR: ANDREW

1. Josephus Flavius quoted in Dov Neeman and Baruch Sapir, *Capernaum*, vii. Josephus's description is from *The Jewish War*, bk. 3, ch. VI, 8.
2. E. A. Wallis Budge, *The Contendings of the Apostles* (London: The British Museum, 1899 edition, 1901 edition, 1935 edition).
3. Edgar J. Goodspeed, *The Twelve*, 99.
4. Michael Maclagan, Thomas Hudson, *City of Constantinople* (New York: Frederick A. Praeger Publishing, 1968), 50.
5. Dorman Newman, *The Lives and Deaths of the Holy Apostles* (London: Kings Arms in the Poultry, 1685), 43–45.
6. Mary Sharp, *A Traveller's Guide to Saints in Europe* (London: The Trinity Press, 1964), 15.

7. The Very Reverend Archimandrite Hariton Pneumatikakis, *The First-Called Apostle Andrew* (Athens: Alexander Matsoukis, Inc., 1971).

8. Anna Jameson, *Sacred and Legendary Art*, 238.

9. Publsher's note: The relics of St. Andrew in Patras are kept in the New Church of St Andrew in a special tomb and are reverenced in a special ceremony every November 30. The cross of St Andrew upon which he was martyred is also kept in the New Church of St. Andrew, near the Saint's relics. Two temples were built in his honor, an old Byzantine-style basilica and a new monumental church completed in 1979.

CHAPTER FIVE: JAMES, THE SON OF ZEBEDEE

1. Anna Jameson, *Sacred and Legendary Art*, 238ff.

2. Vera and Helmut Hell, *The Great Pilgrimage of the Middle Ages* (New York: Clarkson N. Potter, Inc., 1964), 13–14, 16, 28–29.

3. Ibid., 31, 34–35.

4. William Barclay, *The Master's Men* (London: SCM Press Ltd., 1970), 100.

5. Asbury Smith, *The Twelve Christ Chose* (New York: Harper and Brothers, 1958), 40–41, 45.

6. J. W. Taylor, *The Coming of the Saints* (London: The Covenant Publishing Co., Ltd., 1969), 57–58.

7. *The International Standard Bible Encyclopaedia*, vols. I–V (Grand Rapids: William B. Eerdmans Publishing Co;, 1960), volumes III, IV.

8. Hugo Hoever, *The Lives of the Saints* (New York: Catholic Book Publishing Co., 1967), 282.

9. Mary Sharp, *A Traveller's Guide to Saints in Europe* (London: Trinity Press, 1964), 120.

10. *Encyclopaedia Brittanica*, vol. II (publishing date not given), 120.

11. No author given, *Brief Notes on the Armenian Patriarchate of Jerusalem*, (Jerusalem: St. James Press), 10.

12. Arpag Mekhitarian, *Treasures of the Armenian Patriarchate of Jerusalem* (Jerusalem: Armenian Patriarchate, 1969), 9.

13. Ibid., 5.

CHAPTER SIX: JOHN

1. Naci Keskin, *Ephesus* (Istanbul: Keskin Color Ltd., Co. Printing House) and Cemil Toksoz, *The Glories of Ephesus* (Istanbul: Basildigi Tarih: Nisan, Apa Ofset Basimevi, 1967), 16.

2. See Irenaeus's *Adv. Haer.*, II, 22, 59.

3. S. Papadopoulos, *Patmoc* (Athens: The Monastery of St. John the Theologian, 1962), 3–4.

4. Eusebius, *Eusebius' Ecclesiastical History* (Grand Rapids: Baker Book House, 1962), 103.

5. Ibid., 104–107.

6. Asbury Smith, *The Twelve Christ Chose*, 58–60.

7. J. Stevenson, *A New Eusebius*, 145.

8. Eusebius, *Eusebius' Ecclesiastical History*, 114.

9. *The Nicene and Post-Nicene Fathers: Theodoret, Jerome, Gennadius, Rufinus,*

Philip and Henry Wace, eds., 2nd series, vol. III (Grand Rapids: Wm. B. Eerdmans Publishing Company, 1953), 364–365.

10. William Steuart McBirnie, *What Became of the Twelve Apostles* (Upland, CA, 1963), 30–31.

11. See Budge, *The Contendings of the Apostles*, 213; see also Asbury Smith, *The Twelve Christ Chose*, 58.

12. Clement of Alexandria, *Quisdives*, 42.

13. Irenaeus, *Against Heresies V*, 33–34; J. Danielou, *The Christian Centuries*, 41.

14. Cemil Toksoz, Ephesus, 16, 18.

15. Naci Keskin, *Ephesus*, unnumbered.

16. Ibid.

17. Eusebius, *Ecclesiastical History*, 31.

CHAPTER SEVEN: PHILIP

1. Anna Jameson, *Sacred and Legendary Art*, 249.

2. Jean Danielou, *The Christian Centuries*, 40.

3. Robert Grant, *Augustus to Constantine*, 166.

4. Isidore, Archbishop of Seville, *De ortu et obitu Patrum*, cap. LXXIII, 131.

5. Cardinal Baronius, *Annales*: Tom 1, Ann. Christi Claudii Imp. 2, Sec. 32.

6. *British Ecclesiastical Antiquities*, cap.11.

7. Ibid., cap. 2.

8. Freculphus, *Tom posterior Chronicorum*, Lib. II, cap. IV.

9. *Memoire de l' Apostolat de St. Mansuet* (*vide,* 83) par l'Abbe Guillaume, p. II.

10. Lionel Smithett Lewis, *St Joseph of Arimathea at Glastonbury* (London: James Clarke & Co., Ltd., 1964), 112–114.

11. *The Nicene and Post-Nicene Fathers: Jerome*, second series, 372.

12. Emma Zocca, *La Basilica Dei S. S. Apostoli In Roma* (Rome: 1959), 8–9, 23.

CHAPTER EIGHT: BARTHOLOMEW (NATHANAEL)

1. Dorman Newman, *The Lives and Deaths of the Holy Apostles* (1685).

2. "The Armenian Apostolic Church in Iran," a lecture delivered by John Hananian, Consolata Church, Teheran, 1969.

3. Aziz S. Atiya, *A History of Eastern Christianity* (London: Methuen & Co. Ltd., 1968), 316.

4. Edgar J. Goodspeed, *The Twelve* (Philadelphia: The John C. Winston Company, 1967), 97–98.

5. Alexander Roberts and James Donaldson, *Ante-Nicene Fathers*, 10 vols. (Grand Rapids: Wm. B. Eerdmans Publishing Company, no date given), 370.

6. William Barclay, *The Master's Men* (London: SCM Press Ltd., 1970), 104.

7. *Brief Notes on the Armenian Patriarchate of Jerusalem* (Jerusalem: St. James Press, 1971), 3, 5.

8. Arpag Mekhitarian, *Treasures of the Armenian Patriarchate of Jerusalem*, catalogue no. 1 (Jerusalem: Helen and Edward Mardigian Museum, Armenian Patriarchate, 1969).

9. Mary Sharp, *A Traveller's Guide to Saints in Europe* (London: The Trinity Press, 1964), 29.

10. John Julius Norwich and Reresby Sitwell, Mount Athos (London: Hutchinson, 1966), 142.

11. Otto Hophan, *The Apostles* (London: Sands & Co., 1962), 167.
12. Hugo Hoever, Lives of the Saints (New York: Catholic Book Publishing Co., 1967), 333.
13. Mary Cable and editors of the *Newsweek* book division, *El Escorial: The Wonders of Man* (New York: Newsweek Books, 1971), 91.
14. Alban Butler, *Butler's Lives of the Saints*, vol. III, revised and supplemented by Herbert Thurston, S. J., and Donald Attwater (New York: P. J. Kenedy & Sons, 1963), 391–392.

CHAPTER NINE: THOMAS

1. *Souvenir of India, in Honour of the Visit to India of His Holiness Maran Mar Eshai Shimun XXIII*, (Ernakulam, India: Editional Board of the Publicity and Information Committee of H. H. The Patriarch Reception Committee, 1962), 49, 53.
2. Ibid., from the Foreword, 19.
3. Edgar J. Goodspeed, *The Twelve*, 97.
4. John Stewart, Centers of Christian Activity (Trichur, Kerala State, India: Narsai Press, 1928, 1961), 27.
5. Ibid.
6. "Ancient Jewish Colony in India Disappearing," *Los Angeles Times* (August 25, 1971), 1-A.
7. A. Mathias Mundadan, *Sixteenth Century Traditions of the St. Thomas Christians* (Bangalore, India: Dharmaram College, 1970), 38–173.
8. Asbury Smith, op. cit., 103–107.
9. A. Mathias Mundadan, *Sixteenth Century Traditions of the St. Thomas Christians*, 11.
10. Helen Homan, *By Post to the Apostles* (New York: All Saints Press Inc., 1967), 62.
11. Mary Sharp, *A Traveller's Guide to Saints in Europe* (London: The Trinity Press, 1964), 207.
12. D. Balduino Bedini, *The Sessorian Relics of the Passion of Our Lord*, Aloysius Traglia Archiep. Caesarien, Vic., Ger. (Roma: Tipografia Pio X, Via Etruschi 7–9, 1956), 62–63.

CHAPTER TEN: MATTHEW

1. Clement of Alexandria, *Strom.*, 49.
2. *The Nicene and Post-Nicene Fathers*, 362.
3. Merrill Tenney, *New Testament Survey* (Grand Rapids: Wm. B. Eerdmans Publishing Company, 1961), 151.
4. William Barclay, *The Master's Men* (London: SCM Press Ltd., 1970), 66–68.
5. Arturo Carucci, *Il Duomo di Salerno e il suo Museo*, III edizione (Salerno: Linotypografia Jannone, 1960), 66, 69.
6. Ibid., 11.
7. Anna Jameson, *Sacred and Legendary Art*, 142–143.
8. Mary Sharp, *A Traveller's Guide to Saints in Europe*, 152.

CHAPTER ELEVEN: JAMES, SON OF ALPHAEUS

1. Dorman Newman, *The Lives and Deaths of the Holy Apostles*, 1685.
2. Judith Erickson, *Dome of the Rock* (Jerusalem: Israel Publication Services, Ltd., 1971).

3. William Barclay, *The Master's Men*, 115.

4. Ibid.

5. Asbury Smith, *The Twelve Christ Chose* (New York: Harper & Brothers, 1958), 116–117.

6. Aziz S. Atiya, *A History of Eastern Christianity* (London: Methuen & Co. Ltd., 1968), 239.

7. E. A. Wallis Budge, *The Contendings of the Apostles*, 264–266.

8. Edward Gibbon, *The Decline and Fall of the Roman Empire* (New York: Random House, Inc., publishing date not given), 510.

9. Ibid., 508.

10. Mary Sharp, *A Traveller's Guide to Saints in Europe*, no page given.

CHAPTER TWELVE: JUDE THADDAEUS

1. See *Encyclopaedia Brittanica*, vol. II, 120.

2. Constantin von Tischendorf, *Acta Apostolorum Apocrypha* (1851), 261.

3. *Souvenir of India*, 125.

4. Assadour Antreassian, *Jerusalem and the Armenians* (Jerusalem: St. James Press, 1969), 20.

5. Aziz S. Atiya, *History of Eastern Christianity*, 315–316.

6. *Armenian Patriarchate of Jerusalem*, 3.

7. Arpag Mekhitarian, *Treasures of the Armenian Patriarchate of Jerusalem*, catalogue no. 1 (Jerusalem: Helen and Edward Mardigian Museum, Armenian Patriarchate, 1969), 3.

8. Mary Sharp, *Traveller's Guide to Saints in Europe*, 129.

9. C. M. Kerr, *The International Standard Bible Encyclopaedia*, 2964.

CHAPTER THIRTEEN: SIMON THE CANAANITE (THE ZEALOT)

1. Dorman Newman, *The Lives and Deaths of the Holy Apostles*, 94.

2. *Alkhrida*, Precious Jewels (Egypt: Coptic Church, 1915), 56.

3. Otto Hophan, *The Apostles*, (London: Sands & Co., 1962), 285.

4. Eusebius, *Demonstration Evang.*, quoted in *The Bollandistes*, vol. 12 (Paris: Society of Bollandistes, *Acta Sanctorium* De. S. Simone Apostolo et Martyre, 1867), 421–426. Chapter 5, Section 112, Book 3 is quoted.

5. Ibid., 428.

6. Jean Danielou, *The Christian Centuries*, 151.

7. Rt. Rev. Samuel Fallows, *The Popular and Critical Bible Encyclopaedia* (The Howard-Severance Company, 1910), 1590.

8. Dorman Newman, *The Lives and Deaths of the Holy Apostles* (1685).

9. Lionel Smithett Lewis, *St. Joseph of Arimathea at Glastonbury* (London: James Clarke & Co., Ltd., 19640, 117.

10. George F. Jowett, *The Drama of the Lost Disciples* (London: Covenant Publishing Co., Ltd., 1970), 157–159.

11. Theodoret, *Ecclesiastical History*, bk. iv., ch. iii.

12. I. A. Richmond, *Roman Britain*, vol. 1 (Aylesbury, Great Britain: Hunt Barnard & Co., Ltd., 1970), 156.

13. Leonard Cottrell, *Seeing Roman Britain* (London: Pan Books, Ltd., 1967), 186.

14. Ibid., 206.

15. Mary Sharp, *A Traveller's Guide to Saints in Europe*, 198.
16. Ann Jameson, *Sacred and Legendary Art*, 261.
17. Mary Sharp, *A Traveller's Guide to Saints in Europe*, 198.

CHAPTER FOURTEEN: JUDAS ISCARIOT

1. C. M. Kerr, *The International Standard Bible Encyclopaedia*, vol. III (Grand Rapids: Wm. B. Eerdmans Publishing Co., 1960), 1765–766.
2. Herbert Bishko, *This is Jerusalem* (Tel Aviv: Heritage Publishing, 1971), 44.

CHAPTER FIFTEEN: MATTHIAS

1. Hugo Hoever, *Lives of the Saints* (New York: Catholic Book Publishing Co., 19670, 84–85.
2. *The International Standard Bible Encyclopaedia*, "Matthias."
3. E. A. Wallis Budge, *The Contendings of the Twelve* (London: British Museum, 1901 edition), 163–164, 267–288.
4. Ibid., 289–294.
5. *Encyclopaedia Britannica*, "Matthias."
6. Anna Jameson, *Sacred and Legendary Art*, 263.
7. Mary Sharp, *A Traveller's Guide to Saints in Europe*, 153.
8. Dorman Newman, *The Lives and Deaths of the Holy Apostles* (1685).
9. Eberhard Zahn, *Trier: A Guide to the Monuments* (Trier: Cusanus-verlag, Volksfreund-Druckerei Nik Koch), 49, 51.

CHAPTER SIXTEEN: JOHN MARK

1. Louis Cassels, *Glendale News Press* (April 15, 1972).
2. Jerome, *The Nicene and Post-Nicene Fathers*, vol. III (Grand Rapids: Wm. B. Eerdmans Publishing Company, 1969), 364.
3. Aziz S. Atiya, "Origins of Coptic Christianity," *A History of Eastern Christianity* (London: Methuen & Co., Ltd., 1968), 25–28.
4. Ibid., 28.
5. E. M. Forster, *Alexandria: A History and a Guide* (Garden City, NJ: Doubleday Anchor Books, 1961), 86–87.
6. Mary Sharp, *A Traveller's Guide to Saints in Europe*, 148–149.

CHAPTER SEVENTEEN: BARNABAS

1. William A. Smith, *Dictionary of the Bible* (Hartford, CT: S. S. Scranton and Co., 1900), 98–99.
2. Robin Parker, *Aphrodite's Realm* (Nicosia, Cyprus: Zavallis Press, 1969), 13.
3. Mary Sharp, *A Traveller's Guide to Saints in Europe*, 28.
4. For a fuller development of this theory, see W. J. Conybeare and J. S. Howson's *The Life and Epistles of St. Paul* (T.Y. Crowell and Co., 1895), 718.

CHAPTER EIGHTEEN: LUKE

1. A. T. Robertson, *International Standard Bible Encyclopaedia* (Grand Rapids: Wm. B. Eerdmans Publishing Co., 1960), 1936.
2. Joseph Augustine Fitzmyer, S. J., *Encyclopaedia Brittanica*, 475–476.
3. Mary Sharp, *A Traveller's Guide to Saints in Europe* (London: The Trinity Press, 1964), 144.
4. Jerome, *The Nicene and Post-Nicene Fathers*, 364.

CHAPTEEN NINETEEN: LAZARUS

1. G. H. Trever, *The International Standard Bible Encyclopaedia* (Grand Rapids: Wm. B. Eerdmans Publishing Co., 1960), 1860.
2. A. Patsides, *St. Lazarus and His Church in Larnaca* (Larnaca, Cyprus: The Church of St. Lazarus), 2.
3. Robin Parker, *Aphrodite's Realm*, 108.
4. J. W. Taylor, *The Coming of the Saints* (London: The Covenant Publishing Co., Ltd., 1969), 188–189.
5. Ibid., 121–122.
6. Ibid., 106–107.
7. *Roger de Hovedon*, W. Stubbs, ed., vol. III (Longmans, 1868), 51.
8. J. W. Taylor, *The Coming of the Saints*, 108.
9. George W. Jowett, *The Drama of the Lost Disciples* (London: Covenant Publishing Co., Ltd., 1970), 163–164.

CHAPTER TWENTY: PAUL

1. J. Stevenson, *A New Eusebius* (London: William Clowes and Sons, Ltd., S.P.C.K., 1957, 1960), 145.
2. W. J. Conybeare and J. S. Howson, *The Life and Epistles of the Apostle Paul*, 679.
3. R. W. Morgan, *St. Paul in Britain* (London: The Covenant Publishing Company, Ltd., 1860), 60.
4. W. J. Conybeare and J. S. Howson, *The Life and Epistles of the Apostle Paul*, 679–680.
5. Jerome, *The Nicene and Post-Nicene Fathers*, 363.
6. R. W. Morgan, *St. Paul in Britain*, 59.
7. George F. Jowett, *The Drama of the Lost Disciples*, 130.
8. Ibid., 128.
9. Ibid., 179–180.
10. Cecilia Pericoli Ridolfini, *St. Paul's Outside the Walls*, Rome (Bologna: Pfligrafici il Resto del Carlino, 1967), 3, 16.
11. Mary Sharp, *A Traveller's Guide to Saints in Europe*, 173.
12. See *National Geographic* (May 1972), 707.
13. Jerome, In *Isaiam*, c. liv.; also *Epistol.*, xiii. ad Paulinum.
14. Eusebius, *De Demonstratione Evangelii*, lib. iii., as quoted in R. W. Morgan, *St. Paul in Britain*, 108.
15. Ibid., 175.
16. George F. Jowett, *The Drama of the Lost Disciples*, 196.
17. Lionel Smithett Lewis, *St. Joseph of Arimathea at Glastonbury*, 129–130.
18. Ibid.
19. Gladys Taylor, *Our Neglected Heritage—The Early Church* (London: The Covenant Publishing Co. Ltd., 1969), 67.
20. Boyce W. Blackwelder, *Toward Understanding Paul* (Anderson, IN: The Warner Press, 1961), 15–17.
21. J. Stevenson, *A New Eusebius* (London: William Clowes and Sons, Ltd., S.P.C.K., 1957, 1960), 144.

Bibliography

Alkhrida (Precious Jewels). Egypt: Coptic Church, 1915, 1925.

Antreassian, Assadour. *Jerusalem and The Armenians.* Jerusalem: St. James Press, 1969, second edition.

Arnold, Eberhard. *The Early Christians—After the Death of the Apostles.* Rifton, NY: Plough Publishing House, 1970.

Atiya, Aziz S. *A History of Eastern Christianity.* London: Methuen and Co. Ltd., 1968

Badger, George Percy. *The Nestorians and Their Rituals,* Hants, England: Gregg International Publishers, Ltd.

Barclay, William. *The Master's Men,* London: SCM Press Ltd., 1970.

Bede, *A History of the English Church and People.* London: Penguin Books, Ltd., 1970.

Bedini, D. Balduino. *The Sessorian Relics of the Passion of Our Lord.* Aloysius Traglia Archiep. Caesarien., Vic. Ger., 1956, Tipografia Pio X, Via Etruschi, 7-9 Roma.

Benton, William. *Encyclopaedia Britannica*, vol. 14. Chicago: Encyclopaedia Britannica, Inc., 1962.

The Bible Research Handbook, vols. 1 and 2. London: Covenant Publishing Co., Ltd., 1969.

Bishko, Herbert. *This Is Jerusalem.* Tel Aviv: Heritage Publishing, 1971.

Blackwelder, Boyce W. *Toward Understanding Paul.* Anderson, IN: The Warner Press, 1961.

The Bollandistes, Society of Bollandistes Acta Sanctorum De S. *Simone Apostolo Et Martyre, vol. 12.* Paris, 1867.

Brief Notes on The Armenian Patriarchate of Jerusalem. The Armenian Patriarchate of Jerusalem. Jerusalem: St. James Press, 1971.

Brownrigg, Ronald. *Who's Who in the New Testament.* London: Weidenfeld and Nicolson, Ltd., 1971.

Budge, E. A. Wallis. *The Contendings of the Apostles,* London: The British Museum, 1899, 1901, and 1935 editions.

Butler, Alban. *Lives of the Saints,* vol III, revised and supplemented by Herbert Thurston, S. J., and Donald Attwater. New York: P. J. Kenedy and Sons.

Cable, Mary and the editors of the *Newsweek* Book Division. *El Escorial,* The Wonders of Man.

Carucci, Arturo. *Il Duomo di Salerno e il suo Museo, III edizione.* Salerno: Linotypografia Jannone, 1960.

Cassels, Louis. "Two Historical Finds Back Mark's Gospel." *Glendale News Press* (April 15, 1972): 7-A.

Christian Life (November 1954).

Clayton, Rev. P. B. Harvest Thanksgiving service held in the Church of All Hallows-by-the-Tower on October 1, 1954.

Clement of Alexandria, Strom.

Connon, F. Wallace. *London through the Ages.* London: Covenant Books, 1968.

Conybeare, W. J. and J. S. Howson. *The Life and Epistles of St. Paul.* New York: Thomas Y. Crowell and Co.

Corbo, Virgil. *The House of Saint Peter at Capharnaum.* Jerusalem: Franciscan Printing Press, 1969.

———, *New Memoirs of Saint Peter by the Sea of Galilee.* Jerusalem: Franciscan Printing Press.

Cottrell, Leonard. *Seeing Roman Britain.* London: Pan Books, Ltd., 1967.

Danielou, Jean and Henri Marrou. *The Christian Centuries.* London: Datton, Longman and Todd, 1964.

Davis, John D. *The Westminster Dictionary of the Bible,* Philadelphia: The Westminster Press, 1944.

De Toth, J. B. *The Cathedral of the Pope.* Roma: Tipografia Poliglotta Vaticana, 1967.

Dickie. *The Lower Church of St. John Jerusalem.* Palestine Exploration Fund, Quarterly Statement, 1899.

Doppelfeld, Otto. *The Dionysian-Mosaic at Cologne Cathedral.* Cologne: Greven and Bechtold, 1967.

Elder, Isabel Hill. *Celt, Druid, and Culdee,* London: The Covenant Publishing Co., Ldt., 1962.

Erickson, Judith B. *Dome of the Rock. Jerusalem:* Israel Publication Services, Ltd., 1971.

Eusebius. *Eusebius' Ecclesiastical History.* Grand Rapids: Baker Book House, 1962.

Fallows, Rt. Rev. Samuel. *The Popular and Critical Bible Encyclopaedia.* The Howard-Severance Company, 1910.

Gibbon, Edward. *The Decline and Fall of The Roman Empire.* New York: Random House, Inc.

Goodspeed, Edgar J. *The Twelve.* Philadelphia: The John C. Winston Company, 1967.

Grant, Robert M. *Augustus to Constantine, The Thrust of the Christian Movement into the Roman World.* London: William Collins Sons and Co., 1971.

Greek Orthodox Patriarchate, *Short History of the Monastery of Saint John the Baptist,* Jerusalem: Greek Convent Press.

Hananian, John. "The Armenian Apostolic Church in Iran" (Lecture). Consolata Church in Teheran, 1969.

Hell, Hellmut and Vera. *The Great Pilgrimage of the Middle Ages.* New York: Clarkson N. Potter, Inc., 1964.

Henderson, Arthur E. *Glastonbury Abbey, Then and Now.* London: The Talbot Press (S.P.C.K.), 1970.

Henneke, *Neutestamentliche Apokryphen.*

Hoade, Eugene. *Jerusalem and Its Environs.* Jerusalem: Franciscan Printing Press, 1966.

Hoever, Rev. Hugo. *Lives of the Saints.* New York: Catholic Book Publishing Co., 1967.

Homan, Helen Walker. *By Post to the Apostles.* New York: All Saints Press, Inc., 1962.

Hophan, Otto. *The Apostles.* London: Sands and Co., 1962.

The International Standard Bible Encyclopaedia, 5 vols. Grand Rapids: Wm. B. Eerdmans Publishing Co., 1960.

Jameson, Anna. *Sacred and Legendary Art,* vol. 1. Boston and New York: Houghton, Mifflin and Co., 1957.

Jowett, George F. *The Drama of the Lost Disciples.* London: The Covenant Publishing Co., Ltd., 1970.

Kaloyeropoulou, Athena G. *Ancient Corinth, the Face of Greece.* Athens: M. Pechlivanides and Co., S.A.

Keskin, Naci. *Ephesus.* Istanbul: Keskin Color Ltd. Co. Printing House.

Koch, Sharon Fay. "Catch Up on History in Greece." *Los Angeles Times* (April 23, 1972), sec. H 17.

Koumas, M. *Saint Barnabas.* Cyprus: Nicosia, 1962.

Los Angeles Times. "Ancient Jewish Colony in India Disappearing." (August 25, 1971), Part 1-A.

Lewis, Lionel Smithett. *St. Joseph of Arimathea at Glastonbury.* London: James Clarke and Co., Ltd., 1964.

The Life of St. Bartholomew, material obtained from the British Museum, London, pp. 162–163, 178–179, 196–197.

Lokmanoglu, Hayreddin, Rakim Ziyaoglu and Emin Erer. *Tourist's Guide to Istanbul.* Istanbul–HALK–Basimevi: 1963.

Maedagen, Michael and Thomas Hudson. *City of Constantinople.* 1968.

McBirnie, William Steuart McBirnie. *What Became of the Twelve Apostles?* Upland, California: 1963.

Mekhitarian, Arpag. *Treasures of the Armenian Patriarchate of Jerusalem.* Jerusalem: Armenian Patriarchate, 1969.

Meyer, Karl E. *The Pleasures of Archaeology.* New York: Kingsport Press, Inc., 1970.

Mommsen, Theodor. *The History of Rome,* vol. II, bk. iii. 1913 edition.

Morgan, R. W. *St. Paul in Britain, abridged version.* London: The Covenant Publishing Company, Ltd., 1860.

Mundadan, A. Mathias. *Sixteenth Century Traditions of St. Thomas Christians.* Bangalore, India: Dharmaram College, 1970.

Menen, Aubrey. "St. Peter's." *National Geographic,* vol. 140, no. 6 (December, 1971).

Newman, Dorman. *The Lives and Deaths of the Holy Apostles.* London: Kings Arms in the Poultry, 1685.

Norwich, John Julius and Reresby Sitwell. *Mount Athos.* London: Hutchinson, 1966.

Papadopoulos, S. *Patmoc.* Athens: *The Monastery of St. John the Theologian,* 1962.

Parker, Robin. *Aphrodite's Realm.* Nicosia, Cyprus: Zavallis Press, 1969.

Patsides. *St. Lazarus and His Church In Larnaca.* Larnaca, 1961.

Pneumatikakis, The Very Reverend Archimandrite Hariton. *The First-Called Apostle Andrew.* Athens: Alexander Matsoukis, Inc., 1971.

Richmond, I. A. *Roman Britain,* vol. 1. Aylesbury, England: Hunt Barnard and Co., Ltd., 1970.

Ridolfini, Cecilia Pericoli. *St. Paul's Outside the Walls.* Bologna: Rome Pfligrafici il Resto del Carlino, Septembre 1967.

Roberts, Alexander and James Donaldson. *Ante-Nicene Fathers,* 10 vols. Grand Rapids: Wm. B. Eerdmans Publishing Company.

Scott, Thomas. *The Twelve Apostles.* London: Shelf-Mark 4014 bbb 48 (9) of British Museum, 1870.

————*The Apostles.* London: Shelf-Mark 4419 b 34 of British Museum, 1849.

————*Gospel of the 12 Apostles.* London: Shelf-Mark 753 e 27 of British Museum, 1900.

————*The 12 Apostles* (12 Brief Biographies). London: Shelf-Mark 4419 aaa 59 of British Museum, 1874.

Travel Studies on the Apostolic Heroes. London: Shelf-Mark 03127 E 9 of British Museum, 1909.

Sapir, Baruch and Dov Neeman. *Capernaum*, vol. NI/9. Tel Aviv: The Historical Sites Library, 1967.

Sharp, Mary. *A Traveller's Guide to Saints in Europe.* London: The Trinity Press, 1964.

Sieveking, G. de G. *Prehistoric and Roman Studies.* Oxford: The British Museum, 1971.

Smith, Asbury. *The Twelve Christ Chose.* New York: Harper and Brothers, 1958.

Smith, John Holland. *Constantine the Great.* New York: Charles Scribner's Sons, 1971.

Smith, William A. *Dictionary of the Bible,* Hartford, CT: S. S. Scranton and Co., 1900.

Souvenir of India, in Honour of the Visit to India of His Holiness Maran Mar Eshai Shimun XXIII. Kerala State, India: Editorial Board of the Publicity and Information Committee of H. H. The Patriarch Reception Committee, Ernakulam, 1962.

Stevenson, J. *A New Eusebius.* London: William Clowes and Sons, Ltd., S.P.C.K., 1957, 1960.

Stewart, John. *Centers of Christian Activity.* Trichur, Kerala State, India: Narsai Press, 1928, 1961.

Taylor, Gladys. *Our Neglected Heritage—The Early Church.* London: The Covenant Publishing Co. Ltd., 1969.

Taylor, J. W. *The Coming of the Saints.* London: The Covenant Publishing Co., Ltd., 1969.

Tenney, Merrill. *New Testament Survey.* Grand Rapids: Wm. B. Eerdmans Publishing Company.

Tertullian, *Def. Fidei.*

Theodoret, Jerome, Gennadius, Pufinus. *The Nicene and Post-Nicene Fathers,* vol. III. Grand Rapids: Wm. B. Eerdmans Publishing Company, 1969.

————*Ecclesiastical History.* Book IV, Ch. iii.

Toksoz, Cemil. *The Glories of Ephesus.* Istanbul: Basildigi Tarih, Nisan, Apa Ofset Basimevi, 1967.

Vacant, A., E. Mangenot, and E. Amann. *Dictionnaire De Theologie Catholeque.* Paris Librarie, 1931.

Voragine, Jacobus de. *Golden Legend.*

Watts, John. *The Lives of The Holy Apostles.* London: 1716.

Zahn, Eberhard. *Trier, A Guide to The Monuments.* Trier: Cusanusverlag, Volksfreund-Druckerei Nik Koch.

Zocca, Emma. *La Basilica Dei S. S. Apostoli In Roma.* Roma: 1959.

About the Author

Dr. William Steuart McBirnie graduated from Southwestern Theological Seminary and earned seven degrees. His fifty-eight years in ministry included pastoring a church in Glendale, California for twenty-seven years. Dr. McBirnie was knighted twice (Knights of Malta, Order of St. John) and was the second person to receive the Pilgrim's Medal (Israel) since its inception. He did archaeological work in Mexico and the Middle East. He was the president and founder of the California Graduate School of Theology and of World Emergency Relief, an organization that has served people in fifty-two countries.

About the Illustrations

The illustrations used throughout this edition of *The Search for the Twelve Apostles* are the work of nineteenth-century French artist and engraver Gustave Doré. Doré was a self-taught child prodigy who, at the age of sixteen, was the highest paid illustrator in France. His work was extensive—his literary engravings adorned works of Byron, Rabelais, Balzac, and Dante. In 1865 Doré began a series of biblical drawings that would eventually illustrate *Doré's Bible* published a year later. Even though Doré went on to distinguish himself as an oil painter and sculptor, his biblically-themed engravings are his most enduring legacy.

Index